I GOT TICS BOYA
a true story

Written by

Mike R. Devaney

Contents

CHAPTER 1 — THE FIRST FIVE

The sound of water. The chest of a girl in a one-piece bathing suit. She is treading water in a small inground pool surrounded by a chain-link fence. The background is a blur. This is my first memory, one of five, to be exact. The girl is a lifeguard. I don't know who she is or why I am in her arms. This basically sums up my entire life but let's move on.

A three-year-old boy runs through the parking lot of an apartment building made of bricks. I can see this boy from fifty feet off the ground; however, this boy is me. This is a memory about my mom, who I'm sure was not far behind. I run into an apartment with an old couple sitting on the couch. I jump into a closet and throw some coats on top of me. Soon after, I hear a familiar voice. "Hm, I'm sure I could have seen someone run right through this door." I peek through the coats as the old couple plays along with Mom. With nervous excitement, I wait for the inevitable.

A man sits on a couch drinking beer and watching TV. I sit in front of him on the rug. The third memory is of my dad. Ironically, my dad is not one to sit around watching TV with a beer in hand; however, that happens to be my first memory of him. I guess it was a Sunday in the fall.

A dark room. I sit up in bed and look around. The bed sits in the far-left corner of the doorway. To this day, I am not quite sure of this next one. All I can tell you is it's my first memory of fear. I see something across the room. It's unclear what it is; however, it resembles an old lady with long white curly hair. After looking for a moment, the figure moves ever so slightly and breathes. I jump up and run out and into my parent's room. Standing in front of their bed, Mom notices me. "Honey? Is everything ok? " She asks. "There's someone in my room!" I say. "A man?!" Mom yells, now sitting up. "No, it's an old lady!" I say quietly. "Oh, Sweetie, that's just your imagination," Mom says, now relieved. "Huh?!" Dad adds. "It's okay. He just had a bad dream." Mom explains. "Come on, honey." Mom walks me to bed and tucks me in. "See, there's nothing here." She says. "Me and daddy are right across the hall, ok? Now try and get some sleep." "Ok," I say with a kiss. Mom leaves, and I continue to look around the darkroom unconvinced.

A giant oak tree sways in the wind. The leaves are green with red tips, and clouds cover the sky. With my back to a house, I stand in a big backyard surrounded by other large oak trees and a cluster of tall pine trees to my left. The double lot is separated by a driveway that bends to the right. A two-door garage with a shed that connects to the front sits in the back. The house is two stories with siding, the color of dark urine. The back porch has its own lower roof with two windows on the left and a door to the right facing the back of the property. The second story also has two windows. Lastly, an old rusty TV antenna rises several feet above the pointed roof.

A commotion can be heard through the open windows as I scan my new backyard. My focus is currently fixated on something in the next yard. Eventually, my gaze is interrupted by the sound of rattling acorns and snapping twigs. I look to my left and see a girl my age, riding a Big Wheel, the infamous plastic bike from the 80s. She shoots out of a hole in the old rusty fence that divides the backyard directly behind the old urine-colored house. Her Big Wheel speeds directly towards me as the shredded acorns, and twigs get louder. "A girl!" I think to myself. *I mean, I'm sure I've seen one my age before, but this is the first one as far as my memory goes.* The girl pulls the brake and skids to a stop in front of me. She has light brown hair to her shoulders and wore jeans and a light, purple jacket. She had a scrunched-up face that looked tough for a six-year-old. "Hey, kid!?" She shouts. "What ya doing?" I say nothing. "You live here or something?" She asks. "Yea, I just moved here," I say eventually. The girl pauses and then smirks. "The names Hill." She says. "My full name is Anabella Hill, but don't you ever call me Anabella." I think for a moment. "My name's Mike. Me and my family got here a day ago." "How old are ya?" Asks Hill. "You got any brothers or sisters?" "Just a sister," I tell her as the yard gets quiet. "I'm four." Hill doesn't say a word. "In a half," I add. "I got two brothers and one sister," Hill says. "And they're a whole lot older than me." She states. "That's cool," I mention trying to be nice. "Not really," Hill says while wiping her nose on her purple jacket. Without thinking, I look back at what was holding my attention. Hill looks as well. "What are you looking at?" I pick up my hand and point towards the fence. "That." "Oh, that's my brothers," Hill says. "They built it a long time ago." "What is it?" I ask. Hill scrunches her face and turns to me with her answer. "It's a tree fort."

Beyond the ivy-covered fence with overgrowth was a display of trees big and small. One of them was an old oak tree. The branches made a V-shape about ten feet up, and there lay the tree fort. It was shaped like a trailer with one window in the middle and black and dark green paint on half of it that seemed like an abandoned project. The other half was the exposed rotted wood. Ivy ran up the tree's trunk and covered the painted half and the fort's roof.

"A tree fort!" I say out loud. "Yea, you can come over sometime, and I'll take you up there." Hill offers. "Really!?" I shout. Mom comes out the backdoor covered in filth. In a ponytail and gardening gloves, she dumps trash in a bin. A gust of dirt and dust fill the air. Mom coughs and waves her hand in front of her face. She notices Hill, and I look at her. "Hi there," Mom says in a cheery voice. "Hey lady, I'm your new neighbor, Hill." "Hello Hill, I'm Mrs. D, Mike's Mom." Mom adds. "What's your first name?" Asks Hill as she wipes her nose, now with her other sleeve. Caught off guard with the young girl's question, Mom hesitates. "Well, it's Claire, but." "Ok, Claire." Hill interrupts. "Well, I gotta get going. See ya later." Hill puts down the brake on her Big Wheel and zips back across the yard and through the hole in the fence. "Well, I see you've made a friend," Mom says with a smile. "She seems nice." Mom brushes dirt off her arms and heads back to the messy house. I stare out at the hole in the old fence, thinking about what Mom had just said. *Well, that's it—my first five.*

SIS

A three-year-old girl stands in the kitchen of the new house. She watches a ladybug crawl across a screen in the kitchen. *I wish I had a first memory of my sister, but I don't. It's just a mismatch of her getting, well, messed up.* I come up behind my sister in the kitchen and push her to the floor. Mom runs into the room as Cecelia cries. "Mike!" Mom yells. "What did you do?" "It was the wind," I yell.

Sis and I play on the stairs on a cloudy day. I slide down on a newspaper for several steps and bail. Looking at my rug burn, I get an idea. Screams are heard from the bathroom, and Mom jumps out of the shower and puts on a robe. Sis is at the bottom of the stairs crying. With each yell, a small stream of blood shoots from her head. Mom runs past me and grabs Sis. "What did you do!" Mom yells. "Oh Gosh! Get in the car!" We sit in a waiting room. Mom looks down at her bloody, wet robe with Sis in her arms. *Usually, my mom would rather cut out her tongue than to be seen in public in nothing but her bathrobe—desperate times.*

Dad and Uncle Pete move a dishwasher into the unfinished house. Grunting, they put it down in the kitchen. Pete looks around the new house. The front door leads to a large living room with an entranceway leading straight to the dining room. Behind the dining room sits a large open kitchen. The kitchen has two doors. One on the back wall that goes to the back porch and one on the opposing wall that leads to the basement. "Not bad!" Says Pete as he looks around the dining room and kitchen. He then makes a face and sniffs. "Yea, the last owners were not a big fan of personal hygiene," Dad mentions. "No kidding," Pete says. "Smells like old puss..." "Pete!" Mom yells, cutting off Pete as she enters the room. Dad's demeanor changes to a serious face to please Mom as he shakes his head at Pete. "Whoops," Pete says as he lights a cigarette. "The kids can hear you!" Mom adds. "They giving you trouble, Hun?" Asks Dad. Mom shakes her head. "No, they're just brushing their teeth." "Does it work?" Mom asks as she looks over the dishwasher that would go to the trash within the year. "Looks like a piece of shit to me." Says Pete. "I don't know why we need one anyway; they just take up space," Mom complains. "Come on, Hun!" "This baby's the future!" Dad jokes as he smacks the dishwasher on its side. "Put that cigarette out, Pete," Mom asks. "Thought I'd help out with the smell," Pete says while dunking his smoke in a beer can. Dad cracks a six-pack and hands one to Pete as Mom leaves the room.

Sis looks up at a hole in her bedroom ceiling. Mom comes in and tucks us into twin beds pushed together. Boxes and belongings cover the floor. "Your room should be ready soon, Mike," Moms says as Sis points to the big hole in the ceiling. "Mike saw something in the hole." Says Sis. "No, he's just teasing you, sis." Mom claims. "No!" I shout. "I saw something crawling around up there." "That's enough, Mike!" Mom says with a stern voice. "Hill said I can see the tree fort tomorrow," I add, changing the subject. "Oh, that sounds fun!" "Well, until then, get some sleep," Mom tells us as she says her goodnights. Mom turns the light off and leaves the room. "Sleep?" I think to myself. I'm way too excited for that. As Sis focuses on the hole in the ceiling, I lay imagining all the possibilities of the inside of Hills tree fort. Toy boxes, Christmas lights, arcade games, and carnival music. I can see it all.

ADVENTURE ONE

The following day I walk towards the hole in the fence with Hill. The weather is still warm, and the sun peeks through an overcast in the sky. We climb the ladder to her tree fort. Hill comes to the top first, and I quickly follow. We walk across a small deck and through an open doorway that leads into the tree fort. With a grin on my face, I look around. There is nothing. It's empty. *Remember, kids; nothing is how you imagine it.* Still happy to be in the tree fort, carnival or not, I walk around and scan the artwork on the walls. More provocative than I was used to, but nothing too inappropriate. That is until I get to the permanent marker portrait of a massive pair of boobs that cover a wall. Hill picks up a marker and scribbles on a wall by the only window. I join her. "Your house looks like a pig from the back," Hill tells me. "I guess," I say back. "You know how to play?" She asks while holding up a bag of Jacks. I nod, and Hill dumps the Jacks on the floor. As we play, I spot something camouflaged lying on a 2x4. I get up and grab it. "That's my brother's BB gun." Says Hill. She thinks for a moment and stands up. "Come on."

The two of us crouch behind a bush on the side of Hill's yard and look at a large white dog. Hill then looks at a frisbee lying fifty feet from the mutt. "What kind of dog is that?" I ask. "It's a watchdog," she says as she hands me the BB gun. "Her name is Sheba. If she gives you any trouble." "I don't want to hurt him!" I yell. "Nah, it'll just sting a little, is all." Hill states. Hesitant, I slowly make my way to the frisbee. Sheba sees me immediately and starts to growl. I stop for a moment and then continue towards the frisbee. Sheba stands up and lowers her head. I point the BB gun at Sheba as she takes off towards me. I pull the trigger.

"SNAP!" I look at the gun only to realize that Hill had given me a cap gun. Yelling at the top of my lungs, I take off running to the bush. Hill laughs as Sheba jumps on top of me and rips my shirt with her teeth. I somehow get to my feet and jump through the bushes landing back in Hill's yard. I wipe the tears from my eyes and look at Hill laughing as she's getting a kick out of the attack. "It's not funny!" I yell, still crying. "It was pretty funny," Hill says as she helps me up. "Don't worry; she won't bite ya for real." "Really?" I think because that was pretty damn close.

"Come on," Hill says as she walks away. I look at my house and think for a moment. Eventually, I catch up with Hill, and we walk through the greenery and brush towards the fort.

The old oak tree in our back yard is now in full fall colors as I walk to Hills. In pajamas, Hill sits on a rug with her legs crossed while watching the morning cartoons. The room is dimly lit, and the flashes from the TV color Hill as she holds a floppy-eared stuffed animal. She eats a bowl of fruity, dry cereal that sits on the floor in front of her. Also, in pajamas, I walk in her side door and sit next to her in the living room. She slides me the bowl. "Who's that?" I ask as I eat out of the bowl. "It's my favorite stuffed animal. Where's yours?" She asks. "I don't know," I tell her. "I don't have one." Hill turns with a displeased look on her face. "Every kid has a favorite stuffed animal," Hill says. "Don't you know nothing?"

She then slides the bowl back in front of her. I quickly get up and run across Hill's backyard. *I know such a childish decision for a four-and-a-half-year-old means absolutely nothing in a man's life. However, with that said, I promise you down the road, this choice will come into play.* After looking through dark-colored bears and dogs, I reach out and grab a

14

colorful Popple with blue skin, a yellow belly, floppy ears, and a bushy tail. I find Hill still watching cartoons as I sit back down with my new furry friend. Hill looks at us and slides the bowl of cereal back in front of me. I pick out a flake and pop it in my mouth.

It's winter now. Under gray skies, violent winds and rain shake the top of the giant oak tree. The branches are bare in the wet and cold yard. I wake in my own, now finished bedroom. A wooden bed and dresser sit in the room with a yellow wooden rectangle holding: toy guns, a Voltron helmet, Transformer figures, toy cars, and a Wiffle Ball bat. There's a closet next to the door and a second blue closet that sits at the back wall. There are two windows, one across from the entrance and one to its right that looks out into the front side yard. As I look around the darkroom, I can hear the sound of Dad's hammer smacking the wall from the dining room below. "Piece a shit!" Dad yells as he looks down and sees me standing at the bottom of the ladder next to a large hanging plastic sheet.

"Oh hey, bud," Dad says with a smile. "Someone's in my room," I reply. "Well, we better get them out," Dad says as he comes up and searches the room carefully. Let's see, nothing in here." "Wait a sec, nope, no monsters here," He tells me. "It wasn't a monster," I said. It was an old lady, and I think she's dead. "Hm," Dad says. "Well, I guess she came back to life and left because she ain't here. You want the wave?" "Yeah!" I yell as I hop into bed. Dad flaps the sheets over me, making it ripple. He repeats it several times and then lets it float down and over me.

I won't waste time explaining all the scenery in this story; however, I feel it's important to go into detail about a handful of places. One of these locations is my yard. The yard is colorful and calm with green trees and beautifully bloomed plants. I look out the front window towards the side yard, and a bright dogwood sits in the middle. The sides of the front yard are covered in holly and maple trees, with three large pines separating the front and back yard. The front porch is open with four pillars, two windows on each floor, and the roof divides them. The front door sits in the middle of the porch.

Sis joins me at the window, and we run out the front door. A little more than a year later, I find myself in summer. I hold my breath underwater. With my eyes open, I look around as light shines through the water of our large above-ground pool that now sits in our backyard. I'd have to say my favorite age was six because when I turned SEVEN, well, I got Tourette's.

Mom, Dad, Sis, and I sit chatting at the dining room table. We pass servings of food and eat. Mom and Dad sit at each end of the table. Mom's closer to the kitchen, and my back faces the wall leading to the back porch. It's around six o'clock on a sunny day toward the end of August. "The new printer came in," Dad mentions. "It's huge, and I think it's time for a bigger office." "Can we afford it?" Mom asks. "Yeah, why not," Dad says while scooping some rice. "Poopy," I whisper to Sis. She laughs and spits out some rice. "That's enough," Mom yells. "But mom, he made me," Sis says in her defense. "Both of you, stop!" Mom yells again before turning to Dad. "I'd just like it in a better area." "It's not like we're living there, Clair," Dad states. "I don't know." Mom rants. "There's bums, loiterers, and well, I saw that man peeing in the woods by the building right where anyone could see." "It's just a little pee, Hun," Dad replies. As my parents chat, I take my pointer finger and show it to Sis. Her eyes widen, and she shakes her head no. Sis looks down at her food and starts chowing down. I bring a finger to my nose and, before touching it, pull it away. Sis notices and holds back a smile. She grabs a glass of milk and starts to chug. Almost finished her drink, she glances up to see if I stopped. Sure enough, I quickly tap the end of my nose with my pointer

17

finger and hold it there. Sis laughs and spits milk over the table. "That's it, go to your room!" Mom yells for the last time. "But Mom!" Sis pleads. "I said now," Mom says calmly. *My Mom takes a hobby of fishtailing off her sentences, imaginary or not.*

Hours later, Dad works on a workbench in the garage. He cuts 2x4s with a buzz saw. Hill and I sit on hay bundles in a square. In the middle sat two rabbits: one gray and one white. "Hey Hill, check it out," I say, pointing to the night sky out the open wind of the garage. "If you lay right, you can see the dipper." Hill looks up. "Nah, that ain't the dipper, come on." Hill hops off the hay bundles and out the two-door garage as I follow. "Hey, Dad, I'm going to Hills." "Huh? Ok," Dad says without looking up.

Hill and I climb up onto her dad's motorboat that's propped up on some stilts by a shed. We stand on its railing and shimmy down a few feet before climbing on the roof of the shed. Hill and I lay side by side on the rooftop. "Hey, Hill?" I say. "Yeah," she says while we look up at the starry night. "You go to Verncap, right?" I ask. "What's it like?" "Well, probably a lot better than that church school you go to now," Hill answers. "What you scared or something." "Nah," I tell her. "You'll probably Ms. your

friends, though." She adds. "Some of my friends are going," I say quickly.

"Jill, Megan." "Wait a sec!" Hill interrupts. "Don't you have any guy

friends?" "Nick from preschool, and my cousin Matt. "That don't count."

She states firmly. I think for a short moment. "Oh, then no, I guess." Hill

nods her head. "You know what that means don't you?" She replies.

"Gay." "Gay? What's that?" I ask. "My brothers said if a guy hangs out

with a lot of girls, it's gay. Yeah, you like guys." "Oh, ok," I say

nonchalantly. "Wait a sec," I shout, sitting up. "If I hang out with a lot of

girls, don't that mean I like girls? So…It can't be." Already forgetting the

word she had taught me, I scratch my neck. "Well, according to my

brothers, you're gay." I lay back down. "Oh well, guess I'm gay." I think

to myself. I glance up at Hill before moving closer to her and looking back

up at the sky.

  Sis and I eat cereal as Mom runs around the kitchen cleaning up.

Dad enters, putting on his tie. "Ok! First day of first grade and…" He

points at Sis. "7th? Preschool," Sis says as we laugh. "That's it, so are you

excited or what?" Asks Dad. "You guys are going to have a lot of fun

today." Mom chimes in. "Just remember to be polite and have fun. "Well, not too polite," Dad adds. "I know someone will be," Mom says as she fixes Sis's outfit. "Now listen, make friends but remember to stand your ground," Dad tells me. "Don't let anyone push you around." "I won't," I say to him as we shake hands. The back door is heard opening, and I jump out of my seat and towards the back door. "Hey, Claire!" Yells Hill. "Hey Hill, you guys go right to school, ok." HEY HILL!" Sis yells as Hill, and I run out the back door.

We walk down some train tracks with the woods to our right and a long-paved street to our left. "Are we going to play at recess?" I ask Hill as she balances on a rail. "Nah." She sighs. "I can't be seen with a first grader." "Why not?" I ask. "I don't know." Hill shouts as she hops off the rail. "They'll think I'm retarded or something." "Oh," I say, now disappointed. "Hey, Hill. What's retarded?" Hill laughs and puts her arm around me. "Mikey." She says with a smile. "They're going to eat you alive."

THE MIGHTY JEB

A 1988 classroom emits the sound of children talking. I sit in the front row of the classroom, two desks away from the door, four rows in total fill the room. I look around the room for a moment and then back to the front. I hear a rattling thud as my desk shakes. Realizing the person behind me had just kicked my desk, I ignored it. Eventually, the desk shakes again. With no other option, I slowly turn around, meeting face to face with my assailant. It's a boy with a buzz cut. He had brown hair, jean shorts, and a blue-colored shirt. The boy was bigger than most kids in class and was now staring me in the face. After a staredown, I feel satisfied and turn back around. A moment later, my desk is kicked again. This kick was the hardest yet.

A busy lunchroom. I sit at an uncrowded table and eat a bologna and cheese on white bread with yellow mustard. I look up at a crowded table across the cafeteria where the boy who kicked my desk is now sitting. He tells a story animatedly as he waves his hands. I look back down at my sandwich and take a bite. A bell rings, and kids grab their belongings and head out a door in the classroom. The door leads outside to the back of the school, where several different jungle gyms are scattered in a huge dirt lot. Giant oak trees scale the perimeter, and some are sprinkled in the lot. I follow the single-file line out the door; as I reach the exit, the kid who kicked my chair barges through the door and slams into me, nearly sending me to the ground. I catch my balance. Outside the door, I watch the boy running through the playground, yelling and waving his arms as he struggles to keep on his backpack. "I hate that kid," I mutter in my six-year-old frustration. I take a breath. "Maybe I can catch up with Hill." I think to myself as I wipe some sweat off my head and walk towards the back gate.

Sis and I sit in the back seat of a maroon-colored station wagon. Dad drives with Mom at his side. "I thought it'd taste like bananas," I tell Sis while we talk about the host that you receive at church. "What's it taste like then?" She asks. "It tastes like Jesus," I tell her. "That's enough, Mike," Mom says as we laugh. "Some people don't even use their hands," I suggest. "They just open their mouths, and the priest puts it on their tongue." "EW!" Yells Sis. "Yeah, imagine his dirty old fingers touching your tongue?" "Mike," Mom says for my second warning as I continue. "And then they want you to drink out of this old cup with crusty old lady lipstick." Mom's head spins as her eyes turn a ghoulish white color, and she yells with a demonic voice that couldn't possibly come from a human. "I SAID THAT'S ENOUGH!" Sis and I shut up immediately.

An eerie church song plays as we find our seats in the church pew. Old statues, candles, and stained-glass windows surround us. *Church, a place that comforts old people in their remaining years on earth. For a kid, however, It's fucking terrifying. Don't get me wrong; I'm big on faith; it's just sometimes people forget the great thing about faith; it's free.* Money baskets stretch across the pews as the sermon continues, and cash is thrown in. The priest talks from the bible as the people stand and listen. An old man in the row in front of me blows his nose repeatedly in a nasty white hanky. On the third blow, I make a face of disgust. The old man folds up the hanky and puts it in his pocket. The handkerchief, the equivalent of a reusable piece of toilet paper. "Uh-oh," I think. I look around before awkwardly moving down the pew crossing in front of my family. Mom gives me "The Look." It's almost time for the sign of peace, and I want to be as far from old booger fingers as possible.

"We now offer each other the sign of peace." Says the priest. We shake hands with people around us as we utter "Peace be with you" repeatedly. After it seems to be over, Booger Fingers starts to make his way down the pew towards Sis and I. "What the Hell!" I think to myself as people politely let him bye. "It's over! People are kneeling. You really need to climb over seven people to shake my hand!?" I think. He shakes Sis's hand first and then offers it to me. I kneel and ignore. "Mike!" Mom yells in a whisper. Sorry Mom, I say in my head. You can ground me all you want. Mom gives Dad "The Look". Dad quickly elbows me in the shoulder.

Now, with everyone in the church kneeling except for old Booger Fingers, I finally look up and shake his hand. He turns my hand over and puts his other hand on top, sandwiching my hand before patting it. *I'm miserable*. I walk slowly down the aisle to receive communion. I look to my left, where I see the boy from school that I dubbed my worst enemy. The boy is kneeling with his head down, eyes closed, and hands pressed together pointed to the sky as he prays. "God bless grandpa and grandma and Alice." As I pass, he continues to pray with his eyes closed. He folds all fingers in but his middle two. Thus somehow, flicking me the bird. Unamused, I turn forward and continue to walk toward communion.

A few days later, I sit up high in the branches of a large Maple tree in our front yard. As I climb, I hear the sound of a keyboard playing. I look down at two boys I don't recognize. One sits on the curb at my neighbor's house playing a small battery-operated keyboard, the other spins on a "popsicle" shaped skateboard with neon wheels. After watching them for a moment, I continue up the tree.

Later, Sis and I stand on top of the dining room table. I jump off and over the back of a chair, landing on the seat and then the floor. After rolling, I get up and move the chair further from the table. "It's too close. Ok, go." I tell Sis as someone knocks at the front door. As I answer the door, I recognize the boy knocking. It was the boy playing on his keyboard hours earlier. He was about ten years old. He was tall, thin, and had blond hair in a part. "Hey, I'm Tyler the paperboy." He says. "Is your mom or dad home?" "Yeah, hold on," I tell him. "MOM!"

Mom runs downstairs as I open the screen door and let Tyler in. She then brings him to the dining room where her purse is. As I start to close the screen door, I stop. My eyes get wide as I stare straight ahead. "It's him." I think to myself. The boy was looking down at his feet. The same boy who kicked my chair, knocked me over, and gave me the finger was now standing at my front door. His name is Jeb. He looks up, and his expression quickly matches my own. We stare at each other for a few seconds, unsure of what happens next. Jeb's face changes from confusion to extreme excitement as he runs toward me. He throws his hand up for a hi-five, and I quickly do the same.

"You live here?!" Jeb yells. I match Jeb's' excitement if even possible. "Yeah, where do you live!?" I shout back. "Right THERE!" Jeb screams while pointing over to the next block. We continue to celebrate our new friendship while quickly making plans on where it would take us. It's funny, sometimes being a kid. Such a thing as a short distance can make all the difference in the world.

FIRST HOLY ERECTION

Jeb and I sit in the sand under an old wooden jungle gym a month later. We look through small holes in the wooden floor above us as spots of sunlight shine off and onto our faces. "Papa Smurf!" Yells Jeb as we eat our lunch. "No Way!" I shout as I look up. "You gotta love dress day," Says Jeb. "Hey! I bet your peanut butter cups that the next girl's underwear we see will be Cheetara ones!" "Thunder cats on a girl!" I yell quietly. "What you got?" I ask as Jeb goes through his lunch box. "I got some carrots, an apple..." "Carrots!?" I shout. "I'll take the donut." "You're on,"

Jeb says with a handshake. We look up with anticipation until I slap Jeb

on the shoulder. "It's Gem! Yes!" I reach for the donut, but Jeb grabs my

hand. "Double or nothing." He offers. "What's that?" I ask. "Don't you

know anything?" He yells. "Ok, so we bet again, and if you win, you get

double of my snacks, and if I win, then nothing!" "You're on," I shout.

After lunch, I walk across the playground balancing an armful of snacks.

Jeb walks with me, but he's not too happy. I hand him the peanut butter

cups, and his smile quickly matches mine.

Our house is decorated with colorful Christmas lights. It's barely

morning now as Sis and I come running down the steps to only the lights

of the Christmas Tree. The tree is a large blue spruce with small colorful

lights covering it from head to toe. It is draped in beads, colored balls,

random ornaments, and tinsel, lots of tinsel. "The Italian Nightmare," my

dad calls it, mocking Mom. Sis and I run with excitement to the tree in the

living room drenched with presents below. Half an hour later, Jeb knocks

at the door. Opened wrapping paper now scattered on the floor. A

skateboard lays on the floor with a snake painted on the bottom. A girl's

bike and other unwrapped presents lay under the tree. I can make out some toy guns, gameboards, stuffed animals, and a moon hopper. Sis aims the NES light gun at a static screen as Dad and I exchange wires through an old wooden TV stand. Jeb enters.

"Merry Christmas!" He yells in a deep voice. "HOHOHO!" "Merry Christmas, Jeb." The family shouts back as Dad reaches for a cord. "Hey, Jeb, how'd Santa treat ya?" Asks Dad. "Oh, I was super good this year, Mr. D!" "Oh, I'm sure." Dad snickers. "You got one too!? Jeb states as I hold a brand-new Nintendo Entertainment System (NES). "Yea!" I yell. "You have one," Mom interrupts, correcting Jeb's' illiteracy. "Yeah, us too," Jeb adds. "You did?! I ask. "How do you know?" *Jeb took over his older brother's paper route and wasn't allowed to open a single present until he finished delivering all the papers on his route. I know, right? Imagine waking up Christmas morning as a seven-year-old and having to go to work before opening your gifts. Madness. Jeb would save our house for last every Christmas to check out the goods.* "We peeked," Jeb yells. "You peeked!" I scream. "But that ruins it!" "Well, we still GOT one, didn't we," Jeb replies ignoring Mom's grammatical correction. "Who wants pancakes!?" Mom says with a smile.

A priest talks during mass. His voice echoes through the large church as we kneel at a pew in the very back. I'm in a daze as I look past my folded hands at the lady in front of me. She is wearing a short dress that shows her well-defined, cleanly shaved legs glistening from the glow of the church lights. A song starts to play, and people slowly get up around me. I snap out of my daze. Now standing, I open my eyes wide and look down at my crotch. "Holy shit." I think, as my family shoos me out of the pew and toward the alter. I stand and put my folded hands in front of my crotch to hide my now growing dilemma. I step back to let my family out first to the best of my ability. I try to slip back into the pew, but I'm quickly scolded by my mother's stare. I then start my long walk down the aisle. As I pass, Jeb gives me the thumbs up with a smile. I smile back while nodding my head nervously. A pretty red-haired girl from school smiles and waves my way. I manage only to wave a pinky with hands locked below my waist. I look up the line as I get closer to the front.

"Oh no." I think as I look behind me. No one is there. "The body of Christ." Says the priest. I can hear him as I inch closer. It's almost time. I tried to think of anything else to get my mind off it. Pooping, wedgies, kicking puppies, but it was all for naught. The Barbie doll legs of the lady kneeling in front of me are now burnt into the back of my eyelids. My

dilemma wasn't going away any time soon. At this point, you could hang a

small jacket on the end of it. Two more people left. "What do I do!?" I

think. I'm now the last person in line. I step in front of the priest and look

around with desperation on my face. It is now quiet in the church as even

the music has stopped. "The body of Christ." With 'o other option, I

squeeze my eyes shut, throw back my head, and open my mouth. I stick

out my tongue. After a moment, one eye opens, and I see the priest

waiting impatiently. "Stubborn ASSHOLE!" I yell in my head. With my

mouth still open, I attempted to say the word. "AHWEN." The priest

places the host on my tongue and, in slow motion, presses against it with

his thumb before accidentally sliding his fat finger down and onto my

tongue.

    With an utter look of disgust, I close my mouth and walk to my

left, where I still had to follow the long aisle that wraps around the church,

continuing back to my pew. Only my footsteps are heard echoing through

the quiet church. Before walking around the aisle, I tuck my chin in and let

out a loud, dry heave. "Oh no!" I think. If I weren't going to hell for

getting a boner in church, I surely would be, for giving fifty old ladies heart attacks after throwing up our lord and savior on the floor. I look at the front row of white-haired old ladies and smile at them while holding in another heave. I failed. My family and the girl from class, all now kneeling, look up with nervous eyes. Jeb hides his face in his folded hands as his entire body shakes from laughter. "I can make it," I tell myself. My cheeks puff out. No, I can't. I turn right and walk up to the old lady holding the wine cup.

The rag, meant for wiping the crusty lip marks off the chalice, falls off the old lady's arm and onto the floor. "MOTHER FUCKER!" Says a voice in my head as I follow the rag with my eyes. An altar boy picks it up and hands it to her. She wipes the cup only to smear the disgusting red lipstick and saliva across the rim. With a look of disgust, I let out my last dry heave before drinking from the cup. My lips are now on the nastiest part as I gulp it down. I enter my pew and sit down as my family still kneels. I'm miserable. Usually, my mother would demand me to kneel with the rest of the church, but today, I get a pass.

WISH ONE

Dad and I have a catch out in the backyard. It's spring now and the buds of the trees have begun to sprout. "Eye on the ball!" Dad says. I catch his first throw before looking over the fence to Hill's yard. "Come on, stay focused," Dad yells. I throw it back. He catches it and throws it back once again. My attention is somewhere else, and I drop the ball. I pick it up and toss it back to Dad. "Ok, just a little harder now." Dad stops and watches me as I gaze past him and into Hill's yard once again. Dad looks over his shoulder in the direction in which I stare.

The old oak tree that had once held Hill's tree fort has fallen. A large branch is broken, and only ruins remain. Dad looks back at me. Minutes later, construction paper is thrown down on a picnic table by the garage. Rough plans for a tree fort are drawn throughout the papers. Dad points to the plans and then to the trees in our yard. "This one might work with the pine trees," Dad says. I smile with excitement. "Yea!" I shout. "Hmm, they might not be ideal." He adds. "How about those cedars behind them? Might give you some privacy." "Definitely!" I shout.

A week later, I sit in the dining room with Dad, Mom, Sis, Hill, Jeb, and my two cousins Matt and Cassie. I sit in front of an ice cream cake with seven candles placed on top, including a large number

"SEVEN," to display my new age. Everyone sings "Happy Birthday." As they cheer, I can only think of one wish. *Although my wish came true that year, maybe instead of wishing for something I wanted, I should have wished away something I didn't want.*

CHAPTER 2 — A NAME TO THE FACE

Hill and I stand under blue skies that peak over a wooden fence riddled with vines and ivory. A sprinkler from the next yard cranks back and forth, spitting water on the chipped side of my white garage. There are only a few feet between the fence and garage, making this space perfect for hiding. Hill puts on lipstick, shakes her hair, and puts her back against the garage. "OK, kiss me." She says simply as she closes her eyes. I stare at my friend, who, up until this point, I thought of as a tomboy. She has always been a pretty girl, but I hadn't put two and two together until she hid behind a face with lipstick. As I lean forward, Hill laughs. I start over but am interrupted again by her laugh. This time, it comes from her nose. "Come on, I can't do it if you're laughing." "OK, OK." She says. I lean in and peck Hill on her lips. Afterward, Hill opens her eyes. "There, you did it." She says, referring to the conversation that ended with us behind the garage. "What do you think?" "It was cool," I answer. "OK, this time, do it the same, but at the end, stick your tongue out a little." I nod and scratch my head. "What are you doing later?" She asks while applying more lipstick. "Nothing," I reply. "Good!" She shouts. "I found an old swamp."

We come out from behind the garage, and Hill heads home as I walk back into my house. In the kitchen, Mom makes PB and J's while Dad sits at the dining room table, reading the paper. Mom looks at me. "Hey, Honey." "What's that on your lip!?" Mom shouts, interrupting herself. "OH SHIT!" Yells my brain as I wipe the red mark off my lip and look around nervously. "I was, um ahh..." Mom stares me down. "Playing dress up!" I shout. Dad peeks out the side of his paper and gives me his own stair down. "Whoops." I think, looking around the kitchen as if for a sign. "Hill went to kiss me on the cheek and..." I stop talking and hesitate. Dad pops the newspaper back open and continues reading. "The truth Mike." Mom demands with an angry look plastered on her face. The phone rings. Mom and I stare at each other as the phone continues ringing. With no caller ID or answering machine Mom had no other choice but to answer the phone. "You wait right here." She says as she picks up the phone. "Hello. Yeah, he what!? OK, yes! OK, I'll be right there." Mom slams the phone down in a panic. "I have to go! Uncle Pete cut off his thumb." "Again?" Dad asks. "Where are my keys?!" Mom yells. "I'll go." Dad offers as Sis enters the room. "Is Uncle Pete OK?" She cries. "He'll be fine. I'll go. He's, my brother." "You stay with the kids," Mom says while grabbing her car keys. She shouts, "Goodbye." and leaves the house. Dad sits back down and reads the paper while Sis wipes her eyes and goes back on the couch to watch TV. I don't remember exactly what I did next, but I sure as hell know that I got as far away from that kitchen as possible.

BANNED FOR LIFE

A square plastic dot on the NES blinks in the quiet living room. Lights from the TV flash off my face on this cloudy day. My eyes roam the screen. Mario is heard faintly in the background. My right eye slowly starts to close, and I begin to turn my head to the left. I hear the sound of Mario dying and quickly look back at the screen. The sun peeks through a window as I turn off the NES. I jump to my feet from sitting on my knees and run out the door. In bathing suits, Hill and I come running up my driveway in the rain. I jump in a puddle, as Hill holds a towel over her head. We jump up and sit on the side of the front porch as we look at the sky filled with lightning. Thunder crashes as Sis comes out the front door and sits with us. Mom's calm voice is heard through a screen window. "Stay out of the pool now.

Later as the sun sets, Sis draws with crayons at the dining room table. She shows Mom the drawing. "That looks great, honey!" Mom replies. "It's a duck," says Sis as I jump in front of the living room TV. I hit the power button and grab the controller. As I begin to guide Mario through his adventure, my right eye starts to close, and I slowly turn my head to the left. My world turns black as dark storm clouds cover the earth. An eerie wind howls as I come to a cave in a dark forest. The large cave is pitch black and has a red door standing at its entryway. The red door stands alone with nothing but the black of the cave surrounding it. An old-looking door handle turns, and the red door creaks open. I complete the turning of my head and look up to the right before squinting my right eye and closing it. I rinse and repeat several times. Mom enters the room and notices my odd display. I hear Mario bite the dust.

"Damn!" I shout. "Mike!" Mom yells quickly. "Turn it off!" She screams again. "Sorry, I didn't know you were there," I tell her. "It doesn't matter if I'm here or not, there's no cursing in this house, or that thing will go in the garbage!" Knowing full well not to call my mom's bluff, I turn off the NES and head towards the stairs. "Wait a sec." "Come here," Mom says. I walk over and sit on the edge of the ugly gray couch. "What was that thing you were doing with your eyes?" "I don't know," I answer honestly. "You don't know? "Well, you were doing something," she states. "I don't know!" I say, now agitated. "Well then, no more video games until it stops." "But mom!" I complain, standing up. Mom ignores me and heads up the stairs as I plop back down on the couch and sigh. Little did my mom know, she had just banned me from video games for the rest of my life.

That night behind a closed door, Mom and Dad have a conversation in their bedroom. "It was more like a strain. He said he didn't know." "He might have just had something in his eye," Dad adds. "No, it was something else." Mom assures him. "It's probably from sitting in front of that game." She adds. "No, it's just a game," Dad says in my defense.

"He's only on it for like an hour a day. Let me give Ron a call."

A heavy-set man in his forties sits behind a computer, scrolling with the mouse and puffing on a cigarette. He has a button-down collared shirt and black hair which is parted to the side. He picks up his ringing telephone. "Hello. Hey Ron, It's Mick. How are ya!? Not bad, Mick. How about yourself? Good, good. Says Dad. "Me and Clair were just talking about Mike and Cecelia's new NES." "If I remember correctly, Jeb has one too?" "Oh yes." Says Ron. "I do believe Santa brought him an Intendo for Christmas." *Oh, he got one alright, along with every middle-class house in the country. The rich kids got one the year before, and the poor kids will get one next year.* "Well, I was just wondering if you noticed Jeb doing…" Dad pauses. "Something with his eyes." "His eyes!?" Ron yells. "No! Why the hell would he be doing that?!" *See, you have to understand. If there was even a little something wrong with you in the 80s, well, you were fucked.* "No reason," Dad says calmly. "Just something I saw on the news. Well, I hope it's not that CNN," Ron says. "You know they love to gossip. Nope, you know Clair," Dad tells him. "OK, you too. Thanks, Ron." Dad hangs up the phone and shakes his head at Mom. "Can I play now?" I yell up the stairs. "No, honey." "Oh, come on!" I yell again. "Jeb just found a warp to board eight!" "No, just watch TV," Mom blurts out. "Can I watch it while Mario climes the vine to board eight?" "NO!" Mom and Dad yell back in unison.

The following day, Jeb and I walk down the tracks to school. "Ten days left, Dude! Then we're free," Jeb yells. "It's good timing too; I've had diarrhea for like a week. I must be stressed out or something." Jeb looks over at me, but I'm not paying attention. Instead, I pinch my nose. "This walks not helping either." He adds. As a seven-year-old, diarrhea was usually a great conversation piece, so in hindsight, I can respect Jeb's frustration. Jeb looks at me as I pinch my nose. "Hello!" He shouts. "What's with you?" "Huh, nothing," I say. "Why do you keep doing that?" He asks. "I don't know," I tell him. "Well, stop!" I continue to pinch while Jeb tries to ignore it. Also, Jeb has the patience of a squirrel. "Stop it!" He roars while smacking my hand. "I can't!" I yell back as two girls from a class run onto the tracks. "Oh shoot! It's Tia and Sam! Cut it out, man!" Jeb whispers. "I told you, I can't!" I yell. "Then hold it in or something!" Jeb interrupts as the girls catch up. Tia has blond hair, and Sam is a brunette. "Hey, guys!" They say. "Ladies," Jeb states. "What are you guys talking about?" Asks Sam, "Oh nothing, Mike just opened his pool." Jeb

tells them. "Oh wow, can we come swimming?" Asks Tia. "Yeah, sure!" I

shout. "What are you guys doing after school?" I go to pinch my nose, but

Jeb elbows me in the shoulder, and I refrain. "Tia's going to her grandma's,

and I'm going home to play my new Pac-Man arcade." "Wow!" Yells Jeb.

"You got an arcade in your house!?" "Can we play!?" I ask. "You can,

Mike, But Jeb's not allowed over." "Why not!?" Jeb interrupts. "Because

you broke my mom's penguin statue at my birthday party!" "I was trying

to breakdance!" Jeb says in his defense. "Sorry, Jeb." "See ya!" The girls

yell as they take off down the tracks. "Dude!" "You just got a date with

Sam Fresco." "Nah, we're just friends. I tell him. "Besides, I like Tia."

"Tia?" "Then why didn't you ask her for a date?" Jeb asks. I smile before

answering. "Because Tia don't have a Pac-Man arcade!" Jeb and I laugh

and continue down the tracks.

THE TEPPERS

Recess. I stop and look at an old rusty jungle gym at the far corner

of the playground where two boys sit, both with shaggy blond hair. They sit at the top. "Hey Jeb, who's that?" I ask as I pinch my nose. "That's the Tepper brothers, Liam and Mason," Jeb says. "Their second graders and they're bad news." "Come on! You can meet them," Jeb shouts as we head towards the jungle gym. Liam breaks a stick on the metal bars and examines the tip by touching the point. Mason sits at the highest point of the jungle gym with a pack of matches in hand. He presses a match on the flint with his thumb and flicks it to the ground, where a younger kid plays. The lit match sizzles out as it hits the sand. "Are they twins?" I ask. "Nah." Jeb answers. "Liam got left back last year. Oh, and whatever you do, don't say the word divorce." "OK. What's divorce? I ask. Jeb answers quietly as he leans in. "It's when your parents live at different houses so your dad can date the babysitter." "Whoa, I wish I had a divorce," I say. "How come?" Asks Jeb. I whisper loudly. "Have you seen my babysitter!?" Mason watches as the sandbox kid finally attempts to run away before he is quickly smacked on the shoulder by Liam. Liam then nods his head towards Jeb and me as Mason hops to the ground to confront us.

"Hey, guys. This is my best bud Mike," Jeb shouts. "He wants to try out for the club." I look at Jeb with confusion. "It's not a club, Jeb!" Mason says as I hold my hand out. "Hey, I'm Mike." Mason only stares.

He looks at his brother, who gives him a nod. "See this jungle gym?"

"Yea," I answer. "Well, it's ours!" Mason says with a curled lip. "Anyone who wants to go on it has to pass the test." "What's the test?" I ask. "You have to run across them monkey bars and jump to that pull-up bar." He tells me. Mason points to the higher of two pull-up bars as Jeb runs and hops up on the jungle gym. "Wait! You did that?" I ask Jeb with wide eyes. The Tepper's laugh as I point the question at Jeb. Jeb was built more like a lineman. *Don't get me wrong, though; for a heavier kid, Jeb could move.* "Na, Jeb ran halfway across and fell into a bush," Liam says. "We thought it was funny, so we let him in. But you don't look all that funny" Adds Mason. I look at Jeb, who gives me the thumbs up. I make my way to the far side of the monkey bars and climb up and stand on the top. I quickly walk to the other end and catch my balance before looking at the high rusty pull-up bar. I hold my breath and leap. I keep my eye on the bar as I make my way through the air. I grab it tight but miscalculate my momentum, which yanks me off and sends me to the ground. I hit hard, flat on the sand. "DAMN!" Yells Jeb. With no reaction from the Teppers, I gasp for the wind that had been knocked out of my stomach. Eventually, I stand to my feet with a face full of sand. I climb back up the jungle gym once again and make my way to the end. This time I wipe the sweat off my hands with my shirt. I jump, grab the bar, and squeeze the living shit out of it. "Yes!" Jeb yells while throwing a fist. I swing to a stop and drop to my feet. Mason and I stare each other down until he gets another nod from his brother. He then puts out his hand. "Not bad, kid." He says finally, and the two of us shake hands.

THE RABBITS

My sister and I would often make poor decisions that would lead to punishment. Mostly my fault. What we didn't get punished for was saying swear words. The only reason being is because we didn't know any. We didn't know any because my mother would drag us away from them by the arm. Malls, restaurants, the car wash, and even church. By the age of seven, however, I had finally picked up a few, but with that said, there was one word that I had not heard.

I draw with a permanent magic marker on our rabbit cage in the backyard. Sis pets the gray rabbit through the door. "You got a name for him yet?" I ask. "No, but it should probably rhyme with yours, though," mentions Sis. "Good idea!" I shout. "My teacher said if you don't know a word to go through the alphabet." Sis mentions. "OK," I tell her. "Let's get started."

Hours later, Sis is playing with the gray rabbit on the kitchen floor as Dad comes through the front door and puts a six-pack on the dining room table before cracking one open. Mom washes some dishes while I eat a snack. "How's my favorites?" Dad asks. "Good." We answer. "You guys think of a name yet," Dad says while chugging his beer. Sis smiles and pets the gray rabbit while answering. "Yea, he's..." As the following word leaves my sister's mouth, Dad chokes on his beer, and Mom drops a dish in the sink. "Cecilia!" Mom yells. "Where did you hear that word!?" "We made it up," I tell Mom as Sis starts to cry. "You what?" Asks Mom. "It had to rhyme with Digger," I say as Dad wipes his shirt with a rag. "Oh," Mom says, now relieved that we weren't gossiping with skinheads. Mom kneels to comfort Sis. "OK, well, you have to change it. That is a word, and it's a very bad one." "I'm sorry we didn't know." We tell her. "It's ok. It was a simple mistake," Mom says while looking up at Dad. With a fist in front of his mouth, he tries not to laugh at the innocent mistake that could only have come from a child. Mom shoots him a dirty look. "I guess we better fix their name tags," I say as I grab the permanent marker. Mom's eyes widen, and Dad's half-smile quickly fades. The following day the sun rises on our two rabbits Digger and Figger.

MAM, YOUR SON IS HORNY

I stare at a clock on the wall. "Michael." Says a pediatrician as he leans out of a doorway. I continue staring while Mom reads a magazine. "He says it feels like he has to do it," Mom tells the doctor as he examines my eyes. The doctor rubs his chin. "Let me see it again. I do my eye tic, which now looks forced. "Hmm, well, I'm sure it's just allergies." The doctor replies "And pinching his nose?" Mom replies. "Yea, a few allergy medications, and he should be fine." He adds. Mom drives with me in the passenger seat. "Allergies?" She complains. "Even I know it's not allergies."

A day or two later, Mom talks to a Neurologist as I sit in a waiting room. "Well, Ms., you've come to the right place." "Oh, thank God!" Mom says out loud. "You don't know what we've been through. "Every quack on the block, it sounds like." Says the Doctor. "You said it, not me." Mom laughs. The doctor walks up to a life-size poster of a youth's anatomy with a pointer stick. "Well, ma'am." He says. "They have been mistaken. You see, the problem isn't here." He explains as he points to a child's head on the poster. "It's here." The doctor points to the child's crotch on the image. Mom's smile immediately drops to a face of unpleasantry. "You see, Mam." Says the Doctor. "Your son is horny." Mom turns her head slowly from poster to doctor. The doctor's mouth moves, but my mother hears nothing but rage as he continues to smack the crotch of the boy in the poster. I sit in a waiting room with a magazine in front of my face. The faint voice of Mom is heard from the next room as she scolds the doctor for his impossible diagnosis.

Meanwhile, I peek my eyes over the top of my magazine and look across the waiting room at a woman breastfeeding. She fixes herself and throws a shawl back over her boob. I quickly pull the magazine back in front of my face. Mom storms into the waiting room and yanks me out of my seat. "We're leaving!" Mom Yells as If I hadn't figured that part out yet.

"Sicko," Mom mutters on the way home. "I should have known. Obscure magazines, women breastfeeding! I'd never breastfeed in public."

I look at my mom and then out the car window with a disappointed look on my face. It's night now, and Dad and Mom talk in the kitchen as I watch TV in the living room with bloodshot eyes. *At this point, my new shitty companion has been wearing me down. I hold in these tics at school the best I can, but it doesn't seem to matter. They are a consistent bother from morning through night.* "They don't seem to know anything!" Mom says. "It's OK, we'll just keep looking. Someone has to have some idea." Dad tells Mom with reassurance. "Can I climb a tree?" I yell. "Not now, honey." Mom answers. I make an angry face and run out the front screen door. I jump off the porch and run towards the pine trees. I'm not sure exactly what was going through my mind, but I was unhappy. Mom shortly follows. I stop before the pine trees and start to cry. "What's wrong with me?!" I yell as my Mom catches up. She kneels down and hugs me. "Nothing, honey, you're going to be fine. Dad and I just want to make sure we do all we can to see what's going on." "Can I climb?" I ask again. "Sure, just not to the top. OK? It's dark." Dad leans on the open doorway on the back porch with a can of beer in his hand. "You OK, bud?" He shouts. "Yeah," I shout back as I run to the pines. Mom walks up the back steps. Dad puts his arm around her, and they walk back into the house and close the door.

Jungle gym, obstacles, girls, quack doctors, and tics all come in second to a kid's worst enemy, patience. I sit on a pile of stacked plywood in an unfinished tree fort with only two walls up. Dad hammers. "Hey Dad, think we'll finish it soon?" I ask. "It takes time, man. You can help, you know." He tells me. I walk over and kneel next to Dad as he hands him a hammer. "OK, you start it." He says. "I can't," I complain. "What do you mean you can't. Go ahead and start lightly." I hold the nail and tap it until it stands on its own. I slam it down. "Good!" Dad yells. "Now another."

Commercial size printers run at Dad's new office building. Dad throws the last bundle into an old blue van and drives away. "Hey, Mick." Says the owner of a local market. "I got something for you. Hold on." Says the man. "Don't worry about it, Frank," Dad says as he drops off a bundle of papers. "I'll grab it later." Before leaving, Dad sees a row of tear-off tags hanging from a piece of paper that sits above the doorway. The paper reads, Grove studios: Guitar lessons. Dad reaches up and grabs a tag. A second tag falls, and Dad catches it before it lands. With a light

hop, he smacks it back in place and leaves the store.

"Blue skies" plays on a stereo system in a glass case. Inside it

holds a record player, tape decks, etc. On each side was a tall brown

speaker. Mom prepares a meatloaf with applesauce and green string beans.

She yells out the kitchen window over the music. "OK, time for dinner."

It's around Six o'clock, the sun still shines as Sis, and I come out from the

pine trees. Sis washes her hands at the kitchen sink as I sit on the dining

room floor in front of the stereo. Dad enters and says his hellos. He puts

down a filled paper bag and kneels next to me as the guitar solo starts in

the song.

"Sounds good, right?" Dad says. "Yeah," I answer without taking

my eyes off the speakers. "You know what that is, don't you?" Asks Dad.

"A Guitar," I tell him. "Yep, that's the lead guitar. You know you could

play like that someday if you wanted to." Dad says. "Really!?" I shout.

"Of course. You can do anything you set your mind to." He adds. "Can

you teach me?" I say, now intrigued. He pulls out a paper tag. "I can show

you some drumbeats, but if you like the guitar, we should give this guy a

call." Dad hands me the tag with a phone number on it. "Thanks!" I shout.

"It's ready." Mom says as she brings food to the table. I stick the tag under a vinyl record with artwork of a spaceman battling a dragon. The meatloaf smells delicious.

RON VS GANON

Jeb and I run up from Jeb's backyard to his sliding glass door. We open it and come inside the den. Jeb's mom puts dinner on the table. "OK, boys, come and get it." "Hey! No guns at the table!" She yells. Jeb and I take our cap guns out of our pants and toss them on an old chair in the den. Jeb's mom, dad, and brother sit at an oval-shaped table in the kitchen. Tyler finishes and dumps his plate in the sink. "Thanks, mom. I'm heading to Bills." He says. "You finish your homework, Tyler?" Asks Ron. "Yeah, dad, all good." Yells Tyler. "Alright then." Says Ron as he scoops some mashed potatoes. "Bye, Hun. That reminds me, Jeb, you had a lot of homework yourself." Says Cheryl. "It's all done, mom!" *Jeb was one of those smart kids that pissed me off. What took me three hours took Jeb about twenty minutes.* "So, Mikey, how's that ribeye?" asks Jeb's father. "It's really good, thanks! I don't know why but I always eat good here." I reply. "It's because you're surrounded by tubbies!" Ron says sarcastically. The table laughs as we finish up dinner.

That night Jeb and I play on the NES in the back bedroom. The music is heard as we search above ground for the next hidden dungeon. Jeb grabs the controller from me. "It's got to be around here somewhere! I had one more bush!" I complain. "OK, gents, that's enough Intendo for tonight." Says Jeb's Dad. "Aw, come on, dad, just...". "Enough means enough, JEB!" Ron yells. "I should have come back here hours ago! You two sit with little smiles looking at a TV screen when the whole world is turning right out that window." Jeb holds the reset button before turning off the NES. We get up and head out of the room. "That thing will rot your brain, boys, I keep telling ya," Ron adds.

Jeb tosses and turns in the bunk below me. "Hey, you still up?" He asks. "Duh," I reply as I hop down. "Come on. They're definitely asleep by now." He claims. We creep down a hallway to the back bedroom. All the lights are off, but the TV light shines through the cracks of the door to the back bedroom. "Wait!" Jeb whispers. "Did we leave the TV on?" I ask. "No way! My dad would have freaked." Jeb explains as I walk forward. "Stop! Somethings not right." He adds. We crept outside and to the window of the back bedroom. We stand on some trash cans and look inside. As we look in the window, our mouths fall open. Inside the room, Jeb's dad sits on a chair in front of the TV, with the controller in his hand. He was playing Nintendo. Jeb is speechless. "Holy crap, dude!" I whisper, "He's on the 9th board! "He's gonna to beat Ganon!" Jeb says finally. "I can't watch," I tell Jeb as I look away, not to be spoiled by the legendary beast. Jeb stares at his dad, who moves back and forth with the game as he smacks the controller with his thumbs.

Back home a few days later. I yell loudly as I throw books, magazines, crowns, and other miscellaneous items in my living room. "No!" I yell. "I don't want to go!" "Stop!" "It's OK, Mike!" Mom shouts as she grabs me. I pull away and run out the front door. "Let him go," Dad yells. Mom sighs and starts to pick up the mess. "Stop! He'll clean it when he gets back." Mom sits on the couch, puts her hand on her chin, and ponders. The next day we drive to a building in the city. A sign out front reads, Kid's Hospital.

TIC VS TONSILS

Mom and Dad sit in an office with two doctors. "The nose squeeze and the cough." Moms tells them. I sit on a carpet in the playroom as a female nurse hands me a toy that I would never play with. The doctors that Mom and Dad were talking to now stand behind a window in the next room and watch me as I study the stupid toy. "What do you think?" One of the doctors asks the other now that they are alone. "The fuck if I know." The other doctor says. "He does have that cough, though." The two doctors look at each other and smile. *Obviously, I don't know exactly what was said behind that window, but It had to be something close to that, or I would still have my fucking tonsils.*

It's daytime now at the Devaney house. Sis, Hill, and I sit eating ice cream on a three-cushion couch in my living room. Other empty ice cream bowls and popsicle wrappers scatter the coffee table. The phone rings, and Mom answers. "Oh hi Jeb, No, he can't talk. He had his tonsils removed." "His balls?" I hear faintly through the landline. "No! I said his tonsils, Jeb! Don't call here and be crude! No, now you'll have to wait until tomorrow. Bye, Jeb." Mom hangs up the phone and shakes her head. I look back at the TV and eat more ice cream cones.

THE WHISPER OF LIFE

The next day Jeb runs out of his house and grabs his bike in the side yard. It was a blue, two-story house with a connecting garage. He hops on and takes off. I'm sitting in my living room on the carpet when Jeb barges in the front door and plops next to me. Smiling, Jeb lays on his stomach next to me. I glance between Jeb and the TV. "What?" Jeb looks behind his shoulder before whispering in my ear. My expression changes. But then I'm annoyed. "Shut uuuup." I shout. "I swear dude." He replies. "How do you know that?" I ask. "My brother said it. I don't think he knew I was there. I don't know who was on the phone, but it couldn't have been a grown-up. I couldn't really understand everything but..." Jeb says quietly. I had to find out the truth. Even if it meant getting grounded. I hand Jeb the NES paddle and ignore the rest of what Jeb has to say. I stand to my feet and walk to the dining room where Mom has come up from the basement. "Where are you going? MIKE!" Jeb whispers loudly. "Mom," I say out loud. "Does the man put his penis in the girl's vagina to make a baby?" I ask. Mom's face freezes as if I told her the world was ending. She looks at me for a moment with a straight face before answering. "We'll talk about it later." *But we didn't have to. Mom had just given me the answer.* My life flashes before me as I walk back to Jeb, whose face is buried in the rug. "I'm so dead." He mutters. "The penis in the vagina." I think. "Brilliant." *I mean, I'm sure I would have figured it out; eventually, the cavemen did.* But still. With no punishment from Mom, I pick up the paddle and move Mario through Level 8, which is now filled with penis turtles and flying vaginas.

I toss and turn in my bed throughout the night. Now morning, Mom and Dad sit at the kitchen table both reading a paper in their robes. Mom holds an old-fashioned donut and sips her tea. Dad eats a sausage link off of a fork. "OK, time for work." Dad says. "Wait, I think I want a baby," Mom tells him. "You got it, honey." With exaggerated footsteps, the two meet, standing face to face. "Ready?" They say. Mom smiles and nods. They both lean back swiftly until their waists touch. Now looking at the ceiling, Dad looks around smiling. He looks at his watch as Mom sips her hot tea. She tries to take a sip in her awkward position, but it spills on her shoulder and down her arm. "What's for dinner?" Asks Dad. "Whatever Mike hates." Mom answers. "AHHHHHH!" I yell as I jump up in bed. I take a breath and go back to sleep.

Outside an old movie theater in the corner of a strip mall sits a pigeon. It eats an abandoned bag of popcorn in the stairwell of the theater. Jeb, The Tepper brothers, and I come barging out the theater's side door, hooting, and hollering. We jump and throw punches and kicks.

Soon after, we find ourselves at Jeb's house. Inside Jeb's garage, we go through bins and grab material for makeshift wooden swords and nunchucks. The sound of wood clanking, echoes through Jeb's open backyard. An empty lot sits behind Jeb's house and then woods. We clash swords, stabbing and slashing at limbs and torsos until Jeb gets hit in the knee. "AHHH!" He yells. "Sorry," I shout. Jeb slowly stands up and opens his eyes wide before charging me at full speed. I hold up my sword to block as Jeb swings hard. The swords smash together, and the tip of Jeb's snaps off and shatters his first-floor window. "Oh no." Says Jeb. "Jebediah! Get in here NOW!" Cries his mother. Jeb fails to hold back tears and drops the broken sword as he goes inside. *There wasn't a doubt in my mind that Jeb would be using his paperboy money to pay for that window. Every cent.* "Man, he's in trouble," I say as I turn to the Tepper's. "Guys?" I look around to no one. The Teppers are long gone.

It's mid-afternoon now as the hot sun shines through the cloudless sky. I head through a random side yard and into the woods that connect Jeb's street to mine. I walk down a small path that has been developed due to our consistent shortcut. "Mikey!" Yells a familiar voice. "Hey, Hill," I say as she catches up. "Where have you been lately? I haven't seen ya." She says. Jeb's whisper flashes through my mind. "Oh um. Just doing schoolwork," I tell her. "Surly Hill knew about making a baby." I think to myself. After all, she has three older siblings. I wondered why she never told me. "OK, Mikey. Well, if you want to see something cool, come with me." Hill runs towards the dense part of the woods. "What is it!" I shout with excitement. "Trust me!" She calls back. "You're going to want to see this!" I was already running late due to our sword fight, but in no way was going home now an option. "Wait up!" I yell. With a wooden sword still in the back of my shirt, I run towards Hill and the dark green woods ahead.

THE BONES OF OLD LADY MORA

Hill and I climb up and under fallen trees in thick greenery such as thorns, vines, and ivory. An old wooden fence is seen through more

58

foliage in the distance. I take out the wooden sword from my shirt and whack at thorns and tall weeds to make a path. "This is the end, you know?" I tell Hill, who's now behind me. "That fence leads to the road," I add. "Who told you that, JEB?" She says sarcastically as she takes off towards the fence. I stick the wooden sword back in my shirt and run with her. We climb the backside of the fence and peek over. "Wow!" I say out loud with wonder in my eyes.

It was an old mansion. The yard was covered in more vegetation, and the driveway was dirt. Random junk sat in the yard, such as old water heaters, steel car frames, brick piles, etc. The yard was hidden by trees. Eerie, crooked oak trees surrounded the old mansion, and the far front yard stretched out to a wired fence and then a road. The mansion was two stories plus a decrepit attic at the top. The roof was riddled with different layers of ugly brown and green shingles and black tar. The siding was mostly old, exposed wood with some choppy gray paint. Most windows were boarded up, but a few remained intact. The mansion looked as if it had been abandoned for decades.

Hill jumps down, walks over to a hole in the fence, and climbs through. I look through the hole, which consists of a small passageway created by an outer garage wall and an old metal drum with holes in it. We crawl through spider webs, rollie pollies, and black crickets to the other side. We stand up and walk through a side door to the garage, exploring closets and picking up rusty objects as we go. "Is this what you wanted to show me," I ask as we walk across the backyard. "What I want to show you is inside," Hill says with a smirk. "What is this place?" I ask. "It used to be an old hospital a long time ago, but there was a fire, and like 100 people died. "Wow, really!? That's crazy," I say as we wrap around to the side yard, and I gaze up at the old mansion.

The afternoon sun beats down as overcast rolls over the mansion. A crow yells out before flying off an attic window. "This is nothing." Says Hill as she comes to a stop. "See that window?" Asks Hill as she points to the second floor. I nod. "That's the window of Old Lady Mora" I slowly look at Hill, "Who?" "The lady of the mansion." Hill interrupts. "She moved in after the fire and fixed the place up. She never got married. The Mansion was all she had. Except..." Hill pauses. "Except what!?" I yell. "No one has ever found her body." She tells me. "Well, how do they know she's dead?" I shout. "They figured she had finally left the old mansion never to be seen again but other people say that she would have never left.

Not for no reason in the world. Kids my sister knew broke in once, and guess what? They found her!" Hill darts to a basement window. She reaches through a hole in the glass and unlatches it. "I don't know if I want to see a dead body!" I call out as I catch up. "Don't be a wussy; she's all bones now anyway," Hill assures me. "OK, go ahead." She says. "ME! I'm not going myself," I shout. "Someone has to open the basement door." She replies "Why can't you go?" I ask. "I'm too big," she tells me. "Fine," I say as I leave my wooden sword and climb through the basement window. I hang and drop to the floor. The widow barely lights up the room as I look to the doorway to the rest of the dark basement. A foul breath is heard in the pitch black beyond the entrance to the next room. "Miiiiike." It whispers. "Help me up!" I scream as Hill drops my sword. It hits the pavement floor and cracks the loudest echo of all time. "You'll be fine. Just go." Hill says and takes off. *I'm completely terrified, being alone in the dark was my biggest fear.* Now with the fresh story of Lady Mora on my mind, I stand like a statue in the dark basement of the old, abandoned mansion. I bend down and pick up my sword. With no other way out, I feel a shot of adrenaline run through my body, and I take off into the darkness.

Hill heads down the cellar stairs and waits for me at the door. A clatter is heard as something falls from inside. I let out a yell, and Hill starts to laugh. After what felt like an hour, I reach the door and unlock it for Hill. She enters with a smile and pulls some cobwebs off my face. "Let's go, handsome," She says, out of character. We walk up the stairway with no flashlight to explore the dark basement. The large wooden stairway circled up to the attic of the mansion. What used to be an open doorway was now a large wooden door. "Damn-it!" Yells Hill as she turns the handle, "It's locked!" We both look up to the second floor. Without saying a word, we make our way only to find another locked door. "Well, that sucks." She adds. "Hill, look!" I say as I point to the attic, "No door." I head up first. "It doesn't matter now." Says Hill as we reach the attic. "There's no way in from there." The sun shined through a large attic window which lit the decaying room. "She's really there, ya know?" says Hill." With a disappointed face. "I believe you," I tell her. At this point, even I was disappointed. *Telling my friends at school that I found the skeleton of Old Lady Mora would have been legendary.* Through a broken window, a car is heard. "Get down!" Yells Hill as we hit the floor. I quickly crawl to her and lay beside. "Who the hell is that?" I whisper loudly. She puts her finger to her mouth. As the car door opens, we hear low voices. "It might be the cops!" Hill whispers as we cower together on the floor. "Or drug dealers!" She adds. At this point, I didn't know who I was rooting for. "At least drug dealers would just kill us." I think as I imagined the punishment my parents would give me if I was picked up by the police. As we try to listen to what they are saying, the car door closes, and they drive away. Hill and I sigh simultaneously. We stand up and look out the window, but the car is long gone. Hill nods to the steps, and off we go. As Hill and I run into the woods, I look back, knowing full-well that the mansion hadn't seen the last of us.

TICS ELEVENTH HOUR

An old lady with white curly hair writes math problems on the chalkboard. I sit in the back of the class with Jeb. The door opens, and Mason walks in with a teacher. "Hello, Mrs. Cross." Says Mason's teacher. "I have a young man who will be joining this class next year, and I just wanted to introduce him." Jeb and I look at each other with excitement and shake our fists.

As I doodle on some paper, a figure approaches me from behind, as if from a dark corner of the classroom. It's a creature of sorts. It's about the height of a 7-year-old with a potbelly and skinny limbs. It has gray, wet ugly skin with patches of brown hair scattered across its body. It's bald with beady black eyes and a long crooked nose. No lips, really, just a mouth. It wears nothing but a tight red shirt with black letters that read "TIC." It leans over my left shoulder. I ignore it as if I've seen it before. "SMASH IT!" It says as I continue to draw. "Smash it!" It says again as saliva falls from the sides of its brown teeth. "NO!" I say quietly. Tic gets closer. "What did you just say to me?" He says, "Listen here, you little shit, I own you! You do what I tell you to do. Now, take your chin and smash it on that fucking desk!" A loud bang is heard, and the entire class is startled as they turn around and look at me. "Can I go to the nurse?" I say as I hold my bloody mouth. "Of course." Says Mrs. Cross. I hold my chin and mouth as I walk out of the classroom. All I can think of is the red door in the black cave. I hadn't known for sure what opened it. Not until today.

A long stretch of road as far as the eye can see. Farmland on either side. A rodeo sits behind a statue of a giant bison and lumberjack holding an ax. Our maroon station wagon flies by. It's the only car on the road. Inside the car, Dad drives, and Mom sits as his passenger. Mom looks to the back seat. "They're both asleep. Is this about halfway?" Mom asks. "Not yet." Dad answers. "I hope this one's worth it." Mom adds as she looks at the cowboy statue. "It's the best hospital in the world, hun. If anyone can help, it's these guys." Dad replies. "I hope so." Mom answers.

Dad and Mom sit behind a glass window in a doctor's office. Their voices are not heard as they explain their situation to a doctor with short curly light brown hair. The doctor smiles, nods, and answers them. Mom smiles with a huge sigh of relief as she hugs Dad, who smiles back. My feet tap next to Sis. "Michael, they're ready for you." Says a pretty Secretary. I place the walkman in Sis's lap. She puts on the headphones and nods to the metal song that pumps through. A door opens, and I enter the room with my parents and the new doctor. "Hey, honey," Mom says. "Well, hello there, Mike." Says the doctor as I sit with my parents. "So, your parents tell me you've had a rough couple of months recently." He says. I only nod. "Mike, the doctor says he thinks he can help," Mom explains. "Yeah, man!" Dad adds. "He's helping other kids with the same symptoms," Mom says with a smile. "It's true, Mike." Says the doctor. "I do believe we have the answers you guys are looking for. More importantly, we can start helping you feel better. I look up with a fat lip, busted chin, red nose, and dark circles under my eyes. I look at my parents and then the doctor before finally smiling.

On the way home, I sit in the back seat with my headphones on. Mom and Dad chat in the front with a smile. I can't hear them over the music, but it doesn't matter. They were happy with the doctor's proposals, and so was I. I couldn't wait to be the old me once again. Like the doctors, tic had made me a few promises himself. Unlike the doctors, TIC wasn't as enthusiastic about my future. Until then, I stare out the window and turn up "Master of Puppets" on my Walkman.

CHAPTER 3 — GUINEA PIG

A wing in a hospital is dark and empty. On each side of the
hallway is a door with a small square glass window. The bathroom door is
open. Its flickering light reveals the walls covered in smeared feces. The
toilet and floor display more of the same. Banging is heard from the only
other lit room. It's a boy around eight. He starts to yell as he pounds the
small window with his fists. "HEY! Let me outta here!" He screams. A
stream of urine runs under a door and towards a barefoot that is quickly
moved to avoid contact. "Ah!" I shout with a look of disgust. I look back

out the small window at the boy in room three. "Let me out! You mother fuckers."

Someone approaches me from behind as I watch the boy yell. A hand reaches out and grabs me by the shoulder. "Hey, I'm Chris. What's your name?" He says after startling me. "Where are we?" He asks. "Go back to bed, Chris," I tell him. Chris walks to his bed and lays down. He wears a hospital gown that matches mine. "Is this a slumber party?" He asks. The mad boy starts to slam his face against the window as he screams. Blood and mucus smear as two orderlies run in and frantically try to unlock Mad Boy's room with their keys. "I want to go home." Say Chris with a change in attitude. Mad Boy's door opens, and he falls to the floor, swinging his fists as the attendants try to restrain him. "I'll kill you fuckers. AHHHH!" He yells through the hospital wing. "I know, Chris," I say out loud. "You're not alone."

THE YOUNG HAGLER

Two months earlier. The tree fort is finally finished. It's a sunny day, birds chirp, and greenery flows in the light wind. The tree fort is a cube with a roof that sticks over the front and tilts to the back. It sits between three cedar trees. All three stick ten feet or so above the structure's roof.

The fort hovers eight or nine feet above the ground. It has a small window on the left and a three-foot-high cut-out for the door. Each side has a small window, and the back has a long rectangle window from wall to wall. Screens are stapled in all four holes cut out for windows. The plywood is light brown. *It's a masterpiece.*

A red skateboard wheel spins on bumpy pavement. Jeb rides his paperboy bike. The bike's basket holds a lantern, some frail extension cords, and an old wooden pulley with a large rusty hook. I hold the bike seat as Jeb tows me on my skateboard. "YARD SALE!" Jeb yells, and we turn down a street.

As we rummage through stuff at the yard sale, Jeb comes across an old wooden coffee table. It's fairly small and the shape of an octagon. It has a door to store belongings inside. "Mike, check it out!" "Wow, that's sweet," I say. "Damn, it's ten bucks. We won't be able to get the other stuff." I point to the pile of stuff by the bike, consisting of a dartboard, bamboo shades, and a pink rolled-up camping mat. "Hmm," Jeb says as he rubs his chin. "No, we need it." A man with a money belt walks by. I turn and pick up something random while Jeb messes with the coffee table door. "Hey guys, can I help you with anything?" The man asks. "Hey." Jeb points at the man. "Phil." The man says. "Phil! How we doing, Phil?" Jeb asks. "You see, me and my best friend here were looking at this old thing, but ten bucks!? I mean, I know there's a lot of suckers out there, but, come on." Amused by the young haggler, the man plays along. "What do you think it's worth?" "Well, if we even have room in our tree fort, we still would have to get it there, find a way to get it up, so, two bucks?" Two dollars!" Phill complains. "Do you know how much I paid for that thing? Besides, all that other mumbo jumbo isn't my problem. How far do you guys live?" "Eastfield." Says Jeb. "Eastfield. That's not too far. I'll tell you what, five bucks, and I'll even drop it off at your doorstep." "Three!" Jeb yells. "Phil looks at the two of us, who are now looking at him with anticipation. "A tree fort, huh?"

It's a little after noon, and Mom sits on her porch reading a book. A white truck slows down and pulls into my driveway. Jeb and I sit in the truck bed laughing. Looking concerned, Mom jumps to her feet. "Hey, Mom!" "Hey Mrs. D!" Jeb shouts. "Hey, mam, these guys drive a hard bargain," Phil says. Mom smiles and waves. "Ok, it's in the back, so…"

barked Jeb. "No, no," Phil says, interrupting Jeb. "I said the doorstep."

"Alright." Jeb accepts as he hands Phil the three dollars. We take Jeb's

bike, the table, and the other items out of the truck. "What do you guys

say?" Mom yells politely. "Thank you!" Shouts Jeb and I. "Ok, guys.

Have a nice day, mam." Phil says with a wave.

Phil drives off, and Jeb and I grab some stuff from the pile and run

towards the back. "Mike! Come over here." Mom demands. I put my head

down and walk towards my mother. "What have I told you? You don't

get in strangers' cars." "Mom, he was a nice guy." I interrupt. "I'm sure he

was, but you do understand?" "Yeah," I tell her.

The wooden pulley, which looks like it came straight off a pirate

ship, is hooked on a high branch above the tree fort. Jeb and I pull a rope

from the ground. The rope runs up and through the pulley, holding the

coffee table. "PULL!" We shout. The table falls out of the rope and hits

the ground as we fly back and fall to the ground. "No! So close." We

shout before reloading and trying again.

MY FAVORITE DETENTION

On a chalkboard in big bubble letters reads "Welcome to Second Grade." Beneath the sign reads "Mrs. Bird." The class talks among themselves as Mason Tepper cautiously opens the bottom drawer of the teacher's desk. He reaches in his lunch bag and pulls out a bologna sub. He takes out the hefty layer of meat and puts it in the drawer along with a handful of raw onions. Jeb smacks the desk and laughs as we watch. The door opens, and Tepper runs to his seat. A young lady walks in with short blond hair. She drops paper and pens to the floor. The cute redheaded girl from church puts her hands to her mouth and tries not to laugh as the rest of the class giggles.

"Shoot! Oh, hello, class." She puts her briefcase and papers down before standing up straight and addressing the class. "Hello class, my name is Mrs. Bird." "Hi, Mrs. Bird." We all shout with no prompt necessary. "I'll be your teacher this year. It's nice to finally meet you all, and I'm looking forward to getting to know everyone. I know most of you already know one and another, but I have not yet had the pleasure, so I'd like you all to tell me your names and something you did this summer. Let's start with row one. Go ahead, hun." "My name is Delilah, and this summer, I went camping with my grandpa." "Well, it's very nice to meet you, Delilah. I used to go camping with my grandpa when I was a little girl." "My grandpa smells like BOLOGNA!" I shout. The classroom fills with laughter. "Ok class, that's enough." Yells Mrs. Bird. "Young man, there will be no calling out in my class. As you can see on the class rules." Mrs. Bird grabs a wooden pointer and turns to point to the rules on the side of the board. As she does so, a ball of tin foil flies through the air and bounces off the chalkboard, barely missing her face. "HEY, who!? YOU! Principal's office now!" Yells the teacher. I sigh, get up and walk out of the room. "And you can forget about recess." She adds.

I sit on a bench in the principal's office with a look of disappointment as my classmates enjoy recess out the window behind me. The redhead girl in class walks in and jumps up on the bench next to me. "Hey, Lacey," I say out loud. Lacey scoots towards me and sticks her hand in mine. "What are ya doing?" I ask. "You're holding my hand, silly." She says as a roar of laughter and screams are heard from outside. "What'd you do?" I ask. "I got gum in my hair." She tells me. "Gum!? How'd you get in trouble for that?" I ask. "I don't know." Says Lacey. "You didn't throw the foil, did you." "No," I answer. "That's good," Lacey tells me. "But you didn't tattle neither. That's good too. Hey, Mike?" She says after a brief pause. "Yeah, Lace?" I say while looking at her pretty face filled with freckles. "Why do you always do this?" Lacey does a funny-looking impression of my eye tic. It catches me off guard but makes me laugh. "I don't know," I say honestly as Lacey scoots closer and puts her head on my shoulder. Another roar is heard from outside, but this time I'm not disappointed.

Sis and I sit in the back seat of their station wagon as Dad drives while Mom fails to fall asleep. As we pass the giant bison and lumberjack, Sis looks out the window. I throw the Gameboy down and grab the Walkman from Sis. "Hey!" She yells. "I'm not done, stop!" "Give it to me!" "Hey, cut it out!" Mom interrupts. I grab my pillow and punch it before slamming my face in it. Sis takes off the headphones and hands them to me. "Here, I'm done listening to it anyway," Sis says. "Thanks, you want the Gameboy?" I ask. "No thanks, I'll play it later," Sis tells me. To the hospital and back was a six-hour drive every two weeks. And on top of that, I had to see the doctor.

Now home, I sit up with my back against a light brown wooden bedpost. The Bulletin Board to the left is filled with Ghostbusters, Ninja

Turtles, Star Wars, Baseball Card, Garbage Pail Kids, and other random stuff from my childhood. I press the play button on the recorder that I had secretly left under my Phillies baseball cap in Dr. Dickheads office. I picked up a black leather whip coiled around my bedpost with my right hand. I hit play on the recorder. "Well, I'm glad the medicine seems to be working." Says the doctor. I whip a row of green army men off my dresser as I listen to the doctor's voice. "We'll keep the dose as is for now, and in the meantime, I'd like to concentrate on Mike's behavior. I feel sometimes they go hand in hand. I sit up and throw the recorder in my hamper. "Asshole!" I yell as I leave the room.

The sunlight shines through the windows of the tree fort. Inside were two bunk beds made from 2x4s and plywood. A pink camping mat lies on the top bunk with a pillow and a rolled-up red sleeping bag. The bottom bunk has a blue sleeping bag and pillow. On the floor is a gold rug that frays at all ends. It's cut into a square that barely fits on the floor. Bean bags cover the sides of the walls and floor. On top of the table sits a green kerosene lantern and a small portable black and white TV/Radio with a long silver antenna. The dartboard hangs on the wall adjacent to the bunks. Darts and pocketknives stick in random 2x4s, and a felt Guns N'

Roses poster of a skull with a top hat is displayed below the dartboard. On the ceiling, closer to the bunks, is a dark poster of the Ninja Turtles, all wearing red headbands. The bamboo shades hang on the back wall covering the rear screen window that holds back bushy cedar branches. The window views the neighbor's large double lot yard and white two-story house through the window. Last is a deck about three and a half feet wide and roughly five feet long with tall 4x4s at the far end that led to the ground. The balcony had railings and an old wooden ladder between the posts. Laughter and chatter are heard, getting louder as the fort starts to sway. Night has fallen.

The lantern lights the faces of Sis, Jeb, Hill, and I as we sit among the bean bags on the floor of the tree fort. A book of scary stories lays on the floor next to a deck of cards and a Ouija board. I finish up a story and leap forward as everyone jumps and laughs. "They were stupid." Hill laughs. "Ok, my turn!" Jeb states. "No, Hills next," I add fairly. "I'm not going." Says Hill. "Come on! Tell the one about VICTOR!" I shout. "Yea, Hill, tell it!" Says Sis. "Fine," Hill mutters. The following day I wake on the top bunk. I open my eyes and look to my side. Jeb stands an inch from my face with a smile on his own. "It's time." He says.

THE OLD MANSION

As Jeb sarcastically rants about a hole in his underwear, I open a zipper to my blue backpack and shove in what we need. We walk down my street in shorts and a t-shirt on this warm October day. Halloween decorations are displayed from each house on the street. "So, what you going to be for Halloween?" Jeb asks. "I…" "No, let me guess." "Peter Venkman." Jeb mocks in a whiny voice. "No! I'm going as a Zombie Peter Venkman!" I say with confidence. "That's a good idea!" Jeb states, smacking my arm. "How about you?" I ask. "Zombie," Jeb says casually. "Nice," I add as we duck into some tall weeds. An old man in suspenders chops wood in his backyard that hasn't changed since the 50s. Jeb and I peek around the side of his house. As the old man bends down to pick up a log, we make our move. The old man looks in our direction before going back to axing. We crawl through weeds before running into the woods. We make it to the fallen trees, where I hear a growl. I throw my arm in front of Jeb as I notice something in the distance. We dash behind a tree and peek out with a nervous look on our faces. In the distance are two dogs wrestling by a clearing in the woods. Both are medium size black mutts. A third dog lies under a holly tree and chews on what looks like a stick. It's larger than the others with dirty brown fur. "Holy crap! Where'd they come from?" Asks Jeb, "You think they're mean?" "I've seen them before!" I Shout quietly as I recognize the strays. "They go after me and Sis' rabbits, all barking and growling." "We got to go back!" Jeb yells. "Go back!?" I interrupt. "It's twice as far! We just gotta make it to the fence. I got an idea." I take off my backpack and pull out a bag of beef jerky. Jeb grabs for it immediately. "No! Not the jerky!" "Come on, man, let go!" I whisper as we play tug of war. "Fine! I hope they eat you first!" I say as Jeb shoves the Jerky in his back pocket. I unzip my backpack and get what we need. I put sip-ups in my back pockets and hand Jeb the flashlight. A Swiss Army Knife goes to Jeb, and the Buck pocketknife comes with me. I hang the backpack on a broken branch. "On three," I tell Jeb, "One…" "THREE!" Jeb yells, interrupting.

We take off running full speed for the fence. The dogs shred through the woods as their barks get closer. "Ahhhh! Where going to die!" Screams Jeb as we get close to the fence. "Stupid beef, JERKY!" I add to the screams. Jeb and I scurry up the back of the old wooden fence and fall hard to the grass and dirt on the other side. Both in pain from the fall, we gasp for air. I hop up fast and run to a rusty metal barrel. "Jeb, HELP!" I yell as I struggle to push the barrel over to block the hole in the fence. Jeb runs to me with a scream. Our feet slide in the dirt as the barks get closer. The barrel finally rolls over some debris and slams into the fence, covering the hole. The dogs scratch at the fence as Jeb, and I sit against the barrel to catch our breath. "That was close!" we say while giving a high-five. "Give me a sip-up," Jeb says as I check my pocket. "Damn!" "I dropped them," I tell him. "Great," he replies as we get up.

With clouds in the sky, we walk towards the old mansion. By now, I've told Jeb about the bones of Old Lady Mora, so his excitement matches my own. Our plan was to search the entire mansion until we had confirmation of the legend, and what we found that day was just that.

"Wait, Look!" Yells Jeb. "Nope, Not falling for it." I tell him, avoiding the "Made you look." "It's a girl!" He adds. With little hesitation, I look in the direction Jeb is pointing. On the side of the yard was a fence made of wood that ran the length of the property. Standing a few feet away is a girl. She stands in a small grass clearing and stares directly at the old mansion. She wears a long faded blue robe that is covered with yellow stars. She has long brown hair, glasses, pudgy red cheeks, and holds a tall

wooden staff with a crystal ball at the top. She looks the same age as us.

Crickets and birds chirp in the grass as the sun shines down upon

her. "Whoa, what's she doing?" I say out loud. "I don't know," Jeb says as

he walks away. "Where are you going?" I ask. "To say hi!" Jeb states.

"Helloooo!" Jeb waves his hands as we approach the mysterious girl. She

eventually turns her head away from the mansion and smiles at us. "Well,

hello there." She says before looking back at the mansion. Confused, Jeb

and I look at each other as I shrug my shoulders. "Oh my, how rude of

me." She gasps. "Would you boys care for a beverage?"

Jeb and I nonchalantly look at our surroundings of overgrowth and

rubbish as we digest her question. "Sure," I tell her skeptically.

"Wonderful!" "Follow me." She says politely. She turns around and walks

towards an old, dried-up, cement birdbath by the fence. She used the staff

with the crystal ball as a walking stick. Jeb leans towards me and says, "If

she turns that birdbath to water, I'm gonna shit!" She passes the birdbath,

leans her staff on the fence, and lifts up a plank. We sigh with relief and

head towards the fence.

We now walk through a long narrow yard filled with old twigs and acorns. Wind chimes and other decorations hang from the trees that line both sides of the yard. Jeb and I study them as we follow behind our new strange friend. "What's with the robe?" Jeb whispers. "I don't know; maybe she's just excited for Halloween," I answer. "Well, she's a little early!" Jeb says loudly. "SHH!" I say with an elbow. "Hey, you never told us your name," I shout politely. "How silly of me. I'm Jessica. But you can call me Jess if you'd like." "That's cool. I'm Jeb. This is Mike." "Hello Jeb and Mike, it's very nice to meet you. You go to school around here?" I ask. "No, I'm home-schooled." She replies. "That explains everything," Jeb whispers loudly. We reach the back porch of a white two-story house riddled with more twigs and acorns. Jess grabs a plastic jug off of a glass picnic table. She pores two cups of homemade lemonade and Jeb, and I chug it down. "Thanks," I say as I wipe my mouth. "More please!" Jeb yells. "Wow, you guys must have been thirsty," Jess says as she fills Jeb's cup once more. "So, what were you guys up to over there?" "We're trying to find a way in the mansion," I answer. "A way in? Wow, I never thought about going in." "You want to come?" Jeb asks. I give him a look as he chugs his second helping. "Sure! I better change, though, be right back."

"Yea," Jeb mutters as she goes into the house, "you don't want to mess up your robe." "What'd you ask her that for? She can't come!" I complain. "Why not?" Jeb asks. "I don't know. She's a girl." I whisper. "So is Hill!" Jeb argues, making a good point. "Yeah, but..." I had nothing. Jess comes out her back door without her robe. She has on a white long sleeve t-shirt tucked into baggie blue jeans. "Ok, ready!" Jess shouts and runs off the back porch.

"Your house is pretty big. Do you live there yourself?" I ask as we make our way through the mansion yard. "No," Jess laughs. "I live with my mom and little sister." "What about your dad?" I ask. "My dad drives a big truck all around the country. He comes home once in a while with presents, but that's about it." As we come close to the basement stairs, we hear a clatter of debris and head towards the far side of the garage. "It's Tepper!" Mason Tepper pokes through some rubble with a stick. He finds the bottom of an old beer can filled with cement. He picks it up and tosses it through a window of the garage. "Hey, Tepper!" I say. "Yo." He answers. "Where's your brother?" Jeb asks. "Foots broke." He mutters. "Damn, that stinks." Jeb says as he looks over at Jess and adds, "This is our new friend Jess." "Hello, Mason." She says with a smile. "Hey." nods

Mason. "Yo Mike, your sister's here." He mentions. "What!" I yell. "She's at the glass garden." He adds. "I knew I shouldn't have told her!" I mutter.

Sis and her friend dig small holes in the ruins of an old garden house that sits on the far side of the yard. Freshly picked flowers lay beside them. Me and the others approach. "Sis! What are you doing here!?" I ask. "We're gardening," Sis tells me. "How'd you get past the dogs?" "What dogs?" She interrupts. "We came in that way." Sis points out past the front yard of the mansion. "Are you crazy!" I shout. "You can't go in that way; someone will see," I add as Jeb addresses Sis's friend. "Oh, hey, OATMEAL!" "Shut up, Jeb!" Shouts Oatmeal. "Her name is Christy!" Sis adds to her friends' defense. *Jeb is referring to last summer when Christy got to the end of a box of oatmeal cookies before Jeb, and I could taste but one. He's never been the same.* "Hello there," Jess says, breaking the tension. "Hey, want to garden with us?" Sis asks. "She's not here to garden," I tell her. "Come on guys."

The crew heads to the backyard, and Sis and Christy follow. I reach my hand through the broken basement window and hold it open, "Ok, Sis." "ME!? I'm not going down in there!" Sis yells. "Someone has to unlock the door," I reply. "Then you go!" She interrupts. "I'm too big!" I fib as the others turn and head to the stairwell. Jeb and I lower Sis by her arms, and she drops to the floor. As she looks into the darkness of the next room, she hears a foul breath. "Siiiis." Sis looks up with frightened eyes and shakes her head. "You'll be fine." We shout. Sis takes a breath and takes off through the darkness.

After congratulating Sis, we all head to the basement's main room. I reach into my pocket and grab a small domino-shaped keychain flashlight. I squeeze it in the center for light and find my way to a window. I ask Jeb and Mason for help. The now cloudy skies shine through as we pull the plywood from the window. An old pool table and a vintage record player are among the old debris. A dance floor sits a foot higher than the cement floor, displaying an old rug that had seen better days. A cloud of dust explodes as Tepper crashes the Q ball into the remaining balls on the pool table. Jeb joins Mason's simple game. The girls mess with the old record player as I jam a credit card in between the wall and door leading to the mansion's first floor. The card breaks. I take out my pocket knife and again stick it in the door's crack, shaking it impatiently. The girls spin the record as it's scratched by the needle. "Don't play it backward." Jeb whispers. My frustration fades to laughter as Jeb quotes our favorite horror movie.

Jess finds an old book with a faded picture of a dragon on the front. She blows off the dust and opens it. "Hey, I can't hear the music! Turn it up!" Shouts Tepper. Sis turns a knob on the stereo, and the young crowd starts to headbang to silence. "BREAKDANCE!" Jeb yells as he jumps up on the dance floor. A loud clang is heard. "You broke the floor, Jeb!" "Shut up, Oatmeal!" "Did you guys hear that?" I shout as I walk over to the dance floor and look under it with Tepper. He grabs my flashlight and fishes with his other hand. "It's a jewelry box!" Yells Christy. Tepper puts it on the pool table, and everyone gathers around. I slide the blade of my pocketknife through the closed lid and jiggle it until it pops open.

The box is filled with old coins, American and foreign. "We're rich!" Jeb yells as we celebrate. "There's like a hundred bucks in that!" Says Tepper. We pour it out on the pool table and look through it. "That's an Asian coin," Jess says. "My adopted sister has some." "That's so cool!" Sis adds. "Wait, look, KEYS!" I shout as Tepper grabs one and runs up some steps to the door that I had failed to open. Jeb and I pick out the rest of the keys and meet Tepper at the door. As we hand Tepper keys, he throws them over his shoulder with each dud. "We might need them, dude!" I say as keys bounce into the darkness. "We'll get them!" The girls shout as Cristy gets hit by one. "AH HAA!" Jeb laughs. "SHUT UP, JEB!" They interrupt. The quarrel is interrupted by the sound of the door unlocking. Everyone freezes. Tepper throws the last key over his shoulder as I turn the handle.

The creek echoes through the mansion as the door slowly opens. The stale air is heard throughout the mansion's halls as the young adventurers set foot into the main hall. Every movement echoes as we begin to explore. The mansion is more empty than full. Some chairs, bed frames, tables, and other random objects remain. We move into the first room off the hallway. The walls are covered in glass mirrors, revealing torn stickers from the 70s, such as flowers and magic school buses. The floor was a shaggy maroon rug, dirty and ripped.

After the mirror room, we split up into groups, checking drawers and closets. A trunk had been left in the downstairs bedroom. We pull out random treasures left in the mansion, such as scarves, knives, an umbrella, gun holsters, old teapots, and random antiques. Tepper and I throw fallen crystals at a chandelier that hangs in the main living room.

We all meet in the kitchen. This was the perfect time to tell the tale of Lady Mora; however, I feared that it might scare away my companions. This was not an option because I knew there was no way I was going up to Lady Mora's room alone. "Are you guys ready for the upstairs?" I ask as I turn the dry faucets from the sink. "I think I'm comfortable with staying down here for now," Jess explains. Sis and Christy nod. "Yea, I'm not done down here," Jeb adds while looking up the dark stairway. "I'll go," Tepper says. The room grows quiet as Tepper and I climb the staircase to the second floor. The stairs went up to a landing and wrapped around to another flight of steps. "How about Jeb? I guess he was scared, huh?" I tell Tepper. "Ha, yeah," Mason adds as we reach the top of the stairs and look down the hallway. It is darker than the first floor.

"Ha, Yea," I say, now creeped out. We slowly make our way down the hall as I shine my flashlight on decrepit walls. We move into a bedroom and look around until I eventually find myself alone. "Tepper!" I shout with a whisper. I walk across the hallway to a second bedroom where Tepper stands in front of a large wooden closet with an old-style mirror. "Is this it!?" I wondered. "Is this HER room?" I try to navigate the window Hill had pointed to on our previous outing by memory but fail. "What is that?" I ask. "Just a closet, I think." Shrugs Mason Tepper. He puts out his hand, grabs the door handle, and turns. The mirror shakes on the left-hand side as he jiggles and pulls hard on the glass handle. I help Tepper pull on the nob as the mirror continues to shake. "On three." Says Tepper. "One, two, THREE!" The door flies open, and a naked person with long black hair plops halfway out. We fall to the floor, screaming as we grab each other's shirts. After a few moments, we calm down. Tepper stands up slowly and walks to the body. He puts his hand out and pokes it with his finger. "It's a dummy." He says as the black hair of the old manikin sways in the shadows. I stand up and slowly shine my flashlight across the large closet. One by one, more manikins' faces are revealed. Some with dirt or ash. As Mason Tepper and I stared into the closet, Hill's story finally became clear.

Whether or not Hill knew about the old manikin bones is a good question. If I was to bet my allowance on it, I'd bet she planned on scaring the shit out of me. I guess we'll never know. As we walk out of the room, we bump into the rest of the crew with a scream. "What are you guys doing up here?" I ask. "We heard you guys yelling." Jeb answers before

adding, "And there was this crazy animal downstairs! It was foaming by

the mouth and everything. It was gonna eat Oatmeal!" "It wasn't

foaming," Sis adds. Tepper and I explain our screams as we head down

the stairs.

We walk out the basement door and shield the sun from our eyes.

As we turn a corner of the mansion, flashing lights instantly catch our eye.

A cop car is parked in the dirt driveway with both doors open. "It's the

COPS!" Yells Tepper. "Holy SHIT! RUN!" We all shout as we scatter

away. The boys jump on the metal barrel to help boost us over the front

side of the fence. We land in the woods as Sis and Christy crawl through

the small hole in the fence that is now accessible. The six of us run off into

the woods as a cop is heard yelling after us.

Sis, Christy, Jeb, and I lean on an old brick chimney at the end of

the woods. We catch our breath. "That was close. Did the others get

away?" Sis asks. "I hope so," I say, "Where are you going?" "To Christy's

house," Sis answers as they walk away. "OK, don't you tell mom!"

"DUUUHHH!" Sis answers. Jeb leans off the chimney. "I'm starving."

"Me too, let's go to Mill's Market." "Hey, where's that bag of coins?" I ask. We check our pockets and speak at the same time. "Tepper!" "Oh wait, I put some in my shoe! 1, 2,3, $3.87." Jeb counts. "Oh, and this weird one." "Sweet! What's that weird one worth? I ask. "Hm?" Jeb thinks. "I'd say, about a bologna and cheese." The two of us laugh and exit the woods. We had found the bones of Lady Mora. Although synthetic, the adventure was solid.

GUINEA PIG

After another long drive, I find myself back in that god damn waiting room. Dr. Humphries talks to my parents. "He really did it this time." I think to myself. I wanted to kill him; however, I knew I was too afraid of hell to accomplish such a task, but at least I could dream. Today for the first time ever, I would not be joining my family on the way home. Instead, I would stay at this hospital for two whole weeks. The doctors had new meds they wanted to try out and guess who was the lucky fucking candidate. It was the hardest decision my parents had ever made. Tic was still hanging around, and he had gotten stronger.

I play matchbox cars on the floor of the waiting room. The kid I'm

playing with has blond hair. His name is Chris. He's short and a little

chubby. After talking a while, we became friends, and when asked by our

parents if we'd like to be roommates, we say yes. I put my backpack down

in an uncomfortable-looking room. The room has one glass window to the

outside with metal bars, a white tiled floor, white walls, and two white

beds. I chose the bed under the window. Chris enters through a white door

with a silver bent handle and a glass window. "Hey, man," I say as I hop

on the bed. "Hi. I'm Chris. What's your name?" He says with a smile and

his hand out. I pause for a moment and laugh, "Ha, You're a funny guy,

Chris." "Hey, how do you know my name!? Are you going to be my

roommate?" He asks. Now I'm angry. Mom turns from her conversation

with a doctor and sees me yelling at Chris through the window. "MIKE,

stop! Come here," Mom yells as she comes into the room. I follow her

outside the doorway.

"That kid's dumb as hell. I'm not staying with him!" I shout. "Chris

has a memory problem." She tells me. "No crap!" I interrupt as Mom

lightly grabs my arm. "He was hit by a bus." I look back at Mom as I

digest what she said. "What do you mean?" I ask. "He was crossing the street about a year ago and was hit. His memory comes and goes, so he might not remember you sometimes. Is that going to be ok for you?" She asks and I nod. "OK," Mom says, "I know you'll be a big help for him."

Chris watches as I hug Mom goodbye through the room window. Mom holds back her tears, and Dad gives me a smile and a handshake before leaving the room. Mom follows close behind. I walk into my room and jump up to sit on the bed and say, "Hey, sorry I yelled at you." "It's ok," Chris replies. "So, do you remember me now?" I say as Chris studies me and nods his head. "You're Mike, with the tree fort." I smile and shake my head. "So, did you bring a stuffed animal?" He asks, "They told me you could." "Pfff, No," I mutter. As Chris continues to talk. I slide my backpack under the bed with my foot while keeping an eye on Alex's puffy tail, which hangs out the zipper.

This isn't the first time I needed Alex to help me out of a jam.
"He'll be next to you the whole time." The doctors said as they cut out my perfectly working tonsils a year before. I distinctly remember opening my eyes to Alex's goofy face, so I will give the doctors that. But they are still pocket stuffing liars. I mean, wouldn't they check if they were swollen or some shit. "Oh, he coughs? Just take his fucking tonsils." *Anyway.*

"I hope other kids are nice," Chris says, "I wonder what they're all here for?" Chris had asked a good question, for up until this point, I figured I'd be surrounded by kids with Tourette's. "Let's go find out," I tell him. We leave the room and walk into the main hallway, chatting. An orderly in white clothes comes out of a room and interrupts us. "You two! In here NOW!" Chris and I are caught off guard, so we stand and do nothing. "Did I stutter!" He yells. We look at each other before entering the room. We now sit at a round table with five other kids around the same age. Some of the kids mumble quietly amongst themselves. A chart hangs on a chalkboard with the children's names and drawings of kids eating ice cream. They didn't look all that tough. I figured I'd have this place wrapped around my finger by tomorrow. A doctor enters, "OK, listen up. My name is Doctor Quinn. Now, you'll all be here together for a while, so we might as well get to know one another. Before we start the introduction, let me lay down some ground rules. First off, The Rule Board." The doctor picks up a marker and points to each one, "It's pretty self-explanatory. Do what we say when we say it. See those two big guys over there? Ashley and Stacy wave to our new friends." The two orderlies wave with mean faces. They were tall white guys with black hair and biker tattoos. "Yes, they have girl names but make no mistake, they will take you down effortlessly. For those of you who do not know the word effortlessly, I'll say it in words you will understand. They will DESTROY YOU. This chart you see is a reward chart, and It's very simple. If you get enough stars for behaving well, you get ice-cream after dinner. As you can see, you all have a number of stars already earned. These stars are up so we can take them away. The more stars you lose, the more rewards you lose, such as playground time and movie night. If you lose all your stars, well, let's just say you don't want to lose all your stars." Chris' eyes stay wide open as he listens to the doctor talk. "Now, we'll start one by one. Please state your name and a little bit about yourself. Ms. Bloom, would you kindly start us off." He finishes.

The only girl at the table stands up. She has long, coarse blond hair and looks like she's been around the block once or five times. "Hi, my name is Trish. I'm eight years old, and I'm here because I took a screwdriver, and I STABBED MY STEPDAD IN HIS FUCKING EYE!" She ends with a yell. My expression now matches Chris'. "Ok, Thank you, Ms. Bloom." Says Doctor Quinn. "Next, please." Chris looks at the Doctor in disbelief as my eyes stay on the young psycho. The next kid appeared to be Spanish and was the biggest kid in the room by far. He stands to his feet, "Hey, I'm Roberto. I'm seven years old, and I'm here for putting three 6th graders in the hospital." The next two kids stand and talk. Each story was more terrifying than the next, but even worse, I still had to talk. I had nothing. What was I going to say, "Hey, I'm Mike, and I have Tourette's." Even Chris had a better story than me; at least he got hit by a BUS! A small skinny kid stands next to me and speaks, "Hi, I'm Charlie, and I like cats." "Thank god." I think to myself.

"I like to pet them and hold them and see what they look like on the inside." Charlie continues. "Shit!" I say to myself as Norman Bates sits down. I eventually stand and look around the room. "Hey, I'm Mike and…I have Tourette's." I sit back down with a blank stare. Chris stands and looks around the room as if he was going to puke. As he talks, the orderlies begin to pass out dinner. The drawings of the kids eating ice cream slowly but surely begin turning into me and my new skittish friend, bloody and beaten.

I sit in a small bathroom with a sink. My shirt is off, and my clothes are in the corner of the room. *Yea, I poop naked, so what.* "Hey! Why you taking so long?" asked a female orderly. She's a middle-aged black woman that worked the night shift. "I'm going to the bathroom!" I shout. "You been in there for a while, Hun. What are you doing?" She adds. The one place I thought I could get some peace. I hear the jingling of keys. "I'm pooping!" I shout as she opens the door and barges in. She looks around to see if, in fact, I was only pooping. "Ok, Hun. Well, come on out when you're done." I nod.

It's night now as I walk into my darkroom. Chris is asleep. The orderly locks the door and walks away. After hearing the lock, I walk back and jiggle the handle. "Great." I think as I lie in bed and look at the ceiling. The light from the city reflects the raindrops from outside the window. The end of a shit day. At least now I could get some sleep and escape to a dream. I close my eyes. Moments later, I woke to Chris screaming. "Where am I?!" He shouts, "Help me!" I jump to his aid as Chris pulls on the locked door handle. "Chris! It's me!" I yell. I lightly shake Chris by the shoulders, and he starts to settle down." It's me, Mike. Remember?" Chris looks at me and nods, "Mike, with the tree fort." "Yeah, You alright? I ask. "Why? Why are the doors locked?!" He shouts. I put my arm around Chris and walk him to his bed. "Trust me, dude," I say with a smile. "If you could remember dinner, you'd be happy they are."

On a rainy rooftop of a building in the city sits a playground. It's surrounded by an impenetrable fence. Chris and I sit on a picnic table as the others play basketball. Charlie plays in the corner with his stuffed cat. The Orderlies' bullshit by the door that leads to the building. The basketball rolls to Chris. "Hey bitch, throw it back." A loud voice says. Chris goes to pick it up, but I stop him. Roberto walks up to us as I sigh and reluctantly stand up. "Hey, don't make me say it again," Roberto says as he walks up to Chris and gets in his face. I pick up the ball. The rain trickles on my wet face as I stand in front of Chris. "You know his name, Roberto," I say with my chin up. Roberto's mean and scary face slowly turns to me. We stare at one another for a moment. The others watch.

Roberto eventually jabs his hand out with his pointer finger and pokes me in the stomach. "Tickle tickle!" He says with his young deep voice. Startled, I drop the ball as Roberto's crew laughs. "YO, he's ticklish!" He shouts. "Tickle, Tickle! He continues to poke me in the stomach with his pointer finger as I try to block it. "Hey!" I shout. "YO Tickles, get Blondie. We need more people." He adds. "Tickles?" I think,

"Oh well, I guess it's better than Twitches". Roberto picks up the ball and heads back. I wave to Chris, and the six of us play ball in the rain.

That night we watch "E.T." in the movie room as Charlie pets his stuffed cat in the hallway. "Yo, what the hell is that?" Shouts Roberto as E.T. screams and runs through woods on the television. The others break out in laughter, but Chris only smiles. I look around in awe that they have never seen the movie. "YO, where's Charlie?" Asks one of the kids. "He's probably fucking that cat!" Yells Trish. We burst into hysterics except for Chris, who smiles nervously once again. "Yo, you hit Tickle's funny bone!" Roberto yells. It turned out the others had no interest in fighting Chris and me. They seemed to be more focused on the grownups.

The following day Roberto freaks out in the lunchroom as Ashley and Stacy try to restrain him. The other kids cheer as Roberto puts up a good fight. A few days later, Chris and I eat dinner in the dining room. "Well, Mr. Devaney, I see we haven't earned today." Says Dr. Quinn as he hands Chris an ice cream bar. I shrug it off as Chris chows down. The rest of my time there wasn't all that bad, that is until I met Dr. Williams.

GUARDIAN ANGEL

A pretty young Doctor sits with me in an office. "Wow, that sounds like a lot of fun." replies Dr. Williams. "Yea, it was cool," I add. "So, I've also heard you have a best friend named Jeb?" She says with a smile. "Could you tell me a little about him?" I think to myself as a random flashback of Jeb runs through my mind. I see him running towards me screaming, holding me underwater, sitting on my head, yelling, "Smoggle monster!" And a rare fist fight we shared in his backyard. "Yeah, he's my best friend," I say with a smile. "Oh, that's nice," She states. "So, Mike, do you ever have thoughts of causing Jeb harm?" She asks with a strange smile. "What do you mean?" I ask. "Well, Mike. Do you ever want to hurt Jeb?" I think for a moment before answering. "Yeah," I answer simply. "Really?" She replies, now concerned. "Definitely," I add. "Ok, well, can you tell me how often these feelings occur?" "Hmm," I think as I pinch my nose, "All the time." "Really." The doctor states.

Dr. Williams now sits with Dr. Quinn as he reads her report and says, "This can't be right. The boy's here for neurological reasons." "I'm telling you, Bill, he has a dark side." Dr. Williams tells him before adding,

"You should have heard what he was saying about this kid, Jeb." "Well, what do you want me to do, Liz?" Asks Dr. Quinn. "I have strict orders from Humphries, and to be honest, I think you might be overlooking this one. The kid seems harmless." Quinn adds. "Two Days Bill, that's all I need. I'll owe you!" Replies Dr. Williams. Quinn holds up two fingers. "Thanks, Bill!" She says with a smile.

That night I stare out of the bedroom window at the smeared feces and urine on the bathroom floor and walls. Chris holds his ears as the new kid screams and gets restrained. Ashley and Stacey put him back in the room with the bloody window he had smeared minutes earlier.

The next day Mom sits with Dr. Williams as she nicely explains to my mother that her only son is a deranged psycho and also explains the plans set in motion to cure me. I watch through a window from the hall. After hearing the doctor, Mom lunges forward and shoves her finger in the doctor's face while screaming with anger. Ashley and Stacy rush in and get between my mom and the doctor, who is now fearfully backed into a corner. My eyes grow wide as the two large men try to calm down my mother. Throughout my entire stay at the hospital, this was the only time I was genuinely terrified.

I clear my toys off the windowsill. Throwing a metal samurai sword keychain, small transformers toys, a small metal cap gun with a holster, and my small flashlight quickly into Alex's pouch before zipping him up in my backpack. I walk to Chris, who is lying on his bed. "What's his name?" Asks Chris, who is seeing my silly-looking friend for the first time. "Alex," I say with a smirk. "You really leaving?" Asks Chris. "Yeah, man, I gotta get outta here," I tell him. "Well, what am I supposed to do now when I wake up alone and don't know where I am?" Chris asks with a scared look on his face. I put my bag down, unzip it, and pull out the small flashlight keychain from Alex's pouch. I squeeze it on to check if it still works before handing it to Chris. "Maybe this can help," I say as Chris squeezes out the light. "Thanks. So, I guess this is goodbye." He says with his hand out, "Goodbye, Mike with the tree fort." "Goodbye, Chris with the Bus," I add with a smile. We share one last laugh before I leave the white room. I don't look back.

Jeb sits at a desk in his bedroom. In front of him is an old tape recorder. A breeze comes through an open window and taps the open blinds. "Well, that's it for sports. Let's go to Boner for the weather." Jeb says out loud into a microphone. "Thanks, Kyle, well, it's getting horny outside with a chance of vaginas and pee-pees. Here's Assface with your weekly update." Jeb puts his mouth in the palm of his hands and makes a loud fart noise. There's a knock at his bedroom door. "I'M BUSY!" He shouts. He starts the fart again until the second knock. "I'm making a tape for Mike. Tyler, cut it out!" The third knock interrupts Jeb for the last time. Now mad, Jeb gets up and grabs his homemade Bo Staff made from a sanded broomstick with tape wrapped in the middle for grip. He stomps to the door. "I told you to...!" Jeb swings the door open, and I smile and yell. Jeb's anger fades, and he joins me in yelling as we exchange rapid hi-fives. "Your home early! What happened?" Jeb says with a big smile. "I don't know!" I answer, "My mom freaked out on this lady, and we just left." "Your mom!? Damn, so how was it?" He adds. "It sucked ass. They put me in this weird room. It was like pitch black. And this sexy lady doctor did all these weird studies on me." I tell him. "Did she study your wiener?!" Jeb asks. After laughing, we walk out the doorway and towards the stairs. I shake my head, "No, but she hooked me up to this weird thing that helps with anger or some crap." "What'd she do that for?!" Jeb shouts. "Who knows, I'm just glad I'm home," I tell him. "Man, you must have a guardian angel!" Jeb tells me as he grabs his door handle. The door slams shut, and we run down the steps and outside to the sun.

OLDEST PARTNER IN CRIME

Christmas lights hang from my front porch. The different colors stand out on this windy day. As my dad packs the back of the wagon, the rest of the family comes out the front door and he yells, "Let's go, guys, Nan's waiting." Mom has one brother and three sisters, whereas my dad has one sister and three brothers. Both are the second oldest. Mom's side liked to go out to fancy restaurants and things of that nature, minus my Uncle Pete, who would happily dine with a possum. Also, we were rarely ever together at one time. When we did see each other strangely, it would always feel like little time had passed.

Dad's side of the family would cram into a smallish house in North Jersey. We never went out to dinner. We all just hung out at Nan's every time we went up to visit. Gene, Casey, Ryan, Michelle, and Chris, who, although the youngest cousin, is now six foot two inches tall, which for Irish folks it's fucking huge. We'd play video games, read stories and just

103

chill as everyone there got along fine. I swear, I can't remember a single argument between any of us in all our years. Once in a while, relaxing was a nice change-up.

"I found a dirty magazine," Matt says as he holds a lit lighter to the wooden beach steps where we hid from the hot sun. "Really!? Where?" I ask. "In the woods, by the parkway." Matt answers, "It's far, so we'll need our bikes." "Awesome!" I yell while eating my water ice, bottom side up. Aunt May and Mom talk close to the water. "Mike's repeating 2nd grade," Mom says. "How's he taking it?" Asks May. "As you would expect." Mom answers. Matt and I grab our Boogie Boards and head toward the water. "MATT, Get over here!" Yells May, "Now Matt, Aunt Clair is going to take you kids to Mikey's house to swim in the pool, then grandma and pops. Our reservations are at 6:30, so you two better be back by then, you understand? I'm not kidding, Matt 6:30, GOT IT!?" "Yes." We answer. "Good, now go." She adds as we run into the water.

Aunt May looks at a clock that reads 6:20. It hangs on the wall at Grandma and Pops. "I'm going to kill them." She says as she sips her white wine. My Grandpa D passed when I was three. I remember sitting on his knee with Sis as he told us the story of Jack and the Beanstalk.

Besides that, the only old-timer I really had interactions with was Pop. He was a self-righteous man. Stubborn, as most old-timers were. If you did something he thought was wrong, he'd get down on one knee, put his hand on your shoulder, and say, "Bla bla bla." I'm sure as an adult, I wouldn't have taken his words for granted.

The sound of the car engine fades in the distance as Matt, and I watch the brake lights turn at the end of the street. Our faces are completely covered in soot. "Mikey. Let's go!" Matt says as I turn my head. Besides the soot, I look much different now. Several years have passed since the day under the beach steps. For the record, we didn't make it on time that day either. Matt and I have just turned thirteen years old. We quietly open the sliding glass door and enter the house. Our clothes are singed and covered in soot as well. "We really fucked up this time." I think as I look at our attire. We had recently finished building a ground fort in the woods behind Grandma and Pop's house. Inconveniently, the woods were being torn down for housing development. We fought back by shooting out the windows of a bulldozer left behind for the weekend. I was satisfied, but Matt was not. "I told you not to use that much gasoline," I whisper, "What are we gonna do!?" "I got some extra clothes in the guest room." Matt's interrupted by the doorbell, and we jump behind the homemade bar. Pop comes down and opens the front door. "What's Pop doing here!?" Matt Says. "He must have waited for us," I answer. "Awww shit, It's a cop," Matt whispers as he peeks out. I put my head down with disappointment. The cop hands Pop a slingshot. "He's got your wrist rocket." Adds Matt. "Guess I'll never see that again," I say, rubbing my eye full of soot.

Pop shakes the cop's hand and closes the door after he leaves. As Pop turns, he sees the wine glasses move ever so slightly, "Alright, boys, Come on out." Matt looks at me, and with a head nod, we come out with our heads down. Pop looks us over. "Ok, now wash up. We're late for dinner." Matt and I look at each other confused. "Hurry up now." He adds and runs up the stairs.

Pop, Matt, and I walk into a loud restaurant. "Well, look who decided to show up," May says as the family orders dinner. "Well, Pop, where were they?" We were so screwed. Pop wouldn't lie in a thousand years. "The boys showed up as soon as you guys left." Pop answers. "Wow, you two are lucky." Says Aunt May. Matt and I's nervous faces turn to a smile as we join the crowded table. To this day, Pop has never said a word.

Welcome to Bakers Creek

The next day, I sit at a desk in an old-looking classroom. I'm in a little bit of pain as someone pinches the end of my pecker. That someone was me. Not one of my favorite tics. The upside was that I was in a room full of twelve and thirteen-year-old boys, so I fit right in. "Shit!" I yell loudly as I squeeze harder. The class quietly giggles. "Is there a problem, Mike?" Asks the teacher. "Can I go to the bathroom?" I say out loud. "You may." Answers Ms. Lee, "On your way to the office." Quiet giggles are heard once again as I leave.

I stand in between two urinals that reach the floor. A round sink sits in the middle of the bathroom with a black bar that circles it. I breathe heavily with sweat on my face. *I've always enjoyed the callus I'd get on the tips of my fingers from playing the guitar. However, the callus on the tip of my penis was not as pleasant.* Pee shoots in a V, hitting both urinals. After the painful pee is over, I fall forward with my hands up, flushing both urinals. After a short rest, I stand straight and turn around. A small kid with glasses looks at me with bulging eyes. "You have two?" He asks with confusion. "I should have wished for cash," I answer as I pat him on the shoulder. Before leaving, I jump up and stomp on the bar under the sink. The boy watches me leave the bathroom. Crazy noises are heard coming from the pipes. The boy slowly turns to his front and looks down at his own crotch. Eventually, water sprays from all sides of the sink, but I am long gone.

It turns out that getting left back in second grade isn't all that bad. I mean, imagine today being like, "Ya know, I didn't really like that year. I think I'll do it again." The bell rings, and I watch my friends flee to the hallway. I was now the wises in the class, plus I made some new friends. You had HOLLY, spinning a skateboard. SATCH, throwing up a football. LILLY, holding her books to her chest. The TWINS. Preppy girls, one blond and one brunette. TIM, in skater clothes. LEO and PAIGE. Both hippies. And the rest of them.

Maverick slaps me hi-five as he passes. Maverick, well, he's Maverick. The school itself was pretty cool too. At least I thought so. It was old as shit. They built onto it more times than I can count. Empty corridors, dead ends, stairs that led to nowhere, and an entire 3rd floor abandoned due to asbestos.

I'm dressed in black jeans, a skater T-shirt, and Vans. My brown hair is parted in the middle and hangs to the tips of my ears. I hike up my plain blue backpack and look around the halls that are now almost empty of others. After checking for witnesses, I push the doors to the stairs open. Now on the 2nd floor, I stop in my tracks before peeking into a quiet computer class. I look around and see a bouncy ball stuck into a doorstop. I toss it, and the ball bounces around the room. The class erupts as I sneak by with my hand in front of my face. Now today, for good reason, others are accepting of kids with learning disabilities. In the mid-90s, however, it wasn't that simple. I open the door to the next room, and it slowly closes after I enter. The plaque above the door reads "LRC."

"Little Retarded Children," Satch says as he eats a sub by the bike racks in the sun. I strum on an acoustic guitar with my back against a brick wall. Two-dollar bills, some candy, and a handful of loose change cover the inside of my guitar case. A kid walks by and throws in a quarter. Tim eats out of a chip bag to my right. In between Satch and I sit the twins on the broken black pavement in the schoolyard. "That's not what it stands

109

for, Satch," Sav says as she braids Cassidy's hair. "They tried to put me in there last year for English, but my dad came in and cursed out Mr. Ackermann," says Satch with a half-smile. "Maaan I wish I was a fly on the wall that day!" Says Maverick as he tosses a Slammer towards his stack of Pogs. "Ow!" Cassidy Yells. hold still!" complains Sav. I strum my guitar and sing to a girl standing in front of me. "Hey Paula, your dad fights poo as a plumber. Do you recall-a, getting bit by Maverick's dog last summer." The crowd laughs as I continue to sing, "She likes to play in your pool, Tim might be gay, but that's cool. So, throw some change in, cuz you ruuuule." "Thanks, Mike," says Paula. "Whoa, not so fast, Paula, pay the man," Maverick says. "Oh, are you his manager or something?" says Paula. "Your gosh damn right I am!" Maverick interrupts. "Here, Mike, this is only for you." Paula says while placing some change in my case. "Thanks, Paula," I reply. "Yo, Mike, sing about the LRC room." Yells Satch. I hit the G-cord. "Her ass needs a feelin, above Mrs. Lee's ceilin is a classroom full of Special Ed childr-in." The gang laughs, and Satch smacks Maverick on the shoulder. Maverick hands him a dollar, and Satch rolls it up in a ball and shoots it in the guitar case.

Maverick and I sit at different corners of an empty classroom. Mrs. Lee writes on the chalkboard. Maverick points at Mrs. Lee before poking his pointer finger in and out of a circle he made with his other hand. I smile, nod, and give thumbs up. Mrs. Lee has short blond hair, a pretty, round face, and a full figure. "Mike, your late homework is due tomorrow." She says. "I'm leaving early tomorrow," I tell her. "Well, make sure I get it before you leave." She replies. "That's right." A voice says, "You're going to the doctor tomorrow."

Tic emerges from the shadows of the classroom. I hear him but choose to ignore. He continues, "You think they can help you? Hee hee, you're sooo fucking stupid. Probably why you couldn't finish that homework." Another wicked laugh is heard, and my eyes grow wide. A second figure shows itself. It looks similar to Tic but a bit larger. Same short body, pot belly, trollish face, and wet leathery skin. The creature has gray skin with patchy black hair. It wears a red T-shirt that says OCD. "Ahh, I almost forgot." Says Tic, "I have someone I want you to meet. My friend. This is Mike. We hate him. You can pretend all you want to, freak, but we're here to stay." The two creatures' evil chuckles are heard until they fill the classroom.

The next day I sit in a loud, crowded classroom with friends and classmates. "Mr. Reed, can you please send Mike Devaney to the office." A voice says over the loudspeaker. I hear the intercom and grab my backpack before waving to friends and leaving the room. The door slowly closes but does not shut. "Hey, Mr. Reed, why does Mike always get to leave all the time," Paula asks. Mr. Reed looks up from a paper and gets out of his seat. He walks casually through the loud classroom until he reaches the door. He puts his hand out and closes the door, creating a loud bang. The conversations come to a halt as one by one the attention of my friends and classmates falls on Mr. Reed. "You see, class. Your friend Mike has..." All eyes stay on Reed as he pauses, "A DISEASE." *Get in the Ring* plays on my headphones as the family station wagon drives down the long stretch of road to Dr. Humphries office. The tape turns in my Walkman. "Is he going to be ok?" a voice calls out. "I Don't Know Paige." Mr. Reed answers. "What kind of disease?" Asks one of the twins with a valley girl accent. I'm not entirely sure, but I believe it is related to the brain. "What does it do?" Asks another classmate. Reed puts his hands on his hip and takes a breath before answering. "Let me explain."

As the GNR song picks up on my headphones, the station wagon passes the rodeo where Tic and OCD are seen sitting on top of the buffalo statue. They pretend to ride it, each with a cigarette in their mouth. Tic holds a can of beer, and OCD holds a bottle of booze. "THERE HE IS!" Tic and OCD jump off the buffalo, spitting and throwing their cigarettes. Tic's can of beer bounces off the pavement as they run into the street. OCD throws his bottle of booze in the wagon's direction as Tic gives the finger with one hand and grabs his crotch with the other. OCD joins him in verbal fuck yous and nasty hand gestures. I turn around and look out the back window seeing Tic and OCD's display of disgust. I hold a straight face but do not react. Instead, I turn up the song. The lyrics come in as I gaze out to the future with confidence.

"Why do you look at me when you hate me?"-GNR

CHAPTER 4 — LEGENDS OF BAKERSFIELD

The sound of a minibike's engine. It's the end of August now, back in the mid-90s. The hot afternoon sun shines down on Jeb and me as we cruise down a dirt road on Jeb's bike. I sit behind him, my light-colored camo shirt covered in paintball splats. Jeb's attire is similar. Paintball guns hang off our shoulders as we come out of the woods. A dog's turd roasts in the sun. "Thanks for helping me, dude," I tell Jeb as I pick the turd up from the tall grass using a plastic scooper. "If you didn't wait till Sunday, you could have gotten all the yards done yourself," Jeb adds as he scoops one up. "Holy shit!" I yell as I pick up a massive poo, "Damn, dude, what kind of dog does she have?" Jeb replies. "A chihuahua," I kid as Jeb chuckles. We head towards the front yard as Jeb looks towards some long weeds. "I better ask Mrs. Hitler if she needs her grass cut." He says. "Come on, man, I thought we were going in the pool," I add. "Don't you want to make more money?" Jeb asks. "No," I mutter as I knock on a front door. It opens, and a sweet-looking old lady with white hair smiles at us. "Hey, Mam, we're all done," I say. "Thank you, Dear. Here you go." She says, handing me some cash. "Hey, Mam, your grass is getting pretty high back there. How would you like me to cut it for you?" Jeb asks. "Oh, thank you, dear, but I believe a truck full of Wetbacks comes every Tuesday for that." Says Mrs. Hitler. "They're awfully loud, but, oh well, I shouldn't complain. I suppose it could be a truck full of Coons." Adds the old racist. *If there was one person, we didn't mind taking money from, it was Mrs. Hitler.* "Alright, Mrs. Hitler have a nice day," Jeb says as we jump off the front porch. "You too, Hun." She yells. "What's that lady's real name anyway?" I ask Jeb. "I don't have a clue." He answers as he picks up his paperboy bike by its metal basket. I hop on my blue BMX bike. Tim and Holly are seen in the distance approaching on skateboards. They hold their hands up to get our attention. "Here comes your posse," Jeb says sarcastically. Holly was my age because he had also been held back a grade. Tim always hated school; however, he was an intelligent

kid. The four of us cruise down a neighborhood street. Tim and Holly ride

double-decker skateboards while Jeb and I zig-zag on our bikes to keep

up.

THE TREE FORT

The Tree Fort was now in its prime. The outside appears mostly

the same except there is now a small hut on the roof and a silver metal

slide that hangs off the side and ends halfway to the ground. A long rope is

tied to a high branch in an oak tree. The rope leads to the deck of the tree

fort. The other end of the rope is connected to the handle of a wooden bat

with a thick ring of duct tape for grip. The remaining rope from the bat

attaches to a double-decker skateboard deck with no trucks or wheels. The

inside of the fort now has colored Christmas lights stapled around the rim

of the ceiling and down a wall leading to a crummy old outlet strip. All

the plugs are used. The bottom bunk has been turned into a wrap-around

couch with pillows and blankets that end near the round coffee table.

116

A large water jug with a spigot, a big lamp, and an old, knobbed color box TV with an antenna sits atop the coffee table. Posters of Wolverine and Nirvana have now been added to the collection. Homemade nunchucks and wooden swords hang from the ceiling. A butterfly knife joins the others, stuck in the wall. A few girl names and the word "Kerplunk" are written in permanent marker on the walls. A big wooden face of a Jamaican man smoking a pipe also hangs on the wall. The NES and Sega Genesis are crammed on the coffee table with paddles and games stacked behind them.

After a swim in our above-ground pool, we climb the tree and wooden ladder to the deck of the tree fort. Tim sits on the railing drying his hair with a towel. I spin the skateboard swing before holding the bat handle and jumping on. Holly waxes the top of my old swing set for improved grinding. Other tricks on the skateboard swing consisted of holding the bat handle and spinning the board around us, various grabs, and the occasional Superman. This trick could only be performed by Holly, Tim, and myself. Tim turns up a song called *Weenie Beanie* on the boombox, which is buried under various CDs. The grunge song cranks out of the tree fort windows as if creating a montage.

A blanket hangs from the top bunk covering half of the bottom couch. It reads, *7 Minutes in Heaven.* The blanket is pulled open by Satch and Sav. Startled, Leo and Paige stop kissing. I sit on the top bunk with Cassidy as she puts her blond hair in a ponytail. Lilly sits by the coffee table. "Who's next?" Asks Satch. "You ready Lill?" I ask. "Not going to happen, Mike." She answers with a smile. "I'll go in with you, Mike." Says Cassidy as we jump off the top bunk. I take one more look at Lilly before closing the blanket door.

Jeb, Tim, Holly, and I smoke cigs and play poker as Leo pulls out a Playboy. Satch holds an NES paddle while Maverick throws his own paddle at the wall in defeat. Satch waves over the next opponent. Sis and two of her girlfriends hang in the tree fort. Jeb and I climb the tree and shoot water guns through the windows. The girls scream and fight back. Paige, Leo, and I play Ouija board at night while Jeb and Holly hang on the deck with some fireworks. A pack of Black Cats is tossed into the fort. It goes off. We freak. I run and jump off the deck, strumming an air guitar. My shoelace gets caught on a nail, and I fall nine feet to the ground as the lace snaps. Lucky for me, my face broke the fall. As I catch my breath. I see Tim pissing off the deck as Holly passes on the skateboard swing. The pee stream sprays on Holly's grip tape, and his hands slide off the bat, sending him into the pine trees. "Damn, you ok, man?" Yells Matt from the balcony. I wasn't sure who he was talking to, but I nodded my head anyway.

THE NEW KID

A kid gets punched in the face with a boxing glove. It's the first day of school and a group of boys, including my friends and I, make a circle around two boys fighting. We hide from teachers in a lightly wooded part of the massive playground. As we hoot and holler, a young teacher watches from afar with an older teacher smoking a pipe close by. The boys take turns wailing on each other until one hits the dirt. The young teacher pumps his fist in anger and hands the older teacher a five-dollar bill. I gather the boxing gloves, put them in a bag, and hide the bag by an old rec-lodge that sat on the property. Holly helps. As the morning bell rings, kids enter the building. Holly and I happen to pass Satch and Jamal. Jamal's an inch taller than the rest of us, who are all average size and weight for kids our age. "Who's this guy?" Asks Jamal as a boy in jeans and a polo shirt makes his way to the door. He's wearing a chain necklace, and his black hair is slicked back with hard gel. "That's the new kid." Maverick chimes in. "I think he's from the island," referring to a small nearby town on the beach. "He looks like a fucking douche bag." Says Satch. The five of us laugh and head into school.

After lunch, I start to open the door to the stairwell. "Hey, Mike!" Yells Lilly. I abandon the stairwell and continue to walk as Lilly catches up. I turn from the door and walk with Lilly. "I'm glad I found you," Lilly says. "Me too," I shout. "I was thinking Friendly's, but if you want to go somewhere nicer, that'd be fine too." "No." She laughs, "There's a sub for Mr. Ross. The Twins want you to do that Italian guy. What's his name again?" "It's a me, Martino," I say with an accent. "I've got some tasty Meatballs." "Ha, that's the one!" She smiles. "Oh, and Lilly, someday," I say, referring to our date. "Riiiiight," Lilly adds as she walks away. As I walk through the doors to the stairway, I see the new kid smoking a cigarette. "What's up, man?" He says as I give him a head nod. I start to walk up the stairs but stop. "Hey, man, you'll get busted there for sure," I tell him. "For real? You got a better place?" He asks. "Yea, come on." I wave. "Thanks, man."

120

We sit on a long radiator in a dingy empty room on the abandoned third floor. "Over on Ridge," Mitch says as he puffs his smoke. "Me and my brother. I got two stepbrothers, but they're older. I don't see them that much." "You're by Cove Park then," I mention. As I blow out smoke from my cig and pinch my nose. "I never seen a park, but..." Mitch adds. "Nah, it's not a park really, just woods," I tell him, "It's sweet for paintball though." "Word, you guys' paintball?" Says Mitch. "That sounds dope." He adds. "Yeah, man, you can come too if you find a gun," I say as I ash on the dirty floor. "Thanks, man." He says with a head nod. "These old, dude?" I say holding up the cigarette with a cringe. "Na." Mitch laughs. "They're menthol." We head down the stairwell, and both stop at the second floor. Mitch opens the door. "You on this floor too?" He asks. "Oh, um, nah, I got gym." I lie. "Alright, man, thanks again." "No prob." I go to give him a hi-five, but Mitch puts his fist out for a fist bump. Confused, I make a fist too as Mitch changes his up to a hi-five. "Next time," I say with a laugh as we abandon both. I go halfway down the steps before turning and coming back up.

I look at the computer room to make sure Mitch is out of sight and open the door. A teacher in her early 40's writes on the chalkboard. One

121

tall skinny boy, a small boy, and an obese girl sit at a table. "Late again, I see." Says Mrs. Wells. "Yeah, sorry I..." I see a new chair at the table with a body in it. Mitch turns around and looks at me with a smirk. "Well, let's have a seat and get started." Says Mrs. Wells. As she continues to write, Mitch slides out a chair with his foot. I sit in it with a slightly embarrassed face. Mitch faces the board and holds his fist out. I smirk back, and we finally fist bump.

The final bell rings, and I head to the bike rack. As I pull my bike from the rack, Holly comes up behind me and tags my arm. "Got ya last, till tomorrow." "Aw shit!" I shout. "You suck." Holly pulls out the BMX bike next to mine, and we jump on. We ride down a tight hilly dirt trail next to a long pond in the woods. Holly yells as he skids to a stop. *I met Holly in 2nd grade. We weren't friends at first, however. I wasn't avoiding him, really. I just chose to hang out with different friends. He had dark circles under his eyes and always looked tired or something. It wasn't until my mom gave him a ride home from school that he asked me to hang out. As we pulled up to his house, I saw his hot sister jumping on a trampoline in his backyard and said I would come over for the day. It wasn't until she came up to the car window that I realized it was not his sister but, in fact, his mom. We've been friends ever since. Holly also has somewhat of a*

dark cloud. He calls it the Holly curse, and if there was such a thing,

there's no doubt in my mind it would follow him to the ends of the earth.

Another contributing factor is Holly's acute ability to make "good"

decisions.

Outside in a parking lot, Holly bangs on a soda machine. "Piece a

shit!" "Get me a rock." As I get Holly a rock, he notices a cement boulder

on top of a brick fence. It was a little larger than a bowling ball. Moments

later, we carry the boulder down a sidewalk before crossing the street at

the top of a hill. "Put it down." Says Holly. "Thing's heavy as hell!"

"Where are we going with it anyway?" I ask, unaware of our destination.

After putting the round cement ball down, I look around as Holly pushes

the boulder down the steep road and across a small bridge. A car is seen

from afar coming our way. I walk up next to Holly with a nervous face.

The boulder is rolling right towards the moving vehicle. The car pulls into

a driveway at the last second, and the boulder rolls past. I am relieved.

"You gotta warn me before you pull shit like that, man," I tell him. "I

didn't know a car was coming," Holly says aloud as we head back to our

bikes. I shake my head. "Right!"

A 3-year-old girl with brown hair looks down a small hallway in a blanket fort. She crawls down the narrow corridor before hitting a fork in the road. At the end of the path, a teddy bear holds a toy gun. To the left is a towel draped over a piano bench. The girl makes her way down and slowly lifts the towel. "Raaaaar!" Yells Sis. Faith playfully laughs as we come out from the giant fort maze in Sis's bedroom. Mom yells up the stairs, "Ok, time for dinner." Faith was born three years earlier. She has curly brown hair and pudgy cheeks. *After the age of five, I figured Sis would be my only sibling; however, I was mistaken.*

I THINK SHE'S NEBRASKAN

Dad and I drive in a small gray hatchback. My dad freed up some time from work to be the soccer coach for a new team recently formed in the town league. It was his first year as a head coach, and so... "They all SUCK!" I tell dad quietly as I look over the new team on the soccer field. Dad reads from a clipboard. "Dad! We're screwed." "Watch your mouth," Dad says, reminding me of Mom. "They're like the worst kids in school," I complain. "Well, that's who they gave us," He tells me, "So let's just make the best of it. Better get in goal and see what we got." As Dad leaves the car, I hide behind it to pinch the tip of my you know what. I also jump up with both feet and kick myself in the ass. Tic introduced that little number a week ago. *Little shit!* One by one the kids attempt to kick a ball past me, and it's easily blocked, as are the rest of them. Some kids totally Ms. the goal entirely. The last kid fakes me out and scores. "Alright, nice kick." My father says with a smile.

"Not so bad. That Denny kid was pretty good," Dad says on the way home. "Yea, he's ok, but he's like me." I say. "You're good, Mike! When you put your mind to it." Dad shouts. *I was no Allstar, that was for certain. My Dad was right, though. I had fun playing in the games, but I just didn't care most of the time. I guess my mind was always somewhere else.*

The morning sun shines on Mom's newspaper through the dining room window. Dad enters. "Good morning," Mom says, cheery. "Hey Hun, where's the kids." Dad asks. "Sleeping, oh except Mike, he got up early and headed out with Holly somewhere. Said something about playing basketball." Mom tells him. "Did you say basketball?" Dad asks.

"That's what they said." Mom answers. Dad lets out a quiet laugh.
"Right."

As Holly snips a small hole in the barbed wired fence, I stare through to an old basketball court. It's in a big lumberyard with several abandoned large buildings and hangars. With skateboards and a backpack, Holly and I run through tall grass and weeds as we pass the basketball court and make our way to the buildings. Legend had it that an old skate park lay somewhere in the belly of the giant mill. Holly and I had failed to find it on our first attempt, but there was one place that we hadn't checked. The roof. "That's pretty high!" I say as the two of us stop at the sidewall of the tallest building. The building is nearly 50 feet tall. Holly puts the skateboards sideways in a Velcro slot in his backpack. Before handing it to me. "I don't want it," I complain. "I carried it across the yard!" He yells. "So, what. I'll shoot ya for it," I tell him.

We both smack a fist in our other hand two times and yell a word out simultaneously on the third. "QUEEF DANCE!" "DICK FART!" "Damn," Holly says after losing. Holly puts on the pack with the skateboards as I make my way up a tall pine tree with thick, long branches. I balance myself as I walk out on a branch about twelve feet up.

At the end of the limb is a short jump to some pipes on the side of the building. I make the jump and climb. Halfway up, the pipe ends, and I switch to another nearby. Holly follows close behind. At the top of the building is an old rotting 2x4 that surrounds some fans for the heating unit. The plank is only a foot higher but felt like five. A cloud covers the sun as a gust of wind blows over me. *I always hated this part.*

"Come on, man," Holly yells. With two feet on the wall, I leap up from the pipe and grab the 2x4. The wood creeks as I pull myself up and onto the roof. I go to help Holly, but he refuses. Once up, we make our way across the rotten red shingles. We jump small gaps and objects in our way. "Your girlfriend's hot," Holly says. "All exotic and shit. What is she anyway?" "I think she's Nebraskan," I answer. "Where the hell is that?" Holly yells. "I don't know." I shrug. "Somewhere down by the Philippines, I guess."

We eventually stop, and Holly points at an old chimney. We head over and find a narrow hole in the roof. Holly starts to go in, but I grab his arm. "Look!" I point at a hive of hornets. Holly holds some rubble and picks his arm up to throw. "What are you doing!" I yell. "I'm going to take it out!" He states. "What are you nuts! Where we gonna go?!" I ask. Holly hated bees. He also hated Poison Ivy, ticks, and chiggers, which was ironic because we battled all of them on a daily basis. "We'll just have to go down slow," I add. "One, two, three," "DOUCHE DUMP!" "TITY JIZZ!"

After losing, I make my way down first, and Holly hands me the pack. Holly slowly makes his way down the narrow hole as bees buzz by. His face passes inches from the hive. We make our way through what seems to be the attic of the building. At the end is a new room. We jump down to large metal shelves that must have held piles of plywood in its day. I take off the pack and toss it across to the next set of shelves. Holly jumps across the four-foot gap and follows. I put the backpack back on and follow Holly down an aged wooden ladder that ends short. We jump to the floor.

BELLY OF THE WHALE

Pigeons fly as we walk through the seemly endless empty building, covered in dust and rust. Each noise we make seems to echo for miles. I break windows with rocks as Holly tries to pick a padlock to a metal door. "Fuck!" Screams Holly as he throws the lock pick. "I told you, Holly!" I yell, "People take classes for that shit." I say. "Help me move this." He shouts. We pick up a metal slab and drop it on the lock. Holly pulls on it afterward, and it comes loose. "Nice!" We pull up the door to a boarded-up wall. "Aw, what the hell, man!" We complain. Giving up, Holly takes a metal bar and beats the wall as he swears. A piece of wood lands on the floor. "Come on, man, let's go?" Holly mutters as he walks away. "Wait!" I yell while pointing at the broken piece of wood. The backside of the wood has a pattern of spray paint on it. We look at each other before tearing a hole in the rest of the wall. We walk through to the other side. Sunlight peers through the boarded windows and onto the legendary skatepark. Holly and I are speechless as we gaze at its awesomeness. After celebrating, Holly takes out a small boom box from the backpack. An "Ozzy" song echoes through the mill as we cruise on our skateboards up and down wooden quarter pipes that wrap around the large hidden room filled with graffiti.

"Bam, it hit the floor! Haha, you were mad," I say from a tree branch that hangs over a town lake. Holly sits on a lower branch, tying a rope. A soccer ball lands in the water. I jump in, grab the ball and bring it up to a chain-linked fence on the high ground. On the other side is a town pool. Satch meets me at the fence. "Yo Satch." "Hey man, what you up to?" asks Satch, who is also in bathing trunks. "Just making a swing," I answer. "You're crazy." He laughs. "We got an extra pass if you want to get out of the fucking leeches?" Satch adds. I look up at Holly, who notices us talking. "You got two?" I ask. Satch looks up at Holly, who gives him a nod. "Nah, just one." Satch states. "I'm just gonna hang here," I tell him. "Thanks anyway." "Later," Satch yells and heads back to the pool. "Yo Mike, it's twelve." Says Holly. "Let's go." An unfinished housing development. Men eat lunch together at their trucks. Holly and I sneak away carrying a stack of plywood. We pass a sign that reads

LARRY'S CONSTRUCTION

Maverick pulls a name out of a cap by the old rec-lodge at school. Gary has his gloves on, and he's ready to go. We talk quietly amongst ourselves. "You fight yet?" Asks Holly as he wipes the sun off his forehead. "Na, not yet" I say, holding the gloves. "Me neither, man, but I'm ready for anybody," Holly claims. "Maybe not Gary though" He adds. "HOLLY!" Maverick shouts as he holds up the picked name. I smack Holly on the shoulder with a smile. "Go get him, tiger." The two betting teachers take out their money. A bald teacher comes out. From afar, Holly is seen throwing hay-makers at Gary. Gary, with the height-to-weight advantage, blocks each punch and with a right hook takes Holly to the ground. "What the hell is this!" Yells Baldy. "Come on, you two. Take care of it!" The betting teachers reluctantly get off the tree they were leaning on. "Ok, guys, break it up." says one of the teachers as Holly climbs the back of Gary.

The hallways are crowded. Mitch and I open the stairwell doors. The other kids in LRC happen to be behind us, and Mitch holds the door for them. The small kid, Murph, has a backpack three sizes too big for his little body. I hold the rail and kick my ass with two feet. "What the fuck?" Says Mitch. "I'll tell ya later," I say with a smile. "Yo Murph, that's a little big, ya think?" Yells Mitch as Murph passes. "At least it don't have holes in it like Anna's." Says Murph sarcastically. "SHUT UP, ASSHOLE!" Yells Big Anna as she kicks Murphy's large backpack. The pack flies over his head, and he almost goes headfirst to the ground. While trying to catch his balance, his momentum causes him to fall up the entire staircase to the first landing, where he slams into a wall. We break out in laughter as we meet Murphy at the landing. Mitch and I grab him by the arm and help him to his feet.

131

As the school day ends, Jeb and I walk together in the hallway. Jeb stops them at a bulletin board. "Yo D, check it out." *Dance this Friday*. "Sweet. Nice." I nod. Jeb thinks for a moment before nodding as well. "You know what, we should do one." He says calmly. "What, a dance?" I yell. "Yeah, right." "Why not, dude, we got plenty of songs," Jeb argues. "They're all originals." I remind him. "That's what people want, Mike!" Jeb yells with excitement and adds, "Anyone can do covers!" "There's Ackermann. I'm going to ask him." Jeb says confidently. "Pff, good luck," I say sarcastically. Jeb gets Ackermann's attention, and they talk for a brief moment before Jeb walks away and catches up with me. "What'd he say," I mutter. "He said, YES. We're in, dude!" I stop in my tracks while Jeb keeps walking. With a surprised look on my face, I slowly look back at the bulletin board.

The teachers at Bakers Creek Middle School were mostly flower heads from the 60s. A couple even saw some action in Nam. They were pretty laid back, to say the least. On a nice day, they'd extend recess to an hour, and on a really nice day, they'd just say fuck it and take us to Pine Park where they'd send us in the woods to our *Earth Plots* to study nature or do, whatever. A flashback of a bottle spinning is usually attributed to this particular memory.

Denny and I charge down a soccer field at Pine Park. Denny passes the ball, and I kick it around an oncoming opponent. I see an opening and boot towards the goal. Out of nowhere, Satch blocks it with his chest and dribbles it past me and the rest of the team. He scores. I sigh and drop my head. "Alright, good hustle out there!" Dad yells from the sideline. In different jerseys, Satch and I meet while walking toward the dirt parking lot. "You guys' blow." He mutters. "Yeah, I know." "Hey, are you going to the lake tomorrow?" I ask. "My dad's working." He says. "I don't have a ride." "So come with us," I add. "I don't know." He says as I interrupt. "They got a volleyball court..."

LILY PADS

Dad drives the station wagon down an empty road with farmland on either side. Satch and I sit in the back seat with Sis in the front. "I like this song." Says Satch as he looks out an opened window at pine trees quickly passing by. "You know who this is, Satch?" Dad asks. "Nah, Mr.

133

D, who? "Eric Clapton," Dad says with a half-smile. "What's it about?" Asks Satch with a straight face. "Well, it's a sad song," Dad tells the story of how Clapton lost his son. "Wow," Satch says as he digests the story while listening to the lyrics. "That's crazy." Satch cracks his back and looks back out the window. "You think Lilly will be there?" Satch asks me under the music. "Maybe," I answer with a shrug. As if I didn't know. I've only been in love with the girl since 2nd grade. *My mom always claimed that kids can't fall in love. Not that I ever told her I was, but maybe she's right. I will tell you this, though, Lilly put her head on my shoulder once at the ball field, and it was a high that no drug on earth can measure.* "You guys camping in the fort tonight?" Dad shouts over the music. Satch and I look at each other as I wait for an answer. "Sure." He says with a grin. I match it and look out my window. A lake trip, Lilly, and a night in the fort, this just might be the best day ever.

"Thanks, Mr. D." "Thanks, Dad!" "Have fun, guys." Dad drops us off to park the car. We walk past a snack hut and towards the busy lake where people swim and bathe in the sand. "You guys wanna play?" A classmate shouts as Sis runs to her friends. "You coming?" Asks Satch as I look out at the lake where Lilly, Cassidy, and Sav splash in the shallow end. "Yea, in a little bit," I answer. Satch runs off with George, and I head to the lake. "Hey, Mike, how are you feeling?" A younger kid asks, stopping me with his question. "Oh, hey Jimmy, I'm good. How about you?" I answer. "Are you getting better?" He asks. "Better? What are you talking about, dude?" I shout. "You know from your disease." "My WHAT?!" I interrupt. "My brother said some teacher told the class you had a disease." My face turns to shit as I slowly look at young Jimmy. "What teacher?!" "Uumm." Jimmy answers nervously." "What teacher Jimmy?!" "Mr. Reed," Jimmy says finally. I turn my head and look at Lilly in the water. As I watched her laugh from a distance, I think of her and my other friends in that class. "Mother fucker." I mutter. *That Mother Fucker! It was no secret that I had Tics but a disease! Really? What did he think I needed another fucking challenge!?* So much for the best day ever. Jimmy runs away, and I head down and jump in the water.

"Listen up, class." Mr. Reed says early Monday morning. "Tomorrow, a sub is coming in for Mrs. Lee's leave." She is my niece, and it is very important to me that you all show her your best behavior. Otherwise, you will deal with me." The kids in my class all smile and nod. I do not.

The next day a young female teacher stands in front of the class. Students raise their hands one by one as their name is called. Satch looks out the door window at me as I give him a nod. "Mike?" Says Ms. Reed. "He usually comes in late." Satch replies. "Is there a reason?" She asks. Satch sighs and shakes his head. "You see, Ms. Reed, Mike has a disease." "I'm sorry to hear that." Ms. Reed says with compassion. The class starts to smile as Satch continues. "Yes, he tries his best, but well, they say it's eating away at his brain." There's a knock at the door, and Satch gives a sad face as the door slowly opens, and I stand with my head down, holding the door. The teacher smiles and waits for me to come in. Finally, Jeb shoves me from behind, and I hit the floor inside the classroom. The teacher runs to my aid. "Hey, I found this guy in the bathroom looking at the skylight." Says Jeb with some character in his voice. "Ok, thank you. That'll be all." Says Ms. Reed. Jeb whispers and points to his head. "I don't think the cylinders are firing on all 4's if you know what I mean." "OK, thank you, Goodbye!" Yells the teacher. I get up and stand in the corner. Jeb leans into my ear on his way out. "Alrighty then, BYE!" He yells.

Jeb leaves, and the class tries not to laugh once more. Paige lets out a giggle and quickly covers her mouth. "He's so dead." Whispers Sav. "Hi there, I'm Ms. Reed. It's so nice to meet you." I turn around and pick up my head. I look the part and slowly pick my hand up and pet Ms. Reed's face. Finally, I smile, and a mouth full of water pours out the corners of my mouth and to the floor. Paige grabs her laughter once more and runs out of the room. Cassidy puts her head in Lilly's arm as Maverick and Satch bite their smiles.

TIM TALKS FISH

The song *Today* blasts through my backyard out of the boombox in the tree fort. It's late afternoon, and I sit on the fort's roof with my legs hanging over the edge. I squint my eyes from the sun and look out at the pool where Sis and her friend play Marco Polo with Jeb. Tim lays on the roof next to me, playing the air drums. We're both wet and in bathing suits. "You wanna go back in?" I ask as Tim quietly sings lyrics to the song. "Today is the greatest. Nah." He answers. I look down at a pretty

Filipino girl named Cara. She's tanning on a wet towel that lays on the deck of the tree fort.

Nighttime. *My Name is Jonas* plays on the boombox. The colored Christmas lights mixed with the TV glare fill the tree fort, showcasing the posters and other items that hang on the wall. Sis and Tim sit spread apart on the top bunk, Cara and I sit on the couch as I use her lap as a pillow. Tim and I play *Eternal Champions* on the Sega. "Yeah, buddy, take it," I yell as I mash the controller. "Cheap ass move for a bitch." Tim complains. "I got some for ya!" "I'm not even kidding." Sis says. "It was so cute. Of course, I can't keep it because my dad's allergic," She adds with a face. "Aw, that sucks! My aunt's allergic to half the food on the planet." Says Cara. "There it is!" I shout. "Damn, ok, one more for the championship." "That was it!" Tim yells. "First to five! That wasn't five!" I interrupt. "You can't count for shit, dude," Tim mutters. *Besides the pool, Tim and I haven't left the tree fort in three days. I think now it was starting to show.* On the fort wall was an old two-way intercom Sis and I took from Dad's office. "Hello, guys, dinner is ready," Mom says over the intercom. "Thank God, I'm starving," Sis says as she hops down from the bunk. Sis holds a gold button on the intercom and yells, "OK!" I give Sis a head

138

nod. She tries to ignore me, but I nag her by nodding again. "Hey, Mom, can Cara sleepover?" Sis asks. "Sure, it's still summertime." My Mom yells back. "You guys coming?" Asks Sis. "Just bring us something," I tell her. Cara gives me a peck on the lips before following Sis out the door and down the ladder. "You guys are nasty." Sis states. "Manhunt later!" I shout as they climb down the ladder. "Call Oatmeal and Jeb!" "I'm not calling Jeb!" Sis shouts back.

Tim hops up on the top bunk and eats from a chip bag he finds. I grab a VHS that reads *Jackie Chan* written on some duck tape. I put it in the VCR and hop back on the couch as a random fight scene starts to play. "Dude, your girlfriend is sleeping over," Tim says with a grin. "Perks of having a little sister," I say with a hi-five. "What's your plan, man? I'd definitely try a finger if I was you," Tim suggests. "I think I'll just concentrate on my make-out session," I tell him. "Besides, I'd rather have a handy if anything," I add. "A hand job!? Are you nuts!? Fingering a girl is way better than getting a hand job. I can give myself a hand job," Tim claims. *Tim's the most stubborn friend I ever had. He knew he was wrong the second the words left his mouth, but he'd take it to the grave.* "Yeah, well, you can finger your ASS!" I shout before bursting into laughter at

139

my own joke. Tim doesn't flinch. "I got to shit." He says as he hops off the bunk. I take his place and grab the now empty bag of chips. "You're cleaning it up tomorrow," I mutter as he passes the window to the roof.

Holly and I are under cloudy cedar water. The sunlight shines off a metal slab that we pull to the surface. We carry it to a pile of eight at the lake's edge, where a swing hangs. A man walks from the bridge that his crew is working on and counts the slabs. "Seven, Eight. Alright, gentlemen." The man says. "Nice doing business with ya." Holly hands me forty bucks, and we ride off on our skateboards celebrating.

Meanwhile, Tim opens the door to a half-finished basement. There's a card table riddled with empty beer and soda cans. He creeps to a small fridge. He opens it and grabs a soda next to some beer cans. "I counted those fucking sodas, Tim!" Yells his Dad from the upstairs kitchen. "Nice try, though." He adds with a chuckle. Tim and his siblings had a habit of drinking a case of cola in just a few days. Their Pops had put them on a soda limit, and Tim was well over his own. Tim sighs and looks at the beer cans.

The sun shines down on the empty parking lot of the town movie theater. My waterproof watch strikes noon as I ollie over a bag with my skateboard. In the bag are some Hoagies, chips, candy, and soda. Holly attempts to jump a gap on his board but wipes out. Now angry, he smashes his board on the ground as Tim skates up. "Yo dude, lunch is on us!" I tell Tim. "Where'd you get all this shit!" Tim asks. "You know my work ethic, Tim; work hard, play hard."I says. "You got one right," Tim says with a smile as he grabs a random hoagie and unzips his backpack. "YES!! Dude, Where'd you get them!" I ask, spotting the beer. "Does it matter? Yo Holly, you got cigs?" Holly ignores Tim's question. "He fell and crushed 'em," I whisper to Tim.

Holly watches a door inside a diner's waiting room. Tim and I go in the opposite doors, then Tim walks inside the restaurant. "I'll do it. I got to shit." He says as the main door closes. I pump quarters in a cigarette machine that reads 3$. "Hey, what kind of fish you have?" Tim asks, distracting the cashier. "Fish? I don't know, kid." He responds annoyed. "You got some cod?" Adds Tim as he talks fish with the cashier. I put all the quarters in and give a thumbs up. "Ok, thanks anyway," Tim says as he walks towards the bathroom. "Hey, you can't use that unless you order." The cashier tells him. "It's an emergency!" Tim shouts. The heavyset employee shrugs. "Not my problem." He says with a smirk. I pull on a knob to the cigarette machine, but it doesn't budge. Tim walks

out to the waiting room, takes his butt out, and sits on a trash can. "What

are ya doing!?" I ask. " I'm taking a shit." He says simply. "What are you

doing!?" Holly asks as he peeks his head in the waiting room. "He's taking

a shit!" I answer. "Not him, YOU!" Holly yells. "Try another nob." I try to

pull the knob, but the sound of Tim farting in a trashcan makes me laugh

too hard to do anything at all. Tim looks over at a bundle of paper

booklets.

"Dude, look, it's your dad's Swapper!" Tim shouts as he grabs one

and rips a page out to wipe his ass. The irony of Tim's discovery only adds

to my laugh attack. The cashier opens the door, and I quickly pull as hard

as I can. The cigarettes drop, and I grab them as the cashier yells and

chases me out the door. After failing to catch me, the cashier turns to Tim,

who has fallen to the floor. Tim pulls his pants up and runs out the

opposite door. The three of us run for the woods holding our skateboards.

"You little assholes! I'm calling the cops!" Yells the cashier as he waves

his arms. "Eat shit!" Holly screams back as we run into the shelter of the

woods.

Tim and I sit on a long branch and drink beers while we smoke our victory cigs. Three white oak trees sit in a tripod formation in the woods. A wooden three-story tower with low walls. A hole in the first-floor ceiling leads to the second with a makeshift ladder. Holly nails up a wall. "Can I get some help?" He asks. "Relax, man, drink your beer," Tim says. "It's giving me a headache," Holly complains. "That's not till the morning, Holly," Tim shouts. "Come on," I say, interrupting Tim. We hop on the 2nd floor with Holly and grab a hammer and nails.

The next morning, I wake up and head to the shower. "Why in such a hurry?" Asks a voice I had not heard in a short while. I slowly turn around and am face to face with my arch nemesis once again. "Oh, that's right, the big fights today," Tic says with an evil smirk. "Only four people left. Your buddy Satch included. Now there's a winner. Good at sports, good grades, and no Mom to fuck it all up. You're an asshole!" I yell. Tic only laughs. "You'll lose Mike. You will always lose." He tells me as I give him the finger. "Eat shit Tic." "NO!" Tic shouts. "That's your job, you fucking queer! Now DANCE!" I didn't feel much like ticing. I hadn't been sleeping and was exhausted. When Tic is this mad, however, it's better to just do what he says.

LET'S BOX

Ms. Reed's class sits quietly, taking a quiz as she sits at her desk. I haven't picked up my pencil. Instead, I get up and walk towards the board and pick up a piece of chalk. I use my pointer finger to jab hard at what I have written. The teacher looks up at the board that now reads *POOP*. "OH!" Ms. Reed yells as she jumps to her feet. "Ok, let me, um." I quickly undo my belt and start to yank down my pants at the trash can; coutos to Tim. Ms. Reed yells out. "No, Mike, we don't do that here." She says. "I'll take him, Ms. Reed." Satch calls out. "Thank you, Satch." She says with relief.

Satch and I walk in the empty hallway. "How long does a kid with a brain-eating disease take to shit?" I ask. "At least an hour," Satch says blatantly. "Let's hit the attic," I suggest. "The 3rd floor? Isn't there all that poison crap up there?" Statch asks. "Na, they just make that shit up to scare us," I tell him as I open the stair door and head in. Satch looks hesitant but eventually follows. We sit on the long radiator. There are no lights on the third floor, so it's dull and dingy. "My Dad wants me to still play football, but I don't know, I'm thinking soccer." "That sucks. You have to choose." I tell Satch as I smack away something alive. "Why can't you do both like now?" I ask. Satch shrugs as I hop off the radiator and head towards the door. Come on, I'll show you the Hundred-year-old turd. As we walk down the abandoned third-floor hallway, we pass a room where two 8th graders sit and smoke cigarettes. They see us pass and walk to the hall. One was tall, and the other was medium build with longish blond hair. "Hey, You!" "What the fuck you think you're doing up here." "Fuck off, Blondie," Satch says casually. "What'd you say shit head!?" Says Blondie. "Yo, that's Ray's little brother, man." Says the tallboy. "I don't give a fuck!" Says Blondie. "Hey, where do you think you're going?" He yells. "To your mom's," Satch says as we smile. "At least I have one." Blondie states. Satch's eyes bulge as he turns around and runs full speed at the 8th graders. I turn and back up my friend. The 8th graders look caught off guard by Satch's anger, so they run back into the room, shut the door, and give the finger. They hold it shut as Satch pounds and pulls on the handle. "FUCKERS, I'LL KILL YOU!", Screams Satch. He finally stops yelling and walks past me with anger in his eyes. "Satch!" I call out. He heads towards the stairs and says nothing.

The boxing crew hangs in a third-floor room after school. I pull the glove bag out of a cabinet under the radiator. Holly and Tim head into the room as kids talk amongst themselves. "Mike's up today. Think he'll win?" Asks Tim, "Probably.", Holly States, "He's been hitting that bag in his garage for two weeks." "Yea, but bags don't hit back," Tim adds. "Let's pick already! He ain't gonna show. "Satch wouldn't miss a fight," Maverick says through the commotion. "Just pick." Says a bystander. "If it's Satch, they'll just fight tomorrow." Maverick picks a name from the baseball cap. "KEITH!" The crowd is satisfied. Keith was dressed like a jock. He had short blond hair and was slightly taller than me but about the same build. Keith gloves up as well, and we get to the center of the room with our gloves up.

Keith throws a quick jab and hits me in the face. I back up as the crowd starts to cheer. I put my gloves higher this time and move back to the center. Keith throws a combo, but I'm ready this time, and my gloves block his attack. Keith now looks angry. I throw a hard right that is blocked. Quickly I throw my own left-right combo and hit Keith in the face with the left. The crowd again cheers. As Keith charges forward, I put my gloves up and slide back. Most of Keith's blows are blocked, but a couple get through and bounce off my face until eventually I trip over a clump in the ripped rug and hit the floor. The crowd gets loud, and Tim and Holly look bummed out. I feel nothing but disappointment as I quickly get to my feet. With gloves to my side, I walk towards Keith before charging forward and leaving any sort of technique behind. I swing at Keith's face repeatedly as he holds his gloves up. Before Keith is backed into a wall, I spin around with a back fist and hit Keith in the side of the face. He stumbles away and immediately waves his hand to stop the fight. The crowd cheers with a few boos' added in. I throw my hands up in victory as Holly and Tim shake their fists and grin. "Good fight, guys!" Says Maverick. "You're up, Nick." He adds. "Against who!?" Nick asks. "You and Jamal, man. No ones left, and Satch ain't here." Says Maverick. "No way, man, I'm not fighting him." Nick pleads. "Why not cause he's black!?" Maverick yells. The crowd laughs subtly. "No! Cause he's a good fighter." States Nick. "I'll fight him." The crowd gets quiet, and all eyes are on Mitch. "Fuck that Dude. Wait for Satch." Yells the crowd of boys. "I'll take care of Satch later, glove up, new boy." Says Jamal. I get a new pair of gloves out of the bag and hand them to Jamal. I then kneel down and get another for Mitch. "Any rules?" Mitch asks under the voices. "No balls," I tell him. "That it?" He asks while strapping his glove with his mouth. "That's it. Watch his left," I add. Mitch was smart. He might get his ass beat today, but no one's gonna fuck with the new kid who's willing to box one of the toughest kids in the grade.

Mitch and Jamal circle, Mitch stays to Jamal's left. Jamal jabs with his left, and Mitch dodges. Jamal throws another left. Mitch avoids the punch again and counters with a right that hits Jamal in the face. "Ooow," says the crowd as Jamal spits blood on the floor. "You done?" Jamal says but Mitch only grins. A thud is heard, and Mitch bounces off the puke-colored rug.

After school, I sit in Mitch's kitchen at his mom's house. I lean on dark brown wood panels at an open window. Mitch holds a black rifle BB gun. He takes a shot at some bottles lined up by his shed that sit far back in his yard. "Nice shot," I say as he hands me the rifle. "Man, you'd probably love the cabin." "Where's that?" He asks. "Up in the Appalachian Mountains," I tell him as I line up my shot. "My dad takes us up once a year. No running water or electricity. It's sweet. We have a shootout too. For real, though, you should come, man." I pull the trigger, and the far bottle shatters as I hand Mitch back his rifle. "A shootout, huh?" He says. "There's a trophy and everything," I add. "I'm in, dude,"

Mitch says as his Mom walks into the kitchen. "Hey, boys." Mitch's mom

puts some groceries on the table. She's a small woman with short curly

brown hair. *She also had a high-pitched voice that I always claimed*

sounded sexy when Mitch and I broke balls. "You better not be killing

anything." She shouts when she sees the gun. "Na mom, it just stings 'em a

little. Come here, I'll show you." Mitch says as he switches the CO_2. He

takes aim at a squirrel standing upright eating an acorn. "Just stings

them?" I think. The bottles were far, and that thing had no problem

reaching. A pop is heard, and a wad of blood splatters on the garage by the

bay. The acorn falls to the ground, and the headless squirrel topples over.

Mitch's mom starts to scream. While slapping Mitch on the shoulder, she

reaches for a wooden spoon. Mitch and I run out a screen door as Mitch

dodges spatulas and Tupperware that fly by. Mitch's mom stops short at

the door and takes a breath before calling out. "Come back any time,

Michael!" I wave as Mitch, and I disappear into the woods.

Later that day. Before climbing the cedar to the deck of the tree

fort, I hear a girl's voice. It was Hill. She was tanning in her yard while

talking on her portable phone. Hill was only a couple of years older than me, as I've said before; however, in that year, she had quickly transformed into a young lady. Hill hangs up and continues to tan. I put an upside-down trash can at the tall wooden fence that now separates the two yards. I hop up and grab the wooden tips at the top. As I get ready to jump over, I look up; I see Hill talking on her portable phone once again as she enters through her back door and into her house. I watch for a moment as she laughs. I then hop off the trash can and walk back towards the tree fort. *Watching everything unfold at once is obviously more exciting, but the truth was, there would be days or weeks at a time where nothing would happen at all.*

DRAGONS IN THE ATTIC

I lay on the cool floor under a small pink table in my kitchen. In socks, shorts, and a t-shirt, I hang my feet from two screws sticking out of the counter. I stare at the stretching sock. I follow my foot with my eyes as it finally plops to the floor, then I look at my other foot as it hangs. Mom does paperwork on the kitchen table. She hears the second foot drop. "I said go to your ROOM!"

Later that day, I lay on a big bed in a Victorian-style attic that has been taken over by youth. The sheets are covered in dragon artwork, and the oval ceiling is full of a glow-in-the-dark solar system. A Vietnamese girl named Jill plays tag with Sis in the second-floor hallway below us. I sit up and watch a color box TV. An anime plays on the screen. "Man, I can't believe you have a TV in your room," I say aloud. "Coming from the boy who has one in a tree." Says Jess with a grin. "Yeah, but still," I tell her. Jess is coloring with colored pencils on a desk in her bedroom that's filled with small statues and posters of fairies, dragon slayers, and other magical imagery. I look out one of the four windows on each side of the attic.

Through the trees, I can see the old mansion. "Have you been back?" Jess asks. "What since we were kids?" I ask as if it wasn't only a handful of years ago. "Yeah, but..." "But what?" Jess asks as I pause. "I don't know," I tell her as I put my folded arms on the windowsill. "It's not the same. Someone gutted the walls and started clearing the yard. I guess they're trying to sell it." I tell her. "Nothing lasts forever, right?" Jess asks. "I think about her comment before answering. "Nope." As I jump back on the bed, I see a stand with an IV bag hanging. "How you been feeling?" I

151

ask. "I'm good! Thanks, Mike. They got me on some medicine. It makes me super sleepy, but I just take it at night." She adds. "Yea, medicine sucks donkey butt," I say as I squeeze my nose and add, "I get some weird-ass dreams, though. How about you?" "Sure do!" Jess answers, "Sometimes I wake up and get stuck." "ME TOO!" I shout. "I'm looking around the room, waiting for someone to pop out or something." I add. "It certainly is terrifying." Jess laughs. "How's school going?" Jess asks. "It's ok, I guess," I answer. "How about you?" "It's not so bad but kinda far, and some of the girls aren't really all that nice, but I'll get used to it," Jess adds. "Not nice!" I interrupt. "Those little bitches." Jess laughs. "No, it'll be fine. They just gotta get to know me." "Yea, they'll come around," I say, reassuring her. "You want to watch Link?" Jess says. "Didn't they take it off the air?" I interrupt. "I taped them!" Jess adds as she grabs a VHS. "Sweet!" I yell. Jess hopes Indian Style on the bed, and the two of us watch our favorite cartoon. *About a year later, Jess and her family moved out of state. I've never heard from Jess since. Wherever she is, I hope she is happy and well.*

I sit in class as Baldy teaches. I have my head down and quietly smash my chin on the desk. I do my eye tic as well. Today Tic has been a

152

real asshole. "Mike! Will you sit up and join us, please." Asks Baldy.

Now, even more agitated, I ignore him and continue smashing. "Hello,

Mike!" Baldy yells. "I HEARD YOU THE FIRST TIME. DAMN IT!" I

shout. The classroom is now completely quiet as Baldy walks over to my

desk. "You think you're a funny guy, don't you? Guess what." He adds.

"You're not. You'll grow up one day and think, wow, I probably should've

had a plan." "Oh, I got plans," I tell him. "Yea, what, fast food." He yells.

"Actually, I was thinking of becoming a hair model, Ya know, like Fabio."

Baldy's face and shiny head grow so red with anger he can't even speak.

"All that hair," I say as I run my fingers through my own. Paige and a few

braver students start to laugh. Baldy grabs my arm and drags me to the

hallway before throwing me out of the room. I gain my footing in the

hallway and run back to the door that he slams in my face. I punch the

door once. "You FUCK!" I yell before turning and heading down the

hallway. "Bald shithead," I mutter. I can imagine Mr. Baldy later that

evening yelling with his mothers in their apartment, "He don't even know

jeopardy."

BOYS WILL BE BOYS

153

Maverick, Satch, and Jamal hang around a TV cart with a cabinet at the bottom for a VCR. "I'm not going in," Satch complains. "Yeah, man, I'm way too big. You do It," Jamal shouts back. "I'll do It," I state. I didn't know what we were doing until they filled me in, but I needed to let off some steam. Maverick, Satch, and Jamal roll the cart into an almost empty gymnasium. "Make sure you grab Cassidy's." Someone yells. "No, Jamie's!" My friends argue. "How's he gonna know whose who?" Asks Jamal. "Just grab any underwear, PLEEEASE!" Maverick yells quietly.

They roll the cart into an office where a female teacher sits. The boys smile at her as they push it past her and into a door that leads to the girl's locker room. "It shouldn't take three of you, ok boys, that's far enough. Bye!" Says Ms. Gray. The boys smile again and wave as they walk out of the office. Now safely in the quiet locker room, I slowly open the cabinet door of the TV stand. With haste, I quietly go through the lockers and study the bags on the bench. I see a bag that says, Lilly. It's empty but next to it is a pair of plain white panties. Next to them is a second bag. Unlike Lilly's bag, this one is falling apart with crumpled-up dirty tissues, nasty socks, and flies buzzing around it. *Ok, there were no flies, but there might as well have been.* With the white panties lying right in between, I look back and forth at the two bags. I hear the loud voices of classmates coming in from outside, I run by a pink bag and grab some purple panties before getting back in the TV cart, but it won't close. "Shit!" I mutter. The other three boys watch from around the corner of the gym as the girls enter the locker room. "Holy shit!" Maverick yells. The girls chat amongst themselves as the light from the locker room shines through the crack in the door. On my shoulder was a spider climbing towards my face. I swat it, making a noise. Sav looks at the TV stand. "You guys hear that?" From outside the locker room the girls are heard screaming as I barge out the locker room with the panties. I catch up with the others, and we turn the corner of a hallway at full speed. Maverick runs with the purple panties now on his head. "Split up!" As we split up, I turn down a hallway and smack into a teacher. Her papers go flying, and I stop to quickly gather them up. "I'm sorry! We um. Were just ah…" I finally look up and find myself face to face with Ms. Reed. She isn't happy.

Satch, Jamal, and I sit in the office. Maverick sits at the principal's desk. Baldy and Mr. Reed stand in as well. We watch through the glass

155

doors as they are seen asking Maverick something. Maverick shrugs his shoulders as Mr. Reed looks at Maverick's backpack. As Mr. Reed pulls out the purple panties, Maverick grabs them and runs for the door. He is taken down by Baldy. Reed pries the panties from Maverick's hand. Jamal is crying softly as he sits next to Satch and I awaiting our turn. Satch and I sit with dry eyes. I was never really much of a crier. Satch only cried on the ball field. Jamal, though, well, his parents worked hard to get him and his brother into a better neighborhood, so I figured he had a good reason to be crying. One by one, our parents pick us up for a three-day suspension. Mom was seen walking to the school, and I put my head down. The one time in my life I wanted it to be my dad who picked me up from trouble. "My own son, the pervert!" I heard in my head. We drive home in silence until Mom finally spoke. "Boys will be boys." She says. "Boys will be boys. That's IT!? What does that mean?" I wonder. "So, I'm not grounded?" I ask foolishly. Mom only laughs.

I lay on my back, hanging off the side of my bed. I look at the window that is now upside down. *Throughout the beginning of mankind, there has been a common misconception that each generation is spoiled with less hardship than the last. Even on a small level, I believe this may be true. Ya, see, going to my room as a kid was never a treat. There was*

no phone, no computer, and no television of any kind. Sure, I could keep

myself busy for 20 minutes or so but after that, forget it. I play with an old

matchbox racing track that leads to the top of my dresser. I read a

Wolverine comic from the late 80s. I shoot Alex, now in ball form, and he

lands in a tan plastic bin filled with paintballs and BB guns. I lay on the

light blue rug in my room and look at the ceiling. Sometimes I wish they

would just beat me and get it over with. But they were cunning.

BOOBIE TRAP

Matt rolls on a skateboard in my garage as I throw stuff around,

looking for something. I step on a hard object, and it cracks, "Shit."

What's up?" Matt asks as I pull out a broken paintball hopper attached to

the gun. "That sucks. When's your game?" He adds. "Tomorrow. Ahh,

let's go." Minutes later, Matt, Jeb, and I look through Jeb's garage. "Sorry

man, thought I had one," Jeb says as he scratches his neck. "Yo Jeb, this

thing work?" Matt asks while sitting on a motorcycle. "Hell yeah!" Jeb

answers, "I think my brother lost his virginity on that thing." "For real?!"

157

Matt replies with a shout. "Yea, I had Mike smell the seat to confirm." I

crack a smile as Jeb, and my cousin laugh out loud. Usually, I would be

right there with them, but I had the paintball game on my mind and, at this

point, wasn't playing. "You know who probably has one D?" Jeb says as

he remembers. "Yes," I answer, "Yes, I do."

     Matt and I turn off the train tracks and into the woods. Dark clouds

roll in as we walk on a sloppy dirt path. Fishing line zigzags across the

path and up some low branches. Off the line hangs metal hub caps and

random scrap. One of the lines runs to a nylon rope that is tied to a high

branch. The other end in an opposite tree, holds a small punching bag

riddled with nails. Another rope is tied to a crate full of broken glass

bottles that sit on a branch above the path. I grab Matt before he steps on a

doormat that lies on the dirt path. "Don't step on that," I say quietly. As we

walk around it, daylight shines through a hole in the rug, and wooden

spikes are seen in the dirt hole beneath. "This is some Leatherface shit."

Says Matt. "So, what the fuck…" Matt's interrupted by loud paintball

guns that blast off from the trees. We hit the dirt, and the paintballs finally

stop. "Who is it!?" Yells Mason Tepper. "It's Mike!" I shout. The paintball guns go off again, and one hits me in the leg. "It's Devaney, dudes chill! I shout as Mason and Liam are heard laughing from the trees.

The four of us sit on rusty folding chairs on a large wooden floor high up in the trees. Rain drizzles off the green and blue pool tarps, acting as a roof overhead. Mason looks through one of many crates that hold miscellaneous items. "How you doing, Liam?" I ask. "I'm just livin man." He says as he sharpens a stick. "Nice, you guys playing tomorrow?" I ask. "Yup." He says as Matt checks out a homemade flamethrower made from a silly string gun, lighter, and a can of hairspray. Matt pulls the trigger, and a quick flame sprays out. A smile quickly climbs Matt's face. Mason finds a paintball hopper and hands it to me. "Twenty bucks." He says. "All I have is eight." Mason stares at the cash in my hand. "Alright."

After hanging out for a bit, Matt hands me a cigarette, and we light up. "Hey!" Mason says while pointing to a no-smoking sign nailed to the trunk of a tree. Why Mason hated cigarettes so much, I'll never know. "Ok, well, thanks. See you guys tomorrow." I say as Matt, and I walk out of the tarps and across a wooden bridge in the rain. The bridge, which was made of 2x4s, comes to a platform with a trash can nailed to the tree. Three umbrellas with duct tape tightly wrapped around them are in the

159

trash can. A steel wire is tied and nailed to the tree holding the platform. "Is this the way down?" Matt asks as he looks down fifteen feet or so to the ground. "I reckon," I say with some twang in my voice. I hook the curved handle of the umbrella over the wire, hold tight and kick off the platform. As I disappear into the woods, Matt grabs an umbrella and hooks it over the wire. He gives it a light pull, and it comes apart. He sighs and grabs the last one. He hooks it and pushes off the platform. Twigs and branches smack his face and torso as he slides down the makeshift zip line. The other end is nailed to a wood plank divided between two trees. Still, at full speed, the umbrella snags the plank, and Matt flips through the air and slams into a dirty twin mattress nailed to a tree. He then falls five feet or so into a shallow leaf pile. I stand next to the pile of wet leaves as Matt sits up and coughs out an acorn. "Next time, we'll just jump off," I say as I rub my shoulder. "Yeah," Matt says, "Next time."

Rain splashes on Holly's face during the same rainstorm that has lasted a week. Tim and I sit on a log under a holly branch that helps shelter us from the rain. We drink from our beer cans. "Let's go, guys." I signal. "Alright, alright, we're coming," Tim says as he crushes his can and chucks it through the trees. We leave the clearing and head down the thin trail that leads to Holly's tree fort tower. We turn the corner of the trail laughing before stopping in our tracks. Tim and I stand with mouths open as Holly starts to walk forward with a straight face. The three-story tree fort tower is now in pieces. "Holy fucking shit, dude," Tim yells. "Holly man, I'm sorry," I say as words spray through the rain. Holly stops at the foot of the tree that held his fallen fort. He reaches through the rain and picks up a business card floating in a puddle under the tree. It reads *LARRY'S CONSTRUCTION*.

Sis and I argue in the upstairs hallway. "She's going to the dance with me!" I yell. "NO! She's, my friend. Why can't you go with someone in your grade!?" Sis asks before adding, "You and Paige are both class clowns. Go with HER!" "I took Paige last time!" I shout. "Go with one of your stuck-up preppy friends!" I say. "They're not stuck up. At least they won't end up in jail like your loser friends!" She adds. "Holly just got a C+ on his spelling test, so the jokes on you!" I argue. "Oh, yea, what'd he have to spell, SHIT!?" Sis yells as we go into our own rooms and slam the door.

"These idiots," I say as Dad, and I drive to Pine Park. "You showed them everything, and they can't even kick. I bet they can't even win against the 3rd graders." "ENOUGH!" Dad yells. I shut up and look out the window. I stayed silent until the game started.

I block a shot, and my defense takes the ball up the field. It's taken back by the other team, and this time they score on me as I jump for it. I get up angry and see Dad from afar, writing on his clipboard. My anger fades, and I walk up to the kid on my team that cost the turnover. "Hey man, remember what my dad said. You don't have to stop to kick the ball. Use the inside like this. I kicked the ball with the inside of my foot. "Ok, thanks, Mike. I'll get it next time." The boy says and I give him a smile and a hi-five.

TAWANTA LAKE CHAMPIONS OF INFINITY

A week later, we play a night game. It's almost the end of the season, and we still haven't won a single game. Tonight, we play the second-worst team in the league, and I have no intention of losing. "Tonight, my dad coaches a team that wins." I think to myself as Dad addresses the team. Alright, guys, you've all been working hard out there, and these guys know it! Let's put on our game faces and win this one!"

162

The team cheers and hits the field. "Mike, Denny over here," Dad says.

"Listen, the defense is weak. I think if we keep one of you in goal the whole game, we will have a good chance of winning." We nod and run out to our positions. I head to the goal first. The black team gets the ball first and heads down past my defense. They kick past the last defender, but I block the shot. I throw the ball to a teammate, but it's quickly intercepted. The black team dribbles it right towards me. "Great." I think to myself as he approaches. The kid from the black team kicks the ball, and my teammate jumps up and headbutts it away. A girl on my defense gets the ball and kicks it to Denny, who dribbles up the field and scores. Dad and I cheer with the rest of our team. I block two more shots before one finally gets through. "Damn!" I shout. It's halftime, and my team eats orange peels as Dad peps them up. "Alright, keep it down the right side; that seems to be working. You guys got this. Let's GO!"

Our team runs out cheering. Mom, Sis, and Faith cheer from the sidelines. The bleachers are getting packed for the second half. I am now playing center forward. I get the ball and dribble it past the black team. I shoot past the defense, but it's blocked by the goalie. He throws the ball down the field to a teammate, who takes it halfway down the sideline

163

before we steal it back. My teammate passes to a tall girl who takes it up the field. I follow on her right. She passes it to me, but my shot is blocked again. The black team takes it down the field. I run full speed, catching up, and slide tackle the ball away from them. I quickly pop up and get the ball, dribbling it towards the opponent's end of the field. When the black team zones in, I kick it to the tall girl who shoots. The goalie jumps and barely blocks it. The crowd cheers from both sides of the bleachers. Dad smiles and claps. "Yea, Rea. Nice shot!" Rea smiles and runs back down the field to help the defense. The black team gets the ball and shoots on Denny, who blocks the shot. Something was different that night. A feeling I had never felt before on the field. I cared. We all did.

The defense kicks the ball up the field to Rea, who passes it back to me. I dribble it past a black team member and shoot, but it's stopped by the defense. I charge the rebound for the ball. The defender tries to pass the ball but fails as I run full speed and intercept it. Now with the goal in sight, I kick as hard as I can. The ball flies past the goalie's outstretched arms and into the net. The crowd cheers. "Yea, awesome shot, bud!" Shouts Dad. I shake my fist and run back down the field. The scoreboard now reads 2-1, and our team is in the lead. There are only 30 seconds left on the timer. The black team quickly moves down the field and shoots, but Denny blocks the shot and throws it to me. I take the ball and dribble up the field before passing it to a teammate and they head towards the goal. Their defense kicks it out of bounds.

I look at the timer as the black team throws in the ball and see them quickly boot it down the field. I dive headfirst to block it, but the ball is too far away. I land on my stomach and watch with anticipation as the other team gets the ball. They get past the defense and score on Denny. The timer goes off, and I hit the dirt with my fist. "Damn IT!" I call out face first in the earth. There was no overtime. At least at the night games. We tied. The two worst teams in the league, and it ends in a tie. I hear cheering and look up. It wasn't just the black team cheering. It was my dad's team as well. I watch as Dad smiles and gives hi-fives to my teammates, who now are jumping up and down. That's when it hit me. They were cheering, not for a win but rather because they didn't lose. I stand to my feet and smile for the first time on the field. I join my teammates in their celebrations. Dad puts his hand out. "Good job, captain." I shake his hand. "Thanks, Coach," I tell him. "Alright, who wants Friendly's!?" Dad shouts to the team. They cheer once more, and the green team leaves the field for the final time.

A low hum of grunge music is heard coming from Jeb's basement. Jeb on drums, me on guitar, and Leo on bass guitar. The next night we fill the school auditorium with kids as they stand and sit on the old wooden floor. Sis talks to her girlfriends. Other friends and classmates are scattered around the auditorium as we tune up. Cara and some other kids lean on the stage. "It's busted," I shout to Jeb. "Relax, D! Here, try this." He says. I grab the new cord and hook it up. I stand at the mic, looking out at the crowd as Jeb tightens his symbols. "How did Jeb talk me into this?" That's all I could think as I tried to shake the bullshit out of my head. I notice Tic and his companion holding up signs in the crowd, but I ignore them. They probably read something like *Go Fuck Yourself* or *You Suck Dick* but no way I was letting them get to me on this night. "We can't start with *RigorMortis*, we need something more upbeat," I complain. "So, let's start with TICS," Jeb says casually. "I don't wanna start with that." I reply. "Short and sweet man," Jeb says, interrupting. "Alright, ready, Leo?" I ask. Leo gives the thumbs up and gets in position. I lean into the mic.

166

"What's up, Bakers Creek? We're MUTE." Jeb cracks his drumsticks, and I hit the strings. Kids in the auditorium nod their heads as dirty guitar chords and drums blast through the hall. A group of kids form a mosh pit, others lean on the stage and a select few just keep talking to each other loudly over the music. *"Come and comfort me when they drive me insane!"* I yell through the PA during the chorus. After I rip a solo, we all hit the last note in perfect timing. As it rings out, we look out to the crowd for approval. There's a brief moment of silence before a random girl yells out and the rest of Bakers Creek follows with cheers and claps. "Holy shit!" I think to myself. So that's what it feels like. I play it cool and keep a straight face. I nod to Leo before looking back at Jeb. We hold back a smile, and Jeb crashes on the hi-hat as we start the next song. The only cover we knew was *Johnny Be Good.* Jeb slammed on his drums before trashing them in a classy grunge manner as I played the guitar behind my head. Leo shortly followed the chaos. The band on stage was ours, but on that night, it belonged to Jeb.

I work on a light green ball of clay in art class. I take a bite out of it and set it to dry. Later, Ms. Reed is at her desk looking as pretty as always. Girls and a few guys talk amongst themselves. The rest of the boys watch the clock. The bell rings, and they quickly run out the door. Ms. Reed runs to the door and calls out to address the class about homework. I make my move. I pass her with a half-smile as I leave. She doesn't smile back. When the class is finally empty, she sits down at the desk and sighs. She notices a green apple made of clay on the desk. It looks realistic with a leafy stem and a bite taken out of it. Homework with my name at the top is under the clay apple. She picks it up, and now alone in the room, she lets out a smile. *At least, I hope she did. Although Ms. Reed was mad at me for faking the severity of my disability, after that day we always shared a smile.*

Outside in the schoolyard. The boxing crew is in a circle behind the old Rec Lodge. Satch and Jamal stand with gloves on. "Alright, boys, it's the MAIN event," Maverick yells. The crowd cheers as they put up their gloves. Satch throws a hard right jab, but Jamal dodges. He throws another right but Jamal smacks it down, "That all you got?" Satch takes advantage of Jamal's trash-talking and throws a high right-hand jab that hits Jamal in the temple and ear. Jamal throws back a quick combo and hits Satch hard in the face. The crowd cheers out. Satch backs up with his gloves covering his face as Jamal rains down on him with punches. Satch

168

gets hit in the stomach and bends over. Jamal hits him in the face, and Satch pushes him away with his gloves. Now on the move, Satch throws his own attack of quick punches. Jamal blocks them all but the last of the combo, a right cross. Jamal is stunned. He swings blindly, hooking Satch in the face. Satch hits the dirt, and the crowd quiets down.

"He's done." Says Keith. Satch pounds the dirt with his fists before taking off the gloves and throwing them away. "Fuck this." He yells. The crowd gets loud as Satch stands and puts up his fists. Jamal smiles, takes his own gloves off, and tosses them. "Bout time." He says. They meet bare-knuckle. Satch throws the first punch, and the loud sound of bone-cracking bone echoes through the back of the schoolyard. The crowd hoots and hollers as a second crack is heard. Satch catches himself from falling and tackles Jamal to the ground. Both in headlocks, they swing blindly with their alternate hands, hitting each other in the face and torso.

The next day, Mrs. Lee walks into a talkative classroom. She notices Satch with a black eye and busted lip. At the same time, Jamal comes in and sits next to Satch; his face looks about the same. The classroom quiets down. Mrs. Lee looks them over, "You two want to tell me what happened?" "We fell down the steps," Satch tells her. The classroom laughs. "I see; well, someone will talk." She says. "They always do. Ok, class, open to page forty in your textbooks." As the class sighs, Satch puts his fist up. Jamal does the same, and the two friends bump fists.

On the 3rd floor, Mitch and I sit on the radiator and smoke cigarettes. I stick a pack of *Camels* in my gym bag filled with boxing gloves. "So that's it, huh?" Mitch says, looking at the bag of gloves. "Yup, until next year," I answer with a puff of smoke. "You keep them in the fort?" Mitch says, "That thing is dope." "I put them wherever. Some are my dad's. Oh shit, I almost forgot." I yell as I pull a trophy out of the bag. On it was a marksman with gold plaques that would hold our future victories. "Check it out. My dad got it for the cabin. Hope you've been practicing because I plan to be the first name on that bitch." I say. "Damn." "That is sweet." Mitch states, "I hope you're a better shooter than a fighter." "What! I kicked his ass!" I yell with a smirk. "I'm just playing," Mitch says as he flicks his ash. I toss the bag on the ground. "Yea, we'll see," I tell him. "Aww shit, let's do this!" We glove up and trash talk as we spar on the top abandoned floor of Bakers Creek Middle School.

Mitch and I stayed friends throughout high school. Soon after, he, his brother, and some other friends would join the military. On leave, they'd take Jeb and me to the Pine Barrens with M4s and other fun toys they were or were definitely not allowed to have as civilians. We eventually lost touch in our twenties, but I hear that he's now a fireman in Atlantic City. Although I haven't seen or heard from Mitch in years, I'm looking forward to a cold beer with him one of these days.

LEGENDS OF BAKERSFIELD

It's midnight in Bakersfield, New Jersey. A Jack-o'-lantern sits on a counter at the police station. *I've done a lot of stupid, pointless shit that I'm not particularly proud of, and this next one sits towards the top.* A fat cop, with a mustache, walks by holding a coffee. He takes a seat behind the counter, grabs a newspaper, and starts to read. He then hears something and listens closely. He gets up, walks around the counter, and exits out a door that leads to the side of the police station.

Outside, *1812 Overture* plays on an old boombox across the street from the police station. The cop runs down the side steps and to the front yard of the station. Loud bottle rockets and mortar firework rounds explode over the station. As the cop stops in his tracks, a bottle rocket flies over his head and lands on the roof before falling to the ground by his feet. He looks at the dark woods across the street where they seem to be coming from. In the shadows at the edge of the woods is Jeb. He has a lighter in each hand and is lighting the remaining bottle rockets which are stuck in the loose dirt aimed at the station. Tim is next to Jeb with a mortar. He drops a lit firework round, and it launches over the police station before exploding. Holly and I sit in the bushes by the steps holding a smoke bomb. Holly attempts to light the other end.

"HEY!" Yells the cop as he runs back to the side door. "It's busted!" Holly yells. "Hurry, he's coming back!" I whisper loudly. The lighter sparks and Holly lights the wick. I throw it in the door, and Holly shuts it before we hide back in the bushes. The police officer comes back and heads up the stairs and into the door. As the door closes the cop is heard falling into chairs as he walks through the cloud of smoke. "You little fuckers!" He screams and stumbles back out the door. Holly and I run across the street to meet the others as the cop yells in our direction.

"My boombox!" Jeb yells as he remembers. "Just run, Jeb." Yells Tim as we sprint through the dark woods. We come to the opening by the old chimney, but a cop car is sitting in front of the old man's house, and its lights are on. "AW fuck." Jeb yells. "Shit dude, what now!?" Tim says, worried. We instinctively run back the way we came, hop a small wood fence, and land in a giant backyard. We run through a moonlit patch of grass and head towards the back dirt driveway that leads to a side street. A cop car screeches to a stop at the end of the driveway and turns on its lights. The four of us slide to a stop in the dirt and stones, before running back into the yard. Tim heads off in his own direction as the rest of us run to an oversized two-story garage in the back. Holly and I climbed up some old sections of fencing that lean on the side of the garage. We jump up, grab the roof's rim, pull ourselves up, and hop to the second story. We climb to the top of the slanted roof and slide down the other side. The officers shine their flashlights our way, so we climb back up and lay in a dark spot on the slanted rooftop. Jeb runs full speed into an old rotting door next to the garage. He busts through it like a bat out of hell and lands on the dusty floor. Jeb quickly gets up and looks around. After closing the door, he runs up some stairs to the second floor of the garage. "We're fucked, man," Holly shouts. "Any ideas?" I look over at the end of the roof and smack Holly on the shoulder. We creep over to the edge while looking over to a small alleyway. On the other side of the ally is a wooden fence covered in ivy; opposite is a shed in the next yard. The shed roof is low and flat. "Think we can make it?" I ask. "We don't have a choice." Holly states. We put our fists out and shoot for it in a whisper. "Waffle Tits!" "Shit Speckle!" After losing, I put my toes over the edge of the slanted roof, aim through the dark for the gap in the foliage, and jump.

The moonlight shines in my eye for a split second before clearing the fence and landing on the shed. I roll to a stop, and with one hand on the edge, I hop to the ground. Holly gets his footing as I watch from the next yard. He then flies through the moonbeam and hits the shed roof. "Yea!" I yell, "Alright, let's go." As we take off, we hear Jeb shouts my name from where we had just jumped. "It's JEB!" I say. "How'd you get up there!? Holly asks. "Through the window." He yells quietly. "Go back and hide!" I shout. "I can't!" Jeb yells nervously. "OK, man, you gotta just go for it!" I shout in a whisper. "Yeah, man, don't hesitate!" Adds Holly. Holly looks at the roof he is standing on and quickly hops off. He joins me as I watch Jeb get his footing. "He's not gonna make it," Holly says. "He'll make it!" I interrupt. Jeb jumps hard, and his silhouette sores across the full moon that sits in the starry night sky. His momentum slows down as he reaches the lower shed. Jeb lands hard on the edge as shingles fall to the ground. Holly and I celebrate quietly in the dark. Jeb hops off the roof, and my friends and I take off through a backyard and fade into the shadows. "I think we can call it a night, guys," I suggest. "Not yet," Holly says. "We have one more stop."

"It's another hot day out there for October." Says a truck radio as the driver shuts off his engine. He unlocks the front door to an unfinished building in the neighborhood as seven construction workers have a conversation about the materials they'll need for the day. They find the section they've been working on and grab their toolboxes. A big guy with a beard drops his box on a workbench as others sit on overturned buckets on the floor. "He ain't coming in. She's keeping him nice and warm." Says one of the men. "He'll hear from me tomorrow." Says the big, bearded guy as he opens his toolbox to a steamy pile of shit. The big guy yells and turns his head. Each construction man opens their toolbox to the same sight of melted feces that covers their tools. As the smell hits them in the face, they turn away and cover their mouth and nose. A toolbox is kicked,

175

shit, and tools fly everywhere. One of them throws up as they walk away. Another man pulls a wrench out of his box by the handle with two fingers as it drips with diarrhea. The large, bearded guy throws his tool chest. Shit and tools fly through the air, and with clenched fists, he screams in anger. We weren't there to see the outcome at Larry's Construction site, but I like to think the end of the *1812 Overture* played throughout the discovery of Holly's classic revenge.

One for the Razerbacks plays on the Tree Fort stereo. Satch and I play *Contra* on the Nintendo as Tim and Holly watch from the couch bunk. We reach a game over. "Damn!" I yell. "What board was that?" Satch says as he watches me pinch my nose. "Four, I think." I say with an eye tic. "You haven't really been doing that stuff lately, huh?" Asks Satch. "It's there every day, but it comes and goes," I answer. "Yeah, well, hopefully, this time it just goes," Satch adds while I hand my controller to Tim. Jeb and Leo are heard coming up the ladder. "Shit, I got practice," Satch says as he looks at a battery clock. "See ya, man." I say. "Later." Satch says as he moves the plywood door and heads out. A long extension cord is seen going out the door, wrapping around the deck railing and down the side of the cedar tree. Satch passes Leo and Jeb. They say their hellos, and Satch climbs down the ladder as Leo and Jeb enter the fort. They each have a backpack. The friends greet one another as I jump on the top bunk and pick up a camcorder from the late 80s. I hit play and watch through the viewfinder.

Inside is a homemade action movie starring Jeb, Holly, Tim, and I. I watch as blood sprays out and Jeb gives an Oscar-winning death. Gunfights, hand-to-hand combat, and roof jumps follow with more of the same. I take my eye from the viewfinder and hit rewind on the side of the camcorder. "NEXT!" Jeb yells. "Come on. Holly's been waiting all day." I tell Jeb. Jeb sits on Tim's lap as Holly grabs a controller. "Best seat in the house." Jeb says sarcastically. "Aw fuck! Alright, get OFF!" Tim moves and sits by Leo, opening his backpack and showing Tim a bong. The two quietly hi-five as Jeb and Holly play NES. I put down the camcorder with a disappointing look and stare at an empty space on the wall. I cleared that wall for something I planned on hanging up. A priceless trophy that I will never see again.

After Holly's toolbox detour, I had my own motive.

A door at Baker's Creek Middle School was, for whatever reason, unlocked indefinitely. Holly and I made our way to the principal's office.

Under the teacher's mailboxes was a chair that sat fellow misfits and troublemakers throughout the years. Each one had signed their name as a right of passage on the bottom of the wooden mailbox, as did I. To this day, I can close my eyes and see the signatures burnt in my mind. I was so close, as I came several feet away from the trophy that held the Legends of Bakersfield. It was then that Holly and I found we were not alone in the dark hallways of Bakers Creek. Loud footsteps were heard running down the stairwell. Holly took off first while I stood there looking at the door. I bit my lip hard and ran with Holly as the footsteps got louder. Out of all the pointless regrets in my life, that one has stayed with me for whatever reason. We would be the last graduating class of Bakers Creek. A few summers later, they bulldozed the building to the ground as a new building now holds K-8. I couldn't imagine having to spend nine years in one building, but what are ya gonna do?

"What are we going to do, guys?" I ask out of nowhere while sitting on the top bunk. "Oh, come on, Little asshole bazooka BITCH!" Jeb yells over my question. "GUYS!" I shout once more. "About what, Mike?" Holly asks. "I don't know, in life." I add. "Finish school. Go to college." Tim and Jeb state. "Pft, I'm not going to college," I say with a raised eyebrow. "Yeah, fuck that." Yells Holly. "Welcome to the University of D's and C's," I add, getting a laugh from Holly. "What are ya gonna do, push a lawnmower the rest of your life!?" Tim yells over the music. "That's a lot of dog turds, D," Jeb states. The tape in the boombox stops. Jeb loses a life and quickly scrambles to pull a CD from his old backpack. He puts in the disc and hits play before returning to the game. A guitar riff starts up the song as I get comfortable on the top bunk. Seven years I wondered. Where would we be?

I wake up shirtless in my bed. I have short messy hair, and I look disheveled. I look around the bedroom I've had since I was four years old. I crank back my head for my latest tic. I have just turned twenty years old, and I have no school, money, or plans for the future; and in an hour, I'll have no car or job. *With that said, it was possibly the greatest summer I've ever had. However, that was seven years away. So, for now, I'll just hang in a tree with my best friends and listen to the song Loser play on the boombox.*

CHAPTER 5 — THE BARNYARD

I don't know exactly when or where I was going, but I do know I was driving. It was June, and the air was low with the windows cracked. As I watched the road, something caught my eye. I turned my head to the left and saw an old railroad track that ran into a hole in the earth. As I followed the tracks with my eyes, I had a feeling that I had never felt before. It was the feeling of pure happiness. As this feeling ran through me, all the unimportant bullshit in my life had left. I followed the tracks with my eyes for as long as possible until they were covered up by green branches and brush. The tracks were gone. I never did see where they led.

MAGIC BUS

I wake up and put two feet on the floor. The sound of a June

morning creeps through my open window. I stand up, tap my foot and

walk out into the hallway. I'm now standing in the shower with water

running on me. I'm around 5'9 and 165 pounds. I'm thin with a layer of

lean muscle. I turn the shower nozzle all the way to cold and make a face

as the steam leaves the shower. I take three of the same pills and lay them

out. I begin playing Three Card Monty before throwing the last pill in the

garbage, then throwing the other two in my mouth. *Fuckin OCD.* I leave

the bathroom and turn "on" the light. After finishing a bowl of cereal, I

chug a glass of OJ and slam it on the table. I get up to leave again before

coming back and slamming it twice more. Once more trying to leave, but

this time with an angry face, I slam it again. The glass shatters. "FUCK!"

Outside it's a sunny day. I jump off my front porch in shorts, sneakers, and

a collared shirt with my name tag. I hop in a white station wagon with the

windows open and two surfboards sticking out the back of the trunk. One

is an old Hobie longboard, and the other a shortboard. I reach around the

floor for the keys, check the visor and shake my head. "Shit head." I quickly run back into the house and make a call. "Yo, Satch. I need a ride."

Later that day, I find myself working at a local gym. In a small room with a washer and dryer, I look at the reflection in the dryer of the blah face I woke up with. I throw some dirty towels in the washer and notice a brown streak on one of the white towels. I carefully put the last towel in and shut the door before taking a sniff and looking around. I lift my elbow and see someone's smeared feces on my forearm. I want to say something, but nothing comes out. I then fold the towel full of smeared feces and put it in a pile of clean towels before rolling it in front of the guy's locker room. A man grabs one. "These clean?" he asks while not waiting for an answer. "Yup," I say, walking past the front desk, taking my collared shirt, and throwing it in the trash. "See you next time." The counter girl shouts as I walk out the front door in a tank top. I walk to a strip mall pay phone and pop in two quarters.

It's early afternoon now as the wind blows pebbles across an old paved lot that is more sand now than pavement. A small crummy building sits in the lot on the corner of the main road and a side street. The beige color building has a flat roof. Facing the building, there's a dry cleaner on the right and a sub shop on the left. Parked next to the sub shop is a Tie-died Volkswagen bus from the '70s with big letters that read *PHAT'S.*

"Your party was fucking sick," Satch tells me as we park next to the Volkswagen. "Me and Julie Conway talked for like three hours in your shed." Satch tells me. "You bang her?" I ask as Satch smokes the last of his cigarette. "Na, but still, it was worth it. You get rid of those kegs?" He asks. "Yeah, Jeb grabbed them like twenty fucking minutes before my folks got home." Satch laughs at the irony of Jeb's punctuality. "Then how the hell did you get caught." He asks while tossing his butt. "Sis cleaned the shit out of everything, but we forgot about the footprints on the ceiling." Satch shakes his head as we leave his Jeep and adds, "Can't win 'em all."

A jingle bell on the front door rings as we walk inside the old sub shop. Green tile floors, some booths, a soda fridge with sliding glass doors, an old pizza oven, and green countertops fill the shop. A bain marie sits next to the register. Behind that is an open doorway that leads to two rooms in the back. The bigger of the two holds the grill. The smell of fried onions hits me in the face as I'm greeted by a friendly black lab. "Hey, Susie," I say as I kneel down to scratch her ears. I look up to her companion as he carries a wrapped half a sub to one of the booths. "Hey, Uncle Pete." I say. "ONE PUNCH PETE!" Satch shouts; always a fan of the nickname. Satch puts his hands up and gives Pete a soft kidney shot. "You think you still got it?" Pete shrugs, "I hope."

Clark stands at the cash register by the wall phone. He's about the same size as me, with brown hair in a part that almost passes his ears. A smaller kid with brown hair and a full beard sits on a counter behind the bain marie. "Alright, about 20 minutes," Clark says before hanging up the phone on the wall and wiping the sweat off his forehead. With no air conditioning, the sub shop is hotter than a trucker's ass crack in August. Clark gives me a hi-five shake. "Yooo," I say with a grin. "Yo Mike," Clark replies. "What's up Flynn," I say, leaning in. Sitting on a counter, Flynn looks up from his newspaper. "Hey, man. What you been up to?" Clark asks. "Nothing," I reply "I just quit my job." "Nice," Clark says as he hands Flynn the food slip. Flynn takes it to the grill. "Make a whole for Devaney," Clark calls out to the grill. "Miteyyyy!" Obee says while flipping some grilled cheese stakes. Obee was a tall kid with short brown hair. A man in his 30s walks through an old wooden screen door at the back wall. He drops a bag of sub rolls, grabs a remote from the counter, and aims it at a colored box tv in the corner of the ceiling. It turns on to the sports channel. "You guys watching the game?" Pete asks as Satch joins them both. "Mike doesn't watch sports," Satch replies with a chuckle. "He don't?" Pete says before biting his sub. "You didn't know that?" Asks Satch. Pete shakes his head. "You could probably get a job here if you want." Says Clark as he makes an Italian. "Really?" I say with some enthusiasm. Clark grins, "Yea, I mean they hired Obee." "You got an application?" I ask. Flynn hands Clark a piece of paper as he replies, "Um, yea, here." I grab a pen from a metal cylinder by the register and flip over the paper to see a drawing of a naked lady running with a giant dick in each hand. She looks confused as to not know what to do with the rapidly ejaculating penises. Clark and Flynn give a laugh as I chuckle and examine the work of art.

Another guy in his 30s comes out of the back room holding a sub tray. He was dressed like a hippie with a beard and long wavy brown hair that reached his ass. I have seen both men on many occasions, but I couldn't remember their names as usual. "Hey Levi, Mike applied for a job; here are his credentials," Clark says while trying not to laugh. Levi puts down the sub tray and looks at the dick application that was signed and handed to him by Clark. "Niiiice," Levi says, smiling. "Well, we do need a driver on Wednesdays." Obee comes in from the back and throws a rag over his shoulder. "Mity can't drive. He has Tourette's!" Obee shouts. The sub shop erupts in laughter, including the quiet man watching the sports channel.

Clark chimes in, "Soo, you have to hire him." Flynn nods, "It's the law." Obee grabs some Pepper Jack and heads back to the grill. "Go make my sub bitch." I say while throwing a pen cap in his direction. "Should we give him a try, Ted?" Levi asks. "Whatever," Ted mutters back still standing at the TV with his arms crossed. Ted's a ginger with a buzz cut. He had the look of a jock and wore sub-stained gray sweatpants, a white t-shirt, and a white apron that folded and tied at the waist. I have never seen him in anything else at the shop. "Come by Thursday around three. I'll show you the rundown." He says. "Thanks, Levi," I replied while shaking his hand.

It's six pm as me and The Fam sit at our dinner table. We pass helpings of potatoes with cheddar cheese, bacon and green olives, chicken wings, and string beans. If I was ever on death row, Mom's special potatoes would be on my last plate of food. No doubt. I touched the end of my nose while looking at Sis, but she just smirks and downs her milk.

"Hey Faith, you beat Ocarina yet?" " Naa, I'm stuck." She says while

grabbing a wing. "Let me guess, Water Temple," I state while taking a

drink. "No, I'm passed there." She says. "You're what!? Did you look it

up?" I shout. "Na." Faith replies. "Holy poop!" I say in shock. "Yea, she's

been working hard." Mom adds while the sound of metal forks tap on

porcelain plates. "You two have any plans tonight?" Dad asks. Sis answers

first, "Me and Lea are going to the movies." "How about you, Mick?" I

chew some chicken before answering dad's question, "Nothing, I guess."

WHY DO THEY CALL YOU JOHNNY PARTY

It's almost dark now as the last strands of red fade in the sky above

Jebs' house. Jeb's minibike with flat tires sits in the back of his crowded

garage. He rummages through items. I walk in from the twilight through

the open garage doors. I grab a string cheese from an old rusty fridge next

to a gray rotary phone that sits on the wall. "HA!! Hot ya, you little

fucker!" Jeb holds up a random piece of metal with a connected dangling

wire. Jeb had on an old pair of corduroy shorts and a tie-dye t-shirt. "His hair was longer now, about to the bottom of his ears, and he had a goatee. He's still a little taller than me, but he has slimmed down. I nod with a smile as I take a bite of the cheese. "Yo D!" He shouts, acknowledging me for the first time today.

In Jeb's room, he types on a laptop at the desk while I sit on a couch against the window wall and watch TV. Jebs' room has hippy posters, lava lamps, etc. A poster of a zombie hangs next to a bulletin board full of calendars and papers. "You know what we haven't done in a while?" I ask. Jeb says nothing. "Jammed." With still no response, I ask again. "What ya think? Jeb!?" Jeb studies his laptop carefully. This time I try a different approach, "Ya know, sometimes I put on my mom's clothes? Yea, then I hang upside down in my closet and pour milk in my asshole." Jeb bangs the desk and looks at his calendar with a pissed-off face. After looking back at the laptop, his expression changes to shock and excitement as he slowly looks back at the calendar. He finally speaks, "Oh...my....God. We gotta go!" Jeb says getting straight to the point. "Where!?" I say, throwing my arms up. He grabs his keys, cell phone, and wallet as he runs out the bedroom door and down the steps. "Let's Go D!"

He shouts. "Where are we going, Jeb?" "Johnny Party's! It's his birthday; grab my cigs!" I grab a pack of smokes and follow Jeb down the stairs.

It's completely dark now. A white mansion with pillars sits on a nice street. Jeb and I pull up in his maroon station wagon. Jeb lays on the horn. A boy our age comes out of the mansion. He's wearing khakis, nice shoes, a tucked-in button-down collared shirt, and a tie. He's short, has blond short hair in a part, and rosy cheeks. He closes and locks the front door to the mansion, takes a step, and turns back to check the doorknob to make sure it's locked. "Let's go!" Jeb yells. Halfway to the car, Johnny stops and looks at us. "Don't do it! Let's go, Johnny!" We yell. Sure enough, Johnny puts his hands up, turns, and runs back to check the nob. "Was he wearing a tie?" I ask Jeb as he lights a smoke. *I don't really know how to explain Johnny's situation, so I'll just say this...He is the most straight-edge man to ever walk planet earth.* He runs awkwardly to the car. "Oh my, Johnny, lose the tie, bud!" Jeb insists. "But it's my favorite tie, Jeb." Johnny gets in the back seat, and Jeb peels off. "Take it off."

We met Johnny party in high school. Some members of the TV crew found Johnny in the hallway and asked him to show them some dance moves for the morning announcements. They liked his dance move

189

so much that they replayed the ten-second dance video for the entire two-minute morning intro. Now, I know what some people might be thinking. "Oh no, how could they do that to poor old Johnny." Well, what they're not thinking of is the fact that Johnny Party fucking loved it. Every time that video played, he had a big smile for the rest of the day. He'd say, "Hey Mikey did you see my dance moves?" And I'd say, "Fuck yeah I did. That shit was HOT!" Jeb befriended him immediately. He must have knocked ten people over that day just trying to get to Johnny. "JOHNNY PARTYYY!" Jeb screamed as he shook Johnny with joy. "Do I know you?" Johnny asked. Ignoring the question, Jeb threw his arm around Johnny as they walked down the hallway. "Maaan," Jeb said. "I've been looking for you everywhere."

Johnny sits in the backseat of the Volvo and looks around. Jeb bites his nails as he drives and looks at Johnny's tie in the rearview. Another reason the name stuck was because... "Hey Mikey, do you know if there's any parties tonight?" Johnny asks while bending his vowels. I turned around and looked at him before answering, "Do you know where we're going tonight, Johnny?" "A strip club." He replies as I nod. "And do you know what happens at a strip club?" I ask. "Yeah, well, no," Johnny replies. I look at Johnny and simply say, "We smoke cigarettes and drink beer while naked girls jump up and down on our crotch. Now, if that's not a party, I can't help you." "Oh, Ok." He says as he smiles. We sit in silence for a moment before Jeb jumps over the seat and grabs Johnny's tie. I casually grab the wheel, as this was not out of character for Jeb to stop driving while in the driver's seat. I bring us into our own lane as an oncoming car holds its horn as they pass. "Give me the tie Johnny, please!" "No, Jeb, it's my favorite tie!"

A grimy rock song plays in a dingy strip club. Johnny sits between Jeb and me at the edge of the dance stage as we hoot and holler with fists full of cash. A girl dances in nothing but a G-string on the stage. Johnny reaches out his hand to a dancer walking by. She smiles and takes the dollar he had in his hand. As he sits back with a smile, Jeb and I stare at him with confused faces. "What the hell was that Johnny?" Jeb asks. "I'm tipping her, Jeb, Duh," Johnny replies, defending his actions. Johnny knows that we wouldn't treat him any different than we would treat each other. All though light-hearted, we wouldn't skip a beat to try and help break Johnny's shell. I have to give it to him, though; he stuck to his guns. I shake my head as I count out some singles. Jeb puts his hand in front of me. "Nah, I got this." He says. "Here we go, Johnny," I yell as Jeb leans over the stage on his back with three dollars in his mouth and two on his crotch. The dancer straddles his face and climbs down his stomach. She rubs her head on his crotch and shakes her ass an inch from his face. "Oh my God!" Johnny yells with eyes as wide as the sun. As the cheers die down, a dancer comes up and sits in Johnny's lap. "Hey, handsome, you want a dance?" Johnny looks at us for approval. "The answer is yes, Johnny Party," I say with a hand on his shoulder. "Oh wow, why do they call you Johnny Party?" She asks. "You're about to find out, sweetie," Jeb says as he hands her a wad of cash. The dancer takes Johnny by the hand, and they start to walk away. "Whoa, hold up, Johnny, what'd we tell you about stripers?" Jeb asks. "They only like me because of my money." Johnny replies. "Have fun, buddy!" Jeb yells as we nod our heads. "You're an asshole, Jeb." The dancer says with a smile on her face. "I love you, Tory!" Jeb lashes back. "Don't worry, Hunny, Jeb spends more on me than anyone." She says to Johnny as they disappear into the smokey crowd. Still smiling, I turn to Jeb, "You're here every day, aren't you?" "Fuck that!" He says while handing me a cig. We chug our beer and light up.

The place has quieted down now as Jeb, and I sit at the empty bar with an ice bucket containing a few remaining *Honey Brown's*. I crack another. "What'd they start you at?" I ask. "I only drive for Phat's here and there, so I couldn't tell ya," Jeb says. "They usually just throw me some cash at the end of the night." "Hey, aren't we missing someone?" "Yeah, where is he?" I say as Johnny walks up behind us. "Hey, Jeb. Hey Mikey." "Yoo, buddy." "So, how was it?" Jeb asks. "It was good. Do you guys think I can borrow more money?" "More!?" Jeb interrupts. "How much did you give her?" I asked. "Two hundred dollars," Johnny says. "Two Hundred!" Jeb and I yell. "Damn, Johnny, you could have got laid for that much!" I say. "I'll pay you back." He asks. "No, Johnny, we tried to tell you," Jeb says before sighing. "I'm taking a piss." Jeb gets up and walks toward the bathroom. I smirk and hand Johnny some cash. "Thanks, Mikey."

As we leave the strip club, Johnny calls out to the dancers, saying goodbye, name by name. Johnny drives Jeb's maroon station wagon in the dark as I sit in the passenger seat. *I'm drunk.* "So, you have fun, man?" I ask. "Yea, thanks!" Johnny replies. "Good, take a right up here." As I point, Johnny does a double-take, "Right here?" "Yup." As the words leave my mouth, Johnny makes an illegal left at a light and heads down a side street. "I said, right, dude," I say as mellow as possible. "Sorry." He replies. "It's cool. Just keep going. I'll get you there." I reassure him.

Without warning, a cop follows and puts on their lights. "OH NO, MIKEY, IT'S THE COPS!" Johnny screams as if it was *Fredy Cougar*. "Shit, it's ok, Johnny. Just pull over." I tell him. "But I've been drinking!" He yells. "You had one beer like four hours ago!" I yell as I throw some t-shirts and trash over the last six-pack of *Honey Brown*. "What should I do?" He asks me. "Well, pull over for one!" I yell. "Right here!?" He asks for the last time. My reply was simple. "YES!" "OK," Johnny says as he pulls over into a side yard. He runs over lawn ornaments and some trash cans before coming to a hard stop. "Holy shit, dude!" I say as I scramble to cover the beer.

"I have to tell them I was drinking," Johnny says. "Don't do that," I say with a chuckle. "JOHNNY!" I shout. Faster than I've ever seen him move in his life, Johnny flies out the door and directly towards the cop car. "I was drinking! I was drinking!" He yells at the cop, who has barely gotten out of his car. The startled cop puts his hand up and puts his other by his gun. "Stop!" He yells. "Sir, get back in your car!" I watch as

Johnny pleads with the cop. I then look down at Jeb, who is laid flat and snoring in the back seat. I reach down, crack a beer, and chug it down.

SHALLOW GRAVE

Dad pulls up to Pete's rancher in a horseshoe driveway. The place looks a little messy. The yard is wide, and there's an old red faded barn and some chicken coops in the left corner. A roster, chickens, and every other south Jersey barnyard bird roam the yard. Dad shoos them away as he gets out of his white sports car. He checks out a crummy-looking three-man boat with a motor. The name reads *CAPSIZED,* although this boat's name is written upside down. Dad checks out some fishing gear in the boat left out in the rain. "Come on, Pete." He says.

Dad calls out Pete's name as he walks around the house. He sees some dirt flying out of a big hole in the backyard. He looks in the hole and sees Pete. The hole is about four feet deep and shaped like a grave. Susie runs up to Dad, and he pets her and says, "Hey, Pete. We still fishing or what?" "Yup," Pete says as he throws the shovel in the dirt and climbs out to light a cigarette. "You getting a pool?" Dad jokes. Pete shakes his head.

"How's Bobby and Heather?" Dad asks, referring to my cousins. Pete

takes a drag of his cigarette before answering. "Bob's joining the Army."

He says. "No shit!" Dad states, "Good for him! And Heather?" Pete puffs

again. "She moved in with that boyfriend." Dad tries to keep up with his

enthusiasm after Pete's straightforward answer. "Is he treating her

alright?" Dad asks. Pete takes one last drag before flicking his cigarette

butt into the four-foot hole. "Nope," Pete says and walks away. Dad looks

at Pete, the hole, and back at Pete before following him to the boat.

Back at home, I sit up in bed. Within seconds I hear the laughter

that I'm greeted with every morning. "Hey Fuck Face!" Says a familiar

raspy voice. "Aren't you forgetting something?" I immediately blow air

out as I twist my neck. "That's right, you have some catching up to do."

Says Tic with a wicked smile. *For whatever reason, Tic and OCD cannot*

visit me in my dreams. Maybe it has something to do with what side of the

brain or some shit. I don't fucking know, but anyway, I'm not complaining.

"You take it from here," Tic says as he fades into a shadow. OCD points

to the floor with a nod. I ignore his demand and get up; he isn't happy.

Without the ability to speak, OCD grunts and points again. In his left arm

is a bundle of small picture frames. He grabs one and shows me with a mean frown. After seeing his artwork, I sigh and sit back on the bed. I look up at him slowly and tap my foot on the ground. "Happy now, Cunt?" I ask. He nods. After my shower, I come down the stairs, and that's when I see it. Tics' newest associate. In some ways, this little fucker was the worst of the bunch. I felt his presence in bed, but like usual, I could only see him out the corner of my eye. Like OCD, he lets Tic do the talking. The troll-like figure lurks quietly. His red shirt is never fully visible, and I've only seen it read one letter *A*. I'm now shaking in the corner of the living room. It's barely dawn, and I am crouched and sweating. The feeling I have has never been described. Any physical discomforts are heavily outweighed by the mental. Eventually, I find myself in the yard on my hands and knees. The red morning sky is above.

The doctor's office. A man's face. He's bug-eyed and doesn't move a muscle. I sit in a chair across from him and look around the office at the plaques and various awards he has received over the years. Afterward, I stand at a counter as a lady gives me a medicine script. I take it and leave.

I sit on my couch in the living room with a Nintendo-64 controller in hand. I look at a clock that reads 11:15. I pick up a portable phone with a floppy antenna and begin to dial. "This is Tim." Annoyed to get yet another answering machine, I hang up the phone. My dad comes home at noon to eat lunch each day. If he saw me farting around in the middle of the day, he would surely find something for me to do. As I ponder, I hear my Dad pull up outside. I head for the back door. Outside, I hop in the white station wagon and turn the key but hear nothing. I bang the wheel with my fist, get out and slam the door. I walk down a bike path where the train tracks used to be and head into some woods. I'm wearing a tank top, board shorts, and flips. As I walk through the trees. Something lurks in the shadows. I know it's not one of my shitty companions, for they don't have the ability to bend branches. I hear it and stop. It jumps out and onto me, licking my face. I was first startled until I recognized the German Shepherd. I pet him and check his collar. "Damn, dude, you trying to make me shit myself!?" I say before whistling. "Come on, Jack."

THE NINA PINTA AND THE SANTA MARIA

The morning humidity fills the air as I walk up to an old-style rancher. I look through a screen window. I knock on an old wooden screen door before executing a blow tic. "Hey, Paige. You home?" I politely yell through the screen. "Come in!" A girl calls out from inside the house. Jack and I walk in and around to a kitchen where a girl pours lemonade. The girl is thin and about 5'6 with straight, long, bleach-blond hair. She's wearing a long tank top with a bikini under it. "Devaney!" She says with a smile, "What's up, man!" "Hey, Tess!" I say while getting a hug. "Come on in!" Tess says and gets back to the lemonade. "So, how've you been!? I feel like I haven't seen you in forever." Tess adds then grabs some plastic Solo cups from the counter and flicks her hair back, showcasing her natural allure. "I'm good," I reply, "How about you guys?" "We're good, you know?" Tess says before letting out a chuckle that cuts off her girly voice. "Haley's here!" Tess points out. I peek out to a living room where Haley lays on the couch in a tank top. "Hey, Devaney." She says with a sleepy voice. "Yo Haley," I lean on a counter, and Tess slides me a plastic cup of lemonade mixed with *Bankers Club*. "Enjoy." Tess says as I sip it and make a face. "That'll wake ya," I say as Haley comes in and hops on a high stool next to me. She grabs the cup. "Is it strong?" She says before sipping it. "You want one?" Tess asks. "Yeaa," Haley says as she scrunches her pretty face. Haley's a petite girl with short blond hair to her shoulders. "I found your mutt in the woods by the police station," I say.

199

Tess laughs, "Thanks, my dad probably left the fucking gate open again."

"I thought maybe your sister was home," I tell her. "I figured you'd still be in school." Laughing, Haley replies, "It's the end of June, dude." "Damn, already," I say, half kidding. "Yea, we're done with that fucking place," Tess says before getting a look from Haley. "Oh, shit, my bad, Haley," Tess says, forgetting that Haley is a year younger. "I'm not going to make it, guys, all the fake bullshit, I'm done!" Haley states. "Aw, don't worry, Haley," Tess says while pouring the last cup. "You got Devaney." She finishes with a chuckle. "Yeah, man, I'm here for life," I add as I sip my morning brew. "And Paige. Mike, well, your guess is good as mine." Tess tells me, "She packed up a couple weeks ago and took off." "Sounds about right," I add. "For real," Tess says as Haley takes another sip, "You coming with? To the beach, Mike?" "My car's dead, so I'll do whatever," I say while picking through a fruit basket. "Sweet well, soon as Amy gets her ass up, we'll head out," Tess says. "I don't know about the beach though, I'm fucking fried." Tess pulls up her tank top and stretches down her bikini showing her sunburn. "Damn. That sucks." Haley and I chime in. "Devaney, where was that lake you always went to in high school with the swing?" Tess asks. "Shimmer Run," I answer. "Yea, let's hit that up.

At least there'll be some shade," Tess says while being interrupted.

"JUMPSTART!" Yells Amy as she jams her straightened hand up my backside. Her fingertips hit me in the wrong spot, and I lean over the counter to hide the pain. "Aw, what the fuck, man," I say, trying not to go down. Amy's a short girl with long dark brown hair. She has pretty, big eyes and full cheeks. Amy's Korean, although if your eyes were sewn shut, you wouldn't figure it out in a hundred years. Tess takes the floor, "Alright, let's go." "Where are we going? Where!" Amy asks as if she's been up for five hours.

Shimmer Run was a small aquamarine-colored lake in the middle of an assortment of large trees, most of which were pines. Bugs, birds, and other sounds cry out in the summer heat. The wind moves the tops of the trees, causing them to sway as I stand on two thick branches of a pine that leans over the lake. My wet back leans on the trunk. With damp hair, I look through the tops of the moving trees. During meditation, I've heard of people who picture a place in their mind where they would go to escape reality. I was not one of those people. However, if there was such a place, I think it'd be here in this tree. "Jump ya, big pussy!" Amy yells from the raft. As I break from my comfortable slumber, I look down at Amy, slightly annoyed. Amy, Haley, and Tess are floating in the middle of the lake in a big raft. I lean forward and close my feet, instantly falling some forty feet to the lake below. As I come up from the water, I flop on the raft and take a joint that Tess passes my way. I take a drag before handing it to Amy.

"Aw, what the hell," Amy says, "It's all wet!" "Well, we're in a lake, Amy" Tess replies while adding suntan lotion to her shoulders. "Aw, maan," Haley says as Amy throws the roach into the lake and says, "It was out, dude. Where's the rest of it, in the car?" "Na, we smoked it," Tess adds. "All of it?!" Says Amy, " Are you serious? That was supposed to last us all week." "Well, it's gone." Says Tess. "Devaney, you think Jeb has any?" Before I could reply to Amy, a loud, deep voice echoes through the trees. "YOO DEBOO!" Jeb yells while coming through the trees. The four of us on the raft look in the direction of the voice. "What!?" Tess says while covering the sun with her hand to see who's yelling. "No Way!" Amy adds with excitement. Jeb comes onto the sugar sand from out of the woods. He's carrying two homemade Hawaiian slings, two snorkels, and a pair of masks. The raft crew smiles as Jeb jumps into the water. Now at the raft, he jumps out from underwater, and one of the spears accidentally pops a headpiece section of the raft, just missing Amy. She breaks out into laughter. "Holy shit!" She adds. "My Bad," Jeb replies. He hands me a mask. I spit in it and clean it with my finger before rinsing it out. "Hey, Jeb, you got any weed?" Tess asks. Jeb pulls a wooden dugout from his pocket. It's wrapped in a plastic bag with a rubber band around it. He throws it on the raft and swims away. I fall into the water and follow. "Nice." Says Amy while getting it out of the bag. "Thanks, Jeb!" Haley yells as we swim away.

With the cool water on our chest and the sun on our back, we snorkel across the small boomerang-shaped lake. It's fed by a freshwater stream that keeps out the brackish water. Once July hits, though, the place has frequent visitors that stir up the bottom, causing the water to cloud. Today, however, it's as clear as crystal. We spot a largemouth bass swimming through greenery under a large fallen oak tree at the bottom of the lake. We sling up and make our way down with a minute-long breath. I'm not sure why or how Jeb has the lungs of a whale, but I sure as shit know why I do. As a kid, I learned that my shitty companions have a fear of water. Not to say they won't overcome this fear, when need be, but still, at times, water was my only sanctuary.

Three fish with messy holes in them are in a cooler next to Jeb's wagon. A fourth fish is thrown on top. I toss the gear in the back of the wagon as the girls walk by. "Eww," Haley says with her hands on her knees as she examines the fish that have a grimy finish. "You guys going to eat them?" She says. "Hell yeah!" Jeb says as he dumps the rest of the ice over the fish. Haley looks at me with a smile and asks the same question without saying a word. I answer with a shoulder shrug. "Alright, well, if you want some real food, we're going to the clam bar." She says before catching up with the other two girls making their way up the ravine to Amy's four-door. "So, what you up to, wanna hang?" I ask Jeb. "Nah, I gotta work." He answers while loading the cooler in his wagon. I shut his trunk, "That sucks" "Not really." Jeb fires back as he peeks out at the three girls in bikinis walking to the Nissan. "My question's, what are YOU doing?" Jeb asks. I squint my eyes from the sun as I watch the girls climb into the car. "Nah," I reply. "Those ships have sailed, my friend."

MR. P AND THE HANGOVER SOLUTION

Later that night, in a fire hall, Jeb sits behind a DJ table. He opens a giant binder of CDs, pops one in, and grabs a mic. A smoke machine operates as Jeb hits the floor and pumps up the crowd. "Let's go, people!" He yells. "I want to see this floor shaking!" Seeing the empty floor, Jeb grabs a girl by the hand and twirls her onto the dance floor. Girls at a table laugh, and one by one, the tables empty and join her on the dance floor.

The next morning, I open my eyes to darkness. "Where am I?" I think to myself. An air conditioner is on full blast to my left. The next thing I notice is a pounding pain in my head. I sit up and lean on the wall with my face in the cold air. A sliver of sunlight from the window shade peaks through. As my eyes adjust, I see two blond heads peeking out of the oversized comforter that still covers my legs. "I gotta get out of here fast." I think as nausea sets in. With Jack, the dog who got me in this situation at the foot of the bed, I carefully crawl across the two human-shaped lumps before landing on a third with my hand. "Aw shit!" Amy yells. I climb out of bed and make my way to a door made of tiny glass windows. "Sorry, Amy." I whisper. "Where're you going in such a hurry?" She asks. "I gotta puke," I reply. "Well, get me a soda when you're done." Amy flips her pillow and watches my head disappear down the steep case of stairs.

Now in Tess's back bathroom, I kneel wearing only board shorts. As saliva fills my mouth, I wait for the inevitable. "Come on," I think to myself as I stare at the toilet water, waiting for that horrible feeling right before you heave. After puking, I let out a few last dry heaves that reach my colon. I flush and wash my hands. I grab a paper cup off the sink, fill it with mouthwash and rinse. I come out through a living room and into the kitchen, where Tess's dad makes breakfast. "Hey, Mr. P." I say.

"MIKEY!" He replies as he pours some egg batter into a cooking pan. I sit at the same counter where I had my first drink about twenty hours ago. I rub my face. "Damn, You look like shit." He says sarcastically. "Oh, he does not." Mrs. P says as she enters the kitchen and squinches my head with her fingertips. "How ya feeling, Hun?" "You guys were up pretty late. Your head hurt?" She asks. "A little," I lie as pieces of the night before pop into my head. "I think we have some Aspirin somewhere. I'll go grab you one." She adds while walking away. "You're the best," I reply as she leaves the room. "Aw, it's those fucking girly drinks." I tell Mr. P. "That'll do it," He replies and hands me an off-colored drink. "Here, if you can keep this down, it'll help." "Thanks," I say while the smell of sausage and onions hits me in the face. "You hungry," He asks. "Nah," I reply while trying not to think about food at all. "You might as well head back up then. She'll be back there forever. "Why do you say that?" I ask. "Because I ate the last one." Mr. P whispers sarcastically as If running out of breath. "Ha, ok, well, tell her thanks anyway," I say as Mr. P opens the fridge. "Oh, shit," I add. "I forgot; Amy wants a soda." "Well, let's not disappoint that one." He says while tossing me a cola. I thank him and head up the cool staircase. I'm not sure what Mr. P would say to any other boy, but he gives me a pass because I've been around forever. "Pools," I think to myself as memories of the forgotten night finally hit me. "Not one or two. Lots of pools and one angry stranger." comes to mind as I reach the top of the stairs. I turn my head off. Maybe now I can get some sleep.

TRUMP CARD

A few days later, I stand at the bain-marie next to Levi, who shows me how to properly tuck an Italian sub. It's before noon at Phat's, and a woman in her 40s comes in the back screen door. She has curly blond hair and a southern accent that matches her charm. "Well, Willy pissed the couch again." She says before interrupting herself. "Say what?" Says Obee, who has a lineup of stakes on the grill. "My son! He fell asleep drunk on the couch and pissed his gad damn pants! That mother fucker! I told him if he needed to pee, take his little pecker outside and piss off the porch! Is that too hard to understand!?" After Betsy is done ranting about her son, she walks to the back. I look at Levi with a curious smile. Levi shakes his head and continues to work on a cold sub.

"You got Mitey on the bain-marie?" Obee asks. "That's for the girls." In my defense, Levi looks up, "It's for anyone who can make a sub, Obee! "Not uh. Yo Teddy!?" Says Obee. "It's for bitches." Ted answers as he opens a plastic bin of pickles. "You got it, man. Just remember the tuck." Says Levi. "Cool, Yo Obee, where's Flynn and Clark? They said they'd make me their new sub, The Ole Faithful." Flynn's off, and Clarks said he's sick. Levi looks annoyed. "Yea, real sick." He adds.

The sun shines bright outside as Clark and Flynn sit in beach chairs on the sand. They drink beer and smoke cigs. An American flag flows behind them as they fish. Clark reel's in. His bait is gone, "Aw, come on." "Basterds," Flynn adds. The two friends sit on a small piece of land surrounded by water in a runoff in the middle of a strip mall. With a canoe next to them, Flynn opens a cooler and hands Clark, another beer can. Ducks and geese swim in the retention pond as people give strange looks while entering the convenience store. I met Clark and Flynn in high school.

A few years earlier, a night football game plays while Clark and Flynn sneak in the shadows under the bleachers. They take off their backpacks and unzip them. Flynn looks up and points as I am going through a bag of my own just a few yards away. "Yo, dude!" Clark calls as they wave me over. "What are you doing?" Asks Flynn. "I'm going to streak!" I answer. "Us too!" Says Clark as he passes me a plastic bottle of booze. I thank him and chug the bottle before making a face and ask, "What is that?" Flynn takes the bottle and adds, "Gin, wine cooler, and rum." "And Jack!" Clark adds as if proud of their concoction. "You guys going to go naked!?" I ask. Clark and Flynn look at each other before shaking their heads in disappointment. "Yeah, me neither. I got these, though!" I say as I hold up some green field hockey panties. "Whose are they?!" Asked Clark. "Lilly Robertson!" I say, as impressed with myself. "No way!" "How the hell did you get them?!" Asked Flynn. "She gave them to me," I state as I turn around and put on the panties. "Damn dude, your balls!" Clark says as I turn back around. "Damit!" I yell, knowing full well that I can't have my nuts flopping around in front of families and children, for my mother would never recover. "Just wear them over your boxers." Adds Flynn. "Good idea!" I say while doing so. We pack our clothes in our backpacks and put the bags around our shoulders. We come out from the bleachers and jump a fence. The crowd goes crazy.

That next Monday at school, I hear my name over the intercom. "Will Mike Devaney report to the main office." As I enter a door into the office, I see the cheerleading coach sittings behind a desk. I sit while doing my blow tic, "Hey, Ms. Jones Sorry about the cheerleader." "No, no." She says. "Don't worry about her. She'll be fine. Ok, so, everyone is talking about you guys and your, well, you know. Anyway, since it was a big hit, I got to thinking. I didn't have much time but TA-DA!" Jones goes through a bin and pulls out a costume of a bison. "What is that?" I ask. "It's our new mascot!" She says with excitement. "There's only a handful of games left, and I need someone with your oomph to get it off the ground." She looks at me with a big smile as I look at the silly bison costume. "Mrs. Jones, I have a hard enough time getting laid without wearing that," I tell her. "OH, pleeease, Mike?!" It would mean the world

to me. You don't have to change your routine. Just do whatever you do."

She adds. "So you want me to run around the track drunk, knock over

cheerleaders, and beat up the other team's mascot?" I ask half

sarcastically. "YES!" She says with a smile. *People go fucking nuts for*

football. I think it over before saying, "I'm sorry, Mrs. Jones, but..." "OK,

ok, listen." She interrupts, "I probably shouldn't be telling you this, but

there's one more away game, and you'll be riding with the cheerleaders."

"So," I say. "The cheerleaders get changed into their uniforms on the bus."

She adds, throwing in her trump card. I look at the costume one last time.

That Friday at a night football game. The crowd is heard cheering

loudly as I run full speed down the track wearing the bison costume. Clark

and Flynn run behind me in their underwear, pushing over cheerleaders

and taking their pom-poms. I tackle the other team's mascot, and he goes

down hard.

ONE PUNCH PETE

Now back to where we left off. I leave Phat's and stare at the empty parking lot. Forgetting I was car-less, I head back in and wait for a delivery. Pete holds the door to a liquor store for an old lady a few miles away. In his arm is a paper bag full of groceries. He grabs a six-pack of beer and puts the cans on the counter. As he pays, two muscle men walk in wearing tight gym clothes. Pete puts the six-pack in the bag and walks face to face with the two men. Pete laughs before walking in between them to leave. The muscle men look at each other, then at Pete. "Something funny." One asks. "Oh, your uh, girl clothes," Pete states while pointing at their attire. While looking at the two now angry men, Pete's smile fades. *Pete's a piney, but he's no bigot and what he says next is with the utmost and honest sincerity.* "Oh, sorry. You guys are gay. Well, carry on." The cashier hides her frightened face as Pete leaves the speechless muscle men.

Pete walks away from the two unhappy guys and leaves the store. With a slight limp, Pete walks through the strip mall's parking lot to his truck. After lighting up a cigarette, he sees Susie barking out the truck window. He stops and turns around. Muscle man one is behind him, throwing a punch. Pete gets hit in the face and staggers back as his cigarette explodes. He gains his footing and puts up his fists. He then dodges a second punch and counters with a straight right cross to the man's temple, knocking him out cold. Pete leans over him quickly and smacks his cheek to see if he's ok. The second man grabs Pete in a headlock and brings him to his feet. Pete elbows him in the stomach loosening the headlock, and swings around, punching him in the side of the face. The muscular man falls next to his friend. Pete leans over the two unconscious men who can be heard snoring. Pete looks around for witnesses before running to his shattered grocery bag. He grabs only the six-pack and jumps in his truck. *Brown Eyed Girl* plays on the radio as he jumps in his still running truck. Susie licks his face as he peels away.

Waves crash the beach's shoreline on a sunny day. *Brown Eyed Girl* continues plays on a small radio in the sand. With sunglasses on her head, Amy takes a drag of her cigarette as she lounges in a beach chair. "Someone, please change this played-out shit." She asks. Tess sits next to Amy in her own beach chair. Solo cup in hand, she talks to a girl on her other side. The girl's name is Liz. She's stacked and jacked with blonde hair. Next to Liz lays Haley on a towel. She peeks around Amy and sees me coming up the stairs and onto the bulkhead. "Here comes Devaney."

She says after lifting up her sunglasses. "Aw, man." Says Liz. "What's

up." Asks Tess. "Aw, nothing. We made out a little at the party last night."

Liz answers. "So?" Asks Tess. Liz takes a sip of her drink. "I don't know."

She says, "People kept walking by. It was weird. He kept trying to get in

my pants, but I wouldn't let him." "So, tell him you have your period,"

Tess suggests. "Duh." Amy chimes in. "I can't," Liz answers back. "Why

not?" Amy asks, now part of the conversation. "Later, when everyone left,

I made out with Clark and, well..." "He got in your pants," Amy says

before laughing with the others. "Hey Liz, guess who Mike's with," Haley

says as the girls all look back at Clark and me carrying shortboards and

walking in their direction. "What!?" Yells Liz. "Aw, fuck this." Liz gets

up from her beach chair and walks away as the others chuckle. "Bye Slut!"

Her friends yell jokingly.

    "Eh, I don't remember shit," Clark says, answering my question

about the last night's party. "There goes Liz," I say as I watch her leave the

others, "We made out last night." "Nice, you bang her?" Clark asks. "Naa,

I was trying, but people kept walking by. It was weird." I told him. "You

ever get with her?" I ask as we approach the girls. "Nah," Clark states.

"I've always wanted to, but some things just weren't meant to be." We

214

drop our surfboards and towels while greeting the girls and taking off our shirts and sandals. "Hold these?" I say while handing my sunglasses to Amy. "What the hell am I supposed to do with these?" She asks as she takes them anyway from me. "I don't know. HOLD them!" "You coming, Haley?" I ask as we head to the water carrying our boards. "Next time." She answers while looking at her own board lying in the sand. "Ok." I say with a wave, "Later."

Later that day, Amy sits alone at the beach chairs, smoking a cigarette and reading a magazine. I come up, drop my board and sit my wet ass in the chair next to her. I grab one of her cigs out of the pack and light up. Moments go by until Amy breaks the silence with a high-pitched voice, only meant to mock me, "Ya ca-coming with me, H-Haley?" "Shut up, dude," I say, defending myself. "I'll show you how to wa-wa-wax your board." She adds as Tess comes back and sits next to me. I sip the drink she had left and pass it to Tess. "Thanks!" She says. Amy hands me her cup and gets up to get her things together. "Shit, I have work. We still on for tonight, Tess?" Asks Amy. "Aw man, your work party. I'm sorry I have to babysit." Tess answers. "You're kidding," Amy says, now annoyed. "I'm sorry." Says Tess as she looks me over. "Take Devaney!"

Tess adds while pushing me by my shoulder. "You know he's not fucking doing anything." Tess chuckles as I put my arms behind my head with a smile. Amy ponders for a second before answering, "It's at nine. Think you can handle that?" "In my sleep." As I answer her question, Amy starts her way up to the bulkhead. "La-La-La-Later." She mocks. As Amy walks away, I put on a straight face and puff my cigarette while watching her disappear into a mirage. "Hey Tess, we're friends, right?" I ask to prepare her for my upcoming question. "Yeah, man, what's up?" She asks. "Well." As I answer, I chicken out and quickly change tactics. "If me and you were making out and I tried to get in your pants, would you let me?" "Hell yeah!" Tess shouts with a smile as we cheer. "You're a good friend," I add to the sarcasm. Tess takes a sip from her cup and says simply. "No shit."

It's now the middle of summer. Jeb and I walk into a farmers' market on a sunny day. We grab some fruit and bag it up. I bite a peach. "Ya know old people molest the shit out of them things, don't ya?" Jeb says, referring to my unwashed peach. "Nah," I reply with a mouth full. As Jeb looks away, I spit some of the peach out in a small trash can on the floor. A guy our age with long hair and shabby clothes grabs a drink from

216

the market's fridge and walks away to the back. "Yo, did you see that guy?" I ask in a quiet voice, "I think it was Leo." "No way, man, I heard he's in a Cali rehab." Jeb states. Jeb and I pay and leave the store. As we get in Jeb's car, Leo peaks over a shelf of chips and watches his old friends drive away.

FIRST DAY OF COLLEGE

It's morning in the Devaney house as Mom sits at the table in her kitchen. She peeks into the living room, where someone is sleeping on the couch. Sipping her tea, she puts the cup down hard as she coughs. Amy wakes on the sofa. She comes in and sits at the table with Mom. "Hey, Mrs. Devaney." She says with sleepy eyes. "Hey, Amy, how'd you sleep?" Mom replies. "Good." Amy answers. Mom passes her some OJ. "Help yourself." Mom adds. "Thank you," Amy says and pours herself a glass. Later that morning. Sis brushes her teeth as I come out of my bedroom and hop on a dresser in the hallway. Mom comes out of her room. "TUT-TUT!" I tic, "Hurry up, Sis." "Good morning, Mike. How was your night?" Mom asks. "It was ok," I answer as mom folds some clothes. "I saw Amy slept on the couch again. Everything ok?" Mom asks nonchalantly. "Yea, we just drank too much," I answer again, knowing what's coming next. "You guys have been spending a lot of time together. Are you seeing each other?" Sis looks up from the sink with a smirk. "Nah, we're just friends," I state. "Oh, ok, so what are your plans for today?" "Is the Shaggin Wagon ready?" Sis and I give each other a look of disgust. When it comes to anything sexual, my mom never has a clue. "I got work." I tell Mom and add, "The wagons not done yet, though." "You going to need a ride?" Mom says. "Na, Tess is going to pick me up." I say as Mom tries to bite her tongue but can't help herself. "So, are you guys seeing each?" Mom asks. "No, we're just friends!" I add, cutting her off. "You know, in my day, if a boy and girl were spending time together, it meant they were a couple," Mom states in proper fashion before Sis adds to the conversation, "Oh, yea, who steered the dinosaur?" "Ha-Ha," Mom says as Sis, and I chuckle. "So, what are your plans." She says, turning to Sis. "Jeff's picking her up," I answer. "Yea, we're just friends," Sis says instantly, causing the two of us to crack up laughing. Mom shakes her head and goes back to her room with the folded clothes, slamming the door.

As I wait for a ride, I get a visitor. "New job, huh? Good for you." Tic says as he sits next to me on the front porch." As I tic myself, I try to ignore him and put my face to the warm sun. "Sure, hope ya don't fuck it all up with that memory of yours. Remember the ice cream truck, he-he. Oh, and don't get too used to those pretty girls you've been hanging with. I doubt any of them would fuck a retard like yourself." He adds. I turn and smile. "Where are your two girlfriends? I say out loud, "I bet OCD gives great head." I laugh to myself as Tess pulls up. Tic's smile fades to anger as I run to my ride. "You'll pay for that one old friend." Tic says, "Just wait."

It's before noon, and the bright summer sun shines through the open windows at Phat's. A Phish song plays on the stereo as I come through the front door in a hurry, "Sorry, Levi, my ride was late." "Get in the back and finish gutting the bread." He says, finishing up a sub tray. As Levi heads out the back, Ted comes in. "Yo, I'll be back for you at like 5," Levi says to Ted as he walks out the door. Ted nods. "Cool, man." Ted puts a bucket of potato salad in the fridge and turns on the TV. Obee grills some cheesesteaks as Clark messes with the tuna mixer.

A twenty-year-old Mason Tepper comes in and hops up on the counter. I see him through an open window that separates the back room from the front of the shop. "Yo Tepper!" I yell. "What's up, Mike!" He says, eating rolled-up salami and cheese. "I didn't know you worked here," I add. "Yea, I drive sometimes." He responds. A tall skinny guy about twenty-two years old comes in the back door as Flynn loads the bain marie. Flynn looks up, "What's up, Ricky? How was vacay?" "It was sweet, Flynn! I was down in the Keys fishing with my uncle and caught me like four Hammerheads." *Ricky always had a story.* Flynn heads to the back, and Ricky turns and walks up to Obee. "Yo Ricky, how was Maine?" "It was awesome, man, went hunting for some moose, caught me a doe," Ricky says, popping open a big jar of peppers. *The only problem was figuring out which one was real. I will say this, though, on one occasion, Ricky claimed he had a power sail with a motor on it that he would ride across the bay to a local bar. I always said he was full of shit until one day, I helped him move something into his shed, and there it was. A big ass power sail with a fucking boat motor nailed to the back. I never called him out again.*

"Hey, Ted," Clark yells from the back. "I think this thing is broke." Ted turns from the TV and looks at Clark standing next to a mixer and a big bowl of tuna. "So use your arm." Ted answers. "I think it has Poison Ivy," Clark adds while looking at his forearm. "So, use your other arm." Says Ted. "It has ringworm." "Then use your FOOT!" Ted yells before Clark can finish his sentence. Now confused, Clark looks back down at the large metal bowl of tuna. Jeb is seen pulling up through the screen door. He's talking on his cell phone. "You guys have three drivers on!?" Ricky says, looking at Jeb. "Hey Ted, you think you could put one on the grill? My friends are playing paintball later. I'm trying to go." Ricky adds. "Get the fuck back there!" Ted says sarcastically to the Phat's veteran. "Fuck, man." Ricky mudders as he heads to the grill. "Damn," Flynn shouts while reading a text from his Nokia phone. "What's up, dude?" Ted asks. "My friend has an extra ticket to the beach concert," Flynn answers as he puts away his phone. "So take off, man," Ted suggests. "Really Flynn says with excitement. "Yeah, man, we got three drivers," Ted adds while giving Flynn a hi-five. Flynn runs out the back door. "Thanks, Ted." He yells.

Betty comes in as I finish filling the bain marie with lunch meat. "Well, Bear's got hair." She yells. *What Betty is so graciously referring to is her twelve-year-old daughter, who she nicknamed Bear.* "What!?" Ted asks. "Bears got hair down there!" She yells again. Ted makes a face and turns back to working on a sub tray. I look at Mason, who shrugs while Betty continues her rant, "She's got hair on her cooter! I knew it! I knew it was coming. I keep trying to tell Willy; I said you know any day now your little sister is going to be a woman. That dumb mother fucker, he don't listen to shit!" She finally ends her rant. Jeb gets off the phone and heads towards the back screen door. Ted signals to Mason, who is now next to a mop bucket. Not knowing what was coming, Mason slides the bucket over. Ted picks it up, and as Jeb opens the door, he throws the mop water on Jeb's chest, splashing it up to his face. Ted laughs. "Aw, Ted, you asshole!" Jeb yells, "It got in my fucking mouth." "Flynn just finished mopping the bathroom," Ted says with a smile. Jeb dry heaves before throwing up on the side of the building. "That sucks." Says Mason while I make a face at my friend's unfortunate situation. Clark puts a tub of tuna next to me on the counter. He leans in and whispers before walking away. "Don't eat the tuna."

Later that day, "TUT TUT!" I yell while ringing out the mop in the front of the shop. My tic is immediately imitated by random employees in the back by the grill. "What the hell was that?" Asks Ted. "Mike's Tourettes!" Says Clark as Obee chimes in. "I told you guys!" *Inevitably, hearing someone do my tic makes me have to do it again.* I wait a little and "TUT TUT" quieter. Now even louder, the Phat's members Tut Tut away. "I'm fucked." I think to myself as I finish mopping the floor. It's night now, and Levi flips the *Closed* sign at the front door as Obee, Clark, and I finish cleaning the shop. "Alright, boys," Levi yells, "Go clean up and be at my house at Ten. The tap's on me." "Hell, Yeah!" Yells Ricky as he cleans the grill. I hop in the passenger seat of Clark's small truck. "You going to Levi's?" I ask. "You hear of something better?" Clark replies. "Nope," I say as I shake my head. "Yeah, me neither." He adds as we leave the old parking lot lit by a lone streetlight.

Now at Levi's house, Flynn, Clark, Obee, and I sit on a couch, each with a balloon in hand. We're surrounded by people in their 30's. Jeb talks with his brother Tyler. A blond named Tina walks up, and Tyler introduces her to Jeb. She smiles and puts out her hand. Jeb puts down his beer on a pool table and picks Tina up in a hug. Tyler shakes his head with

223

a smile while Tina laughs. Levi enters the room and looks at the four of us on the couch. "My boys!" He says with a nice buzz going. "You guys having fun!?" He asks. The four of us smile and nod our heads. Clark gives a thumbs up. Flynn answers his cell as Levi walks away. "It's Tepper!" He says. "Yo man. Sweet! Alright, later. Ally Fishman's house," Flynn says as the couch crew gets up and heads out the front door.

We park in a crowded yard. Obee and I jump out of his car while Flynn and Clark simultaneously get out of Clark's truck. The four of us walk up together and stop to check out the scene. We all have a smile on our faces. The tiny house is packed with loud nineteen and twenty-year-olds. Two girls make out on the porch as some guys do a beer bong. Another guy is on his hands and knees on the lawn, throwing up as bottle rockets go off in the background. "Nice." Says Clark. Mason comes out the front door as the four of us make our way up and into the house. After Mason gives us hi-fives, he pisses off the porch. The pee splashes off the siding, and hit's the guy puking in the yard as he moans with disappointment.

As clouds overcast the pinelands, Pete feed's the chickens in his yard. His only neighbor comes out of a newly built house and runs towards some chickens that got into his yard. He sees dog poop by the border of the two properties. "Go, get!" He yells as he screams at the chickens. "PETE! Damn it, Pete, I told you to keep these fucking things out of my yard!" Pete ignores him and continues to feed his birds. "I swear, Pete, I'm gonna to start shooting these damn things. And that goes for your dog too. Have him shit in your fucking yard!" The neighbor adds. Pete reaches into the small barn and grabs a 30 Ought Six rifle before walking toward the neighbor. The Neighbor backs up with a scared look on his face. Looking around the chicken coop, Pete finally speaks. "You can shoot the chickens," Pete says before putting a rare look on his face that, to be honest, I have never seen before in my life. "Not my dog." Pete ends before walking back up to the house. He whistles, and Susie follows.

LUNCH OR LAUGHS

It's waking time on Eastfield Ave. Before they have a chance to show themselves, I head into the shower. When it came time to stand under cold water, which OCD demands, I refuse. Instead, I dry off and head to the hallway. Sure enough, I run into my companions. OCD is holding up one of his picture frames. It was a portrait of me with one leg.

I'm in the park, and I'm alone. I walk away only to hear his grunt. I look

back to see a new painting that OCD holds in his hand. This time it's my

Dad, and he is also missing a leg, but he is not at the park. He is in prison

wearing an orange jumpsuit. Why he would ever be in that scenario

matters not. I have seen worse paintings from my shitty little friend, but

still, it was enough to convince me to go back. I head back to the

bathroom and get in the shower once more. This time I turn the nozzle on

cold.

It's noon now back at my house. I sit on my porch watching Jeb,

who pulls up in the empty driveway. He soon joins me and sits in a chair.

"What's up, buddy?" He asks. "Yo," I say as Amy comes out of the house.

"You gonna need my car?" She asks. "Nah, I'm good," I say, looking at

Jeb's wagon in the driveway. "Ok, later. Bye, Jeb." She adds before

climbing in her car and driving away. "BYE, Amy!" Jeb yells before

quieting down and turning to me with a smirk. "Well, what do ya know?

Deebos got himself a girlfriend." He adds. "Na. We're just messing

around," I state. "I don't know. You guys are spending a lot of time

together." He snickers. "You sound like my fucking mom, dude," I say.

"Trust me, Jeb, I'm not wife-ing up crazy, Amy, and I'm sure the feeling is mutual." It's nighttime now as rain drizzles on the trees in my backyard. Amy and I come out of the garage. As she struggles to get her top back on, I kick a puddle at her. She snaps on her bikini and jumps on my back with a laugh. I quickly spin her around before putting her down for a kiss. As the rain grows heavy, we run towards the pool.

It's eleven o'clock in the morning, and I turn the sign to open. A friend named Cliff comes into Phat's. He lives around the corner and plays the meanest Bass Guitar around. "BARNYARD!" He says. "Yo Cliff! I got you!" Obee yells back as he hits the grill. *What's a Barnyard? Well, I'll tell you. First, you put down a full portion of cheesesteak meat, then a full slab of chicken cheesesteak, add some bacon, top it all off with some Pepperjack cheese and a large squirt of Ranch dressing. Finally, cut a fresh south jersey sub roll, slap it all in, take a bite, and then, well, someday, you'll just have to find out for yourself. I don't know where the idea came from, but it was a must-have at Phat's.*

The lunch rush is over. Tess and Haley sit across from each other at a booth. "S.A.T's don't even matter, Haley," Tess says after swallowing a chunk of sub. "Uhg!" Haley mutters. "Besides, your score is way better than most," Tess adds. I toss a basket of fries on the table and sit next to her. "Here's some Ricky fries," I say while wiping my sweaty head with my forearm. "What'd you get on your SATs, Devaney?" Tess asks. "I don't know. I always wrap that shit up." "I didn't say STDs, MIKE. Tess says with a smile, "I said SATs." "Oh, I never took those" "Really?" "How come?" Asks Haley. I toss a fry in my mouth and answer, "Hey, If you can't swim, don't jump in the river." "WHOA!" Clark yells from the back. "Words of wisdom from Devaney." He adds to the chuckles. "Yea, Haley, poets don't take SATs." Flynn chimes in as he sits on a counter and grabs the newspaper. Meanwhile, Amy and Liz hop out of a truck and into the shop. "Oh shit, I almost forgot," Tess remembers. "Guess who I ran into yesterday?" She says while looking in my direction. "Yourself," I answer, getting a laugh out of Haley due to Tess's sometimes ditsy yet charming personality. "Blake," Tess says quickly. "Oh shit!" I forgot about that chick." Haley adds with a smirk that once again is in my direction. "Whatever happened with you two? You guys were meeting up for a WHILE!" "Well," I answer, "I'm pretty sure she was meeting up with everyone." Haley pats my shoulder as Tess laughs at my luck. "HEY! Sup y'all." Amy and Liz say as they join the table. "Hey, you girls are just in time," Tess says. "For what?" Liz asks as she hops the booth and grabs a fry. "Devaney's game," Haley smirks. Amy joins in while dunking a fry in some cheese sauce. "Hey, I'm Mike." Amy mocks. "Will you ba-ba-BLOW ME!?" The table explodes, and Flynn and Clark join in from the back. "What are you laughing at, Liz?" Tess asks. "Yeah," Amy replies quickly as if rehearsed. "It almost worked on your drunk ass." Once again, the table erupts in laughter as Clark bangs a metal pot with a spoon adding to the nostalgia. As Liz hides her face in some Ricky's fries, Amy heads to the back bathroom. "Don't forget to piss on the lid!" I shout, referring to an inside classic. As Amy flicks a middle finger, I throw my arm around Haley. "At least Haley likes me," I say in my comedic defense. Haley leans in with a smile full of sub. "Always." She adds, trying not to choke on lunch or laugh.

It's late afternoon as the wildlife chirps through the open windows of the shop. I mop up a broken ketchup bottle next to a booth. As I do so, Ted comes out from the back bathroom and picks up a tuna sub at the counter next to the TV. He takes a bite. Jeb watches through the screen door in his car as Ted eats from the sandwich, which is now filled with Jeb's revenge. Jeb smiles and drives away. Like an elephant, Jeb never forgets. *Years ago, I played a prank on Jeb. One of many, but this one sticks out particularly well. Jeb bided his time, and a few weeks later, I spent the entire school day with apple butter soaked in my would-be clean pair of socks.* As I mop, Obee talks to two girls at the counter. I don't know if I mentioned this, but Kyle O'Brien, better known as Obee, is Tim's younger brother. When we were kids, I could just throw him into a wall. As young adults, I refrain.

"Is his name Mike?" One of the girls asks him. "You guys know Mitey?" Obee says with a smile and adds, "You know he has Tourette's? Yeah, his dick is huge!" *For whatever reason, Obee thought that by some mutant miracle, having large genitalia was a direct result of being born with Tourettes.* On the one hand, he called me out. On the other hand, he announced to local talent that I had a whale cock, so, It's a wash. "Yeah, you guys want to see!?" He asks before getting an answer. "Hey, Mitey, they want to see it! Come on to the back." "What about your boss?" Asked one of the girls. "Ted!?" "I'm sure he's seen it by now," Obee adds as they make their way to the back. I shake my head and continue to mop the floor. As Ted watches TV, he glances over at me. At second glance, he speaks. "What the fuck are you waiting for!" I shrug and take off my apron before putting it on the counter. "Get back there." He adds as I walk past and make my way to Obee and the girls I have never met.

Obee drops me off at my house at dusk. I run up to the bathroom and open the door to see Sis putting on makeup. "You scared the shit out of me!" She screams, I thought you were mom." "What is that!?" I ask, looking at her getup. "A dress," she states. "You know what mom would say?" I add sarcastically. "That I look like a whore." Sis answers as the front door of the house is heard opening. "Oh shit, I'm so dead!" Sis says in a panic. "Just go down the antenna." I remind her. Sis climbs out the window and down the rusty old tv antenna on the side of the house. She jumps to the bottom and grabs her high heels from the grass. She crouches down by the front porch and looks in the window. Mom, Dad, and Faith have their backs to the window as they watch me tell a story with big waving hands motions. Sis smiles as her girlfriend pulls up. Faith turns around, and Sis puts up the "Shhh" sign with her finger. Faith gives the thumbs up. Sis hops in the car, and they drive off.

THE PEARL

Nothing seems to be going on tonight, so I head to bed. The house phone rings, and I grab it quickly. It's 11:30, and I don't want it to wake the rest of the house. "Hello? Ok." I hang up and grab my dad's car keys. Minutes later, I pull into a parking lot and park in front of an old dive bar with purple neon lights. I notice two guys my age arguing out front as I search for some cash in the glove box. None of us were twenty-one yet, and considering I couldn't even grow facial hair, I was not yet into the bar scene. However, there was one place that I never had a problem getting into. The Pearl. *The building does not exist today, but recently I had a discussion with a friend about this night, and we laughed our asses off. For that reason, only I tell it now.*

I grab a ten-dollar bill and get out of my car. As I do, so I hear a crack and quickly move out of the way as one of the boys arguing comes flying my way. He takes out my side mirror and hits the pavement. As the mirror bounces on the ground, the guy still standing calls out. "You got something to say!?" He says. "Hey, Laff," I say aloud as I pick up my Dad's side mirror. "Devaney!" Laff says, now recognizing me. "Oh man, did I do that?" He asks as I study the mirror. "Kinda," I answer as I throw it in my open window. "I'm sorry, Mike! Let me buy you a beer." He says with a slur. "I thought you were leaving?" I tell him as I point in the direction he is going. "Leaving, no, I just got here." He says while slapping my shoulder. The two of us walk into the bar as Lenny takes a nap in the parking lot.

The bar is crowded with another fifty people I know, including Mason Tepper, Clark, and Flynn. Laff hands me a pink drink that matches the drink in each person's hand. I don't know what's in it, but it's topped with Bacardi 151, tastes delicious, and is limited to two per person. *You can throw up, punch people and have sex in the bathroom, but if you order three Zombies, they get pissed and tell you to leave.* I mingle with some friends from high school. Most of them went to college, so the summer was the only time I'd really see them. There's Mutt, the Conner twins, Clay, and Bella, just to name a few.

A live band plays on stage in the tight noisy one-room bar. I don't remember the band's name, but I do know that it was "Cat-something" because they were all dressed up as cats. Not a Halloween outfit either. I'm talking about real cat outfits like they just got off of Broadway. They kind of sucked, but any live rock music is good if you ask me. As Clark runs the bubble hockey table, Flynn makes out with a girl. Tepper, well, it

233

looks like he's dancing, I guess. To be honest, I could have been doing any of those things, but I just finished my second Zombie, so who knows.

The next thing I remember is smoking a cigarette with a cat person. At first, Clark, Flynn, Tepper, and I were getting along with the cat people as they packed up their van. Then out of nowhere, we were not really getting along with the cat people. They weren't very nice people. I do remember that. I guess if you want to be a cat, you should probably not be that nice to anyone. As Clark and some other friends get into a yelling match with the cat band, Tepper hops in the driver's seat and hits the pedal. As he does so, keyboards and symbols fall out the open doors and onto the ground. The cat people scream and chase him as he comes my way. I've never stolen a car before, but the two Zombies and I thought it was a good idea at the time. I run and jump up and through the passenger side window. "Where we going!?" I shout to Tepper. He looks at me and yells. "Mexico!" Just like that, Mason Tepper and I were on our way to Mexico. Unfortunately, we didn't get far. Actually, we never made it out of the parking lot. Tepper hit some trash cans, and we got the fuck out of there.

A few nights later, Amy and I lay out on the oversized couch in my living room. It's the end of summer, and friends are slowly disappearing back to college. "What are you up to tonight?" She asks. "Satch has tickets to a rock show. I'll probably go with him. You?" I ask. "Me and Tess are going over to Randy's to get high." She says. "Randy's?" I think to myself before saying it out loud. "Yup," She says. "Your ex?" I ask, now concerned. "Unfortunately," Amy says out loud as I interrupt. "You're not going there!" As the words leave my mouth, I instantly regret them. "What the hell was that?" I think to myself as the magazine Amy was reading slowly comes down from her face. "Oh, I'm not?" She asks, now with an attitude. I quickly change my demeanor to humor. "No," I say. "And why not?" Amy asks, still unsure of what just happened. "Because" I say as I finally look up. "You're hanging with me." Amy's attitude changes and a smile climbs her face. "What about the show?" She asks as the sound of a song enters my front yard. I've heard the song a hundred times, but the name escapes me. I hop up and out the screen front door before answering Amy's question. "Satch don't care."

Satch pulls up in a green Jeep. His tires scrunch some sand and pebbles as it comes to a stop. "Yo man, I gotta bail. Sorry," I say as I lean

235

on his Jeep with my elbow. "It's cool, brotha." He says casually. After a quick conversation, we hi-five before he pulls away. As Amy stands on the porch, I turn to her, and we share a sincere smile. And that was that. For the first time in my life, I had fallen in love with a girl. As I walk to join her, the song on Satch's stereo fades in the distance. Now in silence, the name of the song finally comes to mind. "Oh yeah." I think to myself. *Certain Tragedy.*

THE BARNYARD

The New Jersey Pine Barrens. Pete pulls up in his dirt driveway to head into the house. He whistles at Susie, who lies on the dirt path. When she doesn't come, he checks on her. "Hey girl, let's go." Susie whimpers. Pete gets on one knee and studies her. He picks her up and brings her inside. "Yeah," Pete replies, answering someone on the other end of his house phone. "I don't know. She just keeps throwing up. Can you guys look at her? How much!? Just to walk through a door?! No, she's an old girl. Poison? No, my kids aren't stupid; they wouldn't." Pete stops mid-sentence. He looks out a window at his neighbor's house before hanging up his phone.

Pete's barn doors are now open as he walks out, holding something in his hand. Susie lies next to some flowers several feet from the chickens and other birds surrounding his barnyard. Pete puts some of Susie's toys around her. He gives her a kiss on the face. "You're a good dog." He says with tears filling his eyes. Unable to bear Susie's suffering, Pete stands up and loads a round into his gun. A shot is heard as blackbirds fly from the tops of the pine trees.

The next morning. Pete's neighbor makes some coffee and takes the mug out to his back deck. As he looks in his yard, he drops his mug and immediately starts searching with frightened eyes. He goes back into his house, slams the sliding glass door, and locks it before closing his shades. Chickens roam Pete's neighbor's yard around a shallow grave-shaped hole that now sits in the middle of his green grass. I have no clue what Uncle Pete was doing at the time of his neighbor's frightening discovery. I like to think he was looking at an old picture of himself and a pup while listening to *Susie Q* on his record player.

CHAPTER 6 — CRYING BLUES

A crying three-year-old boy in nothing but underwear sits on the floor in a motel. Other kids are heard crying around him. An Albanian woman tries to quiet the three-year-old as two men talk to each other in a foreign language. They are not happy. The three grown-ups sit in this crummy motel filled with crying children. One of the men grabs a dope syringe and goes to the three-year-old who cries the loudest. The lady shakes her head in the toddler's defense, but the man yells, and she gives in. An older boy with black hair and a blue shirt runs to the crying child's aid by hitting the man in the face. "NO! Leave my brother alone!" Yells the four-year-old. The man with the syringe quickly backhands the boy, who crashes through a glass coffee table and snaps his leg. The man holding the needle sticks the crying boy, and he quickly falls asleep.

It's nighttime, and everyone in the motel room is asleep. The front door explodes open, and a SWAT team barges in. As screams and cries are heard, one of the men puts their hands up while the other gets off the couch and runs for a bed. As he tries to lift the mattress, a SWAT member shoots him with a round from a shotgun. He goes down, and they cuff him as he cries in pain. "Shut up!" Says the officer. "You're lucky they weren't lead." The place is now a busy crime scene. An Italian man tries to break through the yellow barrier but is blocked by police. "My boys are in there!" The man yells. "Let me through!" The three-year-old is now in sweatpants and a t-shirt. The two brothers are being taken care of by medics. Their blankets fall to the ground as they see their father and run to him. "Daddy!" yells the older boy. "Let him through." Says one of the policemen. The father takes one step and falls to his knees in tears as the two boys run into his arms.

WELCOME TO NEW JERSEY

A moving van sits in front of a small apartment building in the city. The two boys from the motel are now around seven and eight years old. Ray and his younger brother sit in the backseat of a car as Lou drives. The boys fight over baseball cards in the back seat. "Hey!" Lou yells to his two sons. "Cut that out!" The car eventually passes a sign that reads "WELCOME TO NEW JERSEY." A small house sits on the rounded corner of a street. Lou unpacks a box in their new kitchen as the boys play soccer in the hallway behind him. "Alright, wash up!" Lou yells while reading the ingredients on a box of cookies. He thinks for a moment and throws them in the trash.

A few days later, the two brothers sit in the office of a grade school. "Ray." Says a teacher softly. Ray punches his brother in the arm before he's taken out to his classroom. The younger brother is led to his class shortly after. *Pee-Wee's Big Adventure* plays on a box TV that sits on a cart in a dark classroom. A lady from the office opens the classroom door and waves at the teacher who sits behind her desk. "Ok, find a seat."

240

"After the movie, Ms. Green will introduce you to the class." Now

separated from his older brother Ray, the boy nods and finds a seat. A

bubble is heard popping next to him. "Hey, can I have one?" The new kid

asks while rolling his shoulder, which will soon have a bruise from his

brother's punch. The boy chewing gum hands a piece to the new kid.

"Thanks." says the new kid while popping the gum in his mouth. "I'm

Mike," I whisper while holding out my hand. The boy thinks for a moment

with a serious face before putting his hand out and shaking my own. "I'm

Satch." Says the new kid. After shaking hands, my new friend and I watch

the rest of the movie with a mouth full of gum.

Satch is now back where we left off, 20 years old and standing at

shortstop on a baseball field in Pine Park. The other players, also in

regular clothes, are around the same age as Satch. Bob, the second

baseman on his team calls out to Satch. They don't seem to be getting

along. "Yo Satch." He says. "I heard that scholarship went to shit. What

happened, man?" "Na, It's all good." Satch answers, "I'm just doing my

thing." "Liar, your brothers got free room and board while you're sucking

Lenny's dick AND making the Subs." Steve, the left fielder, laughs as the

pitcher strikes out the batter. "How about you shut the fuck up and play

241

some ball," Satch suggests. "Mmmm, I bet it tastes like cheesesteak." Says Bob. "Go ask your girl Trish," Satch says quickly. "I heard she likes every other dick on the block." Both teams start the ooo's and aaaw's. "WHAT!? You talk about my fucking girl like that again, and you get popped," Bob replies as Satch drops his glove and approaches him. "Aw, Mr. Tough Guy, now." As the words leave his mouth, Satch hits him in the face with a straight punch. He falls back and puts up his fists. The other team starts to cheer. Bob then throws a counter punch at Satch and hits him in the eye. He throws another, but Satch dodges it and throws a quick combo. Both fists hit Bob, who falls violently to the dirt. Out of nowhere, Steve sprints in and tries to tackle Satch, but he moves, and Steve flies through the air. Satch uppercuts him in the ribs and sends him to the ground. Satch gets on top of him and starts to punch his face. As the rest of Satch's team runs in and tackles him off his teammates, the other team bangs on the dugout fence and goes wild with cheers. After the brawl, Satch gives a bow to the crowd and walks directly to his car, never to play again.

It's eleven am on a sunny summer day. Satch pulls up in his green Jeep. The tire cover on the back is a picture of the Cleveland Indians Mascot. He beeps the horn, and I come out in board shorts, sneakers, and a tank top. A punk rock song plays on the stereo. I hop in and look at Satch, who has a black eye. "What happened to you?" I ask. "I fought some douchebags. He mutters as we pull away. "Now parked, Satch and I each smoke a cigarette. Satch eats a big burrito, and I eat a hot dog with too much ketchup and mustard. We each sip an energy drink. Satch speaks, "Yea, man, my boy put on like twenty pounds of muscle in a month." "20 pounds!" I yell. "Holy shit!" "Yea, I got to get some," Satch adds. I wipe my mouth before asking a question, "Where at?" "That fat dude at Rock Arm has 'em," Satch says while puffing his smoke. "What guy?" I ask. "You know." Satch answers while chewing. "The guy that's always checking you out while he eats his lunch." I laugh and look at the store he speaks of. I point out the window and ask. "That place right there?" I ask. "Yea, It's like eighty bucks, though," Satch says. "For twenty pounds of muscle," I add. "Shit. I'd let that guy eat sushi off my boner." Satch chuckles as he bites his burrito. "Aw, man, I'm done, dude. Ready?" We put out our smokes, finish our energy drinks, and exit the Jeep. We head straight towards the gym.

ITS NOT A CARTOON IT'S ANIME

The doctor's office. The bug-eyed doctor looks at me. "I'm still getting the fucking attacks!" I shout out of nowhere, now agitated. "The meds don't do shit! Can't you give me something as needed?!" The doctor doesn't budge. Now at the front desk, a secretary hands me a script. "Ok, so here's your Lex..." She starts. "Save it!" I interrupt, "I'm done with that shit." "Oh, um, well, what about the Lorazepam?" She asks. "The what!?" I say. I take the script and shake my head as I walk away. Amy gets up from a chair in the waiting room and rubs my back as we walk out. Four years of telling that prick doctor about my panic attacks, and I had to ASK for the right meds myself? What the fuck was I paying him for? I never went back.

I grab two beers out of my fridge, and when I close it, I'm face to face with Tic. He is holding a small box. It is blue with a red ribbon tied into a bow. "This is for you when you're ready." He tells me. Confused, I shake him away and return to the living room. Amy and I sit together on my couch and watch TV in the dark. "Alright, I guess I'll sleep at my house tonight," Amy says while getting up from the couch. "You sure?" I ask. "Yea, I'll hang with my mom. I'm sure yours is sick of seeing me."

"Come on, my family likes you more than my ass," I say, trying to comfort her. Amy gives me a kiss and heads out the door. "Night," Amy says goodbye as I stretch my neck and do a blow tic. "Later." I watch as Amy pulls away from the house before heading out the door to my wagon. I start it up and drive away.

I park at a motel and look around before walking up some steps and finding my room. I look around nervously before opening the door and walking in. I sit on the bed and stare at a wad of cash on the table. "I can't do this," I say aloud while standing up. As I grab the cash, there is a knock on the door. I regain my composure and answer it. The top of a blond girl's head is seen as she enters. Her bottom half is seen wearing fishnet stockings and high heels. She puts her purse down on the table and sits on the bed. "Hey. Sorry, I'm kind of new at this." I say. "It's two hundred, right?" The girl softly says yes and pats the bed with her hand, and I eventually sit next to her. "We can take it slow, Mike." She says. "Damit, Amy, come on!" I yell. "What's wrong?" Amy asks with a face full of cheap makeup. "I didn't tell you my name yet," I say, half sarcastic. Amy sits on the bed and takes off her blond wig. "Sorry I forgot. Should I go back out?" She asks. "No, it's over," I answer as humor sets in. Amy rubs my head. "It's my fault, I know." "We still have that weird cartoon you like. Want me to put it on? "It's not a cartoon, Aim. It's Anime," I state. "Yeah, I guess." Amy walks to the TV as I get comfortable on the bed. She hits play on the VCR and joins me in a cuddle as I pass her a bowl of popcorn.

This was a good week for the two of us. Not one fight. *I believe the hot and cold of our relationship would be better told in a montage. From smiles under the stars to yelling and smashing things until the cop's show. Now, this was all a long time ago, and although it doesn't matter now, the cold was mostly my own fault. Ya see; The second I had feelings for the girl, I became "somewhat" possessive. Although unnecessary, I believe this was due to Amy and I's friendship prior. This did not help us, for the memories of that friendship would bleed into the memories we made as a couple. This would slowly continue until, eventually, I couldn't tell them apart.*

DOUCHEBAG

"You're not going!" I say as I drive Amy's car down a bridge on the causeway. The windows are down, and the day's hot air dries our bathing suits. It's been a year now since our decision to be together, and for the most part, we've been inseparable. "Why do you care so much!?" Asks Amy. "Are you serious!?" I yell, "You and five of your girlfriends in a house for three days on the beach." "So what!?" She says. "They're all fucking single!" I say as I put on the air conditioner and roll up the window. "So, you don't trust me?" Amy says in the quiet car. "I trust you," I add. "Just not the fucking douchebag's that'll be around." Now annoyed, Amy lights a cig and cracks her window. "I don't know, Amy," I say. "Maybe if you made better decisions in the past, you'd..." I stop mid-sentence, but the damage was done. Amy turns to me with a look of shock. She then looks away and out the window. She tries to hold back her tears, but some run down her face. I know what a douchebag move it was, but I said it all anyway. The rest of the car ride was silent.

I knock on a front door before walking into a small rancher to see Obee and Vin, a smaller kid with short black hair. Vin pops up from the couch. "Yo guys," I say while giving Vin a bro hug. "Watch out. He'll give you Tourette's!" Obee yells. "Shut the fuck up, Obee!" Vin shouts to his friend. "Don't worry, Mike." Says Vin, "I'll take your Tourettes any day."

"Thanks, bro," I say while heading to the back of the house. "Tim's in his

room," Obee says as he throws Vin a beer. "Good luck getting him out."

I open Tim's bedroom door to about ten ashtrays filled with

cigarette butts. Some are seen in a drawer. A still skinny Tim, now with

short hair, sits on a small couch playing Xbox. He is wearing only shorts.

"Yo, buddy." I shout. "What's up?" he answers. "So you ready or what?" I

ask. "For what?" Asks Tim while he lights up a cigarette. "Camping. I told

you all week, dude." I tell him. "Today? Shit, what is today?" Tim asks,

standing up. I think for a moment before answering, "Wednesday." "It's

not Wednesday!" He argues. I think again and reply, "It's not? Oh, I don't

know then." "Na, I'm good, man." Tim states. "Come on!" I say quickly.

"What the hell are you going to do here?" As I say it Tim smiles with his

hands out. "Anything I want. Aw, wait, damn it. I told Ella we'd do

something tonight." Tim tells me. "That high school chick?" I ask. "She's

eighteen." Says Tim avoiding the question. "That eighteen-year-old high

school chick," I ask in the same manner. This time Tim laughs, "Yup."

"How's that going?" I ask. "Good, man." He says while grabbing a hoodie.

"Nice. You guys coming with me?" I ask. "Na, we'll meet you." I head out of Tim's room and down the hallway. As I turn the corner, I run into a girl with brown hair to her shoulders. The girl is short and a bit voluptuous for lack of a better word. Her face was most noticeable; however, I've always been a sucker for a pretty face. "Whoops, ha, sorry." She says. "Whoa, you, ok?" I ask as we move around each other in the small hallway. "Tim's in his room. I'll ah, see you guy soon." I say. "Ok, thanks!" She says with a smile as I walk away.

THE TRACKS

It's night now in the woods. Crickets, bats, and other creatures act as a hidden orchestra as my friends, and I put up our tents. A short walk from the makeshift tent sight is a small beach of sand that sits on the edge of a narrow bay line. A trash can fire burns next to a picnic table. Sitting on the table, I strum my acoustic guitar and sing out some originals, including *Summer High*. Also, I play a few crowd-pleasing covers, one being a song titled "Age Six Racer," which symbolizes the end of summer for the girls who sing along. Haley, Tess, and Amy sit on beach chairs below in the sand with a few other friends I have not yet mentioned. They talk amongst themselves as Jeb and Satch try to light the larger fire pit. "What is that, dude? No, give it to me," Jeb yells. "You have to make a tepee." He adds. "What are you, a fucking Indian?" Say Satch, "It doesn't matter." "It matters!" Jeb yells again. Also in beach chairs are Sis, one of her girlfriends, Clark, and Flynn. They sarcastically discuss how bad Sis's friend's feet smell. "Man, your feet stink!" Claims Clark as I sing the word *SIIIT* I abandon the song's next line to chime in on Flynn and Clark's foot discussion. "*And Gabby's feet, SMELL, LIKE, SHIIIT!*" Tim and Ella join the laughter as they sit on a log.

     The large fire is now lit, and Jeb and I jam out "HEY JOE" on our acoustics. The beer cooler is half empty now, and a bowl of herb is passed around the campfire. Clark smokes a cig. Some of the girls and Satch sit around the fire in hoodies. The rest of us are in T-shirts. "I got to pee." Says one of the girls, and just like that, the rest follow into the dark woods. As Amy gets up, I gently grab her hand. "Hey, sorry about earlier," I say as Amy leans down for a kiss. "Me too." She adds. "Barf." I hear from Tess as Haley chuckles. Tim gets up and walks through some trees to the bay. As he pees in the water, Jeb puts his arm around Tim and asks with excitement, "How you been, man?!" "Chill, dude!" Tim laughs as Jeb shakes him by the shoulders. As I chuckle and turn away from Jeb and Tim, Ella looks at me through the fire. I smile and raise my can of beer. She does the same.

It's now late October at my parent's house. Trick-or-Treaters scurry off the front porch as Amy texts on her Nokia. She sits on the couch in a demon costume with horns and a tail. Mom and Sis talk about how cool Faith looks in her witch costume. Amy reads her text that says, "Mike's not gonna want to go there." "Maybe we'll all meet after." Amy hits send and joins in on how awesome Faith's costume looks. I Jump down the stairs, my hair is spiked, and a cigar sits in my mouth. Three homemade claws stick out from each hand. I wear a "wife-beater" t-shirt, jeans, and boots with a dog tag around my neck. "What's up, bub?" I say as Mom compliments my costume.

Later, on the porch. Amy sits in my lap as we wait for Jeb. He pulls up in his new Grand Marki as Amy laughs at a comment I make. "Finally." I say, and with the car still running, Jeb gets out in a spot-on recreation of John Goodman from *The Big Lebowski*. As he does so, a kid stops dead in his tracks. "I'm sorry, officer!" Says the kid. "I'm on my way home now." As the kid says this, I quickly put it all together. It's 9:00pm,

251

and Trick-or-Treating is over. Jeb, who already looks intimidating due to the costume, fake handgun, and Cruiser, also he looks like an off-duty cop. "YOU!" Jeb yells, quickly adapting to the situation as always. Now terrified, the boy backs up, and before he can speak, Jeb yells again. "Give me your candy, Right NOW!"

Amy and I watch in tears as Jeb, who, though only playing, did not see the magnitude of what he's just done. The kid holds out his bag of candy that he had worked all night for. As Jeb snatches it out of his hand, a girl intervenes and grabs it from Jeb while smacking his arm. "Stop it, Jeb!" Yell's Jeb's girlfriend who had been sitting in the passenger seat of the Grand Marki. "I'm just playing around!" Jeb yells while taking off his shades. "It's ME!" Says Jeb as the kid grabs his bag of candy and runs away. "He was scared to death!" Says Jeb's girlfriend as they meet us on the porch. "Na." interrupts Jeb, "It's my neighbor." "See ya, Billy!" Jeb calls out to the ten-year-old, who is now nowhere to be seen. "Let's Go," I shout, and the four of us head to a party for Halloween.

I didn't know exactly when or where I was going. I do know it was June because the trees still had some weight to them. The air is on low, and the windows are cracked. As I drive, something out the window

252

catches my eye. It's a set of train tracks that run through a hole in the earth. I follow these tracks with my eyes for as long as possible. I was sure at some point; I would see through to sunlight on the other side. Eventually, the tracks were camouflaged by leaves and greenery. The tape in the stereo has flipped, and I am in silence no more. I put my arm out slowly and turn down the song. Amy is asleep on my shoulder. She looks comfortable, and I don't want to wake her.

It's late winter now, and the trees are barren. Rusty clouds fill the sky on this windy day. I wake in my bed alone and look to my side before getting up. I come down the stairs. No one else is home. In pajama pants and a t-shirt, I open the fridge and grab the OJ that is almost empty. I stand and look out the window in the living room as I chug down some juice. Something catches my eye outside. I open the front door and see a box outside on the curb. A hoodie hangs out and flaps in the wind. Also seen sticking out is a video game controller, a ukulele, and a picture frame. In it is a picture of Amy and me. After seeing the box, I turn around, head back inside and close the door.

THE SWAPPER VS THE INTERNET

Mom works in a classroom with a disabled child as a teacher and a second aid in the class talk at a desk about something boring. As Faith got older, my mom got a job as an aid in a special needs school. It was the first job she had, had since college. My Dad, however, still has the same job since I met him. On the other side of town sits my Dad's office. It's an old one-story building, which as a child, was a place to explore.

Dad walks through the office building holding a folder. He waves at someone through a doorway. A man sitting at a desk greets Dad as he walks into the room. The man looks a little shot out. "Hey Dan, how we doing?" "Yo Mic," Answers Dan, "What do you have for me? "Not much today." Answers Dad. "Yep, Swappers slowing down alright." Dan puffs on a cigar. "Computers are kicking our ass out there." He says. "Hey, nothing beats a face-to-face, Dan," Dad says half sarcastically. "The swapper though, well, I give it another year at best." *Now I don't know exactly how this went because I obviously was not there, but I know it went something like this.* "You know Mic, I was thinking." Says Dan. "The people buying ad space think there's two bundles a store, right?" "But really, there's no way of checking. I mean, even if they did, there would be no telling how many people already grabbed." Dad interrupts by saying, "Leave one bundle, save money on ink and paper." "Yea, but there would be one problem, Dan." Dad interrupts. "What?" Dan asks. "Then I'd be a liar," Dad states. "Hey, you said a year at most." "I'm just saying," Dan adds.

Later that day, Mom and Dad sit at the table in the dining room. "Oh, you wouldn't do that." Says mom after hearing about Dad's discussion with Dan. "I'm just saying, Hun, it's a possibility, and we'd save a lot of money." Says Dad. "It's dishonest, and you wouldn't do it." States Mom. "I'll make that decision myself, Clair," Dad says, ending the conversation.

Weeks later, Dad signs over the Swapper to Dan. They shake hands and say their goodbyes. On the way home, Dad stops at a food store. He fills a small bag of groceries and pays. As he walks out of the market, he sees an old crummy board on the wall with flyers pinned to it. He checks it out. A few weeks later, Dad sits in his new office, talking on the phone. Large nice-looking boards are leaning on the walls of his office. "That's right, ok, sounds good. I'll have it to you by Friday." Dad hangs up the phone and grabs a dart from a dartboard. He spins around in

his chair and throws it at a picture of a vacation place in the tropics. He
hits his mark.

THE BEEF BALL

A small cabin sits on the edge of a large blueberry field. Jeb
quietly opens the front door to his cabin. He closes it and checks the only
bedroom where his girlfriend sleeps. He smirks and heads to the main
room. Jeb's hair is now longer, and he has a full beard. Two medium size
dogs follow him. One black and the other white. He loads a wood-burning
stove before sitting on his couch and grabbing a GameCube controller. He
turns on his TV and smokes from a glass pipe filled with weed. After
putting the pipe down, he looks up at a mantle above the TV. The wood
stove lights up the cabin and a picture of Jeb's father with the black dog
rests on the mantle. Jeb looks back down at the TV with a sad smile and
continues playing his game.

It's rush hour at Phat's, and the crew works fast to keep up. I take
an order from the phone while making a sub. "A roast beef?" I ask, "Ok,
that it? Meatball sub." "Yo, Mike, get that tuna done first." Yells Ted. I

hand a slip to Flynn and look up at all the orders of cold subs lining the board. My eye tic has been at me all day, and now it's on crack. "TUT!" I yell. With no comments, it's as though my friends have adopted the tic as well. Levi sees my aggravation, grabs a slip, and puts it on the cutting board. "One at a time, Mike." He says. I nod and get to work. Obee looks at my slip, smacks Clark, and they start to laugh. "BEEF BALL!? Yo Ted, look at this!" Obee says as Ted glances and laughs. "What the fuck is a BEEF ball!? Yo, Flynn! Get in here." Yells Ted "Mitey!" Obee shouts, "You got any Beef Balls out there!?" Flynn comes back and joins the charade. The line of people at the counter are not pleased, and neither am I while making the subs. The laughter from my friends continues until, eventually, I crack a smile that turns into a laugh.

It's night now, and the shop has slowed down. Clark, Flynn, and Ted play cards in the back by the grill while I wrap up the bain marie. "Yo Mike, you in?" Asks Ted as I look at my pair of sevens. "Yeah," I answer. "What you got, boys?" Asks Ted as they throw their cards down. Clark has two Ace's, Ted has three Jacks, and Flynn has a flush. "DAMN it!" They yell, minus Flynn, who takes the pile of dollar bills with a smile. Jeb heats up some leftovers in the microwave and sits out by the front. "How's

Sis?" He asks. "Good," I answer. "Where's her college again?" Asks Jeb. "I forget the name. Somewhere in the mountains of Maryland," I say as I split up the tips.

The jingle bells ring as Ella opens the door to Phat's. She looks in the fridge of sodas. "Aww, maan." She says out loud. "Something wrong?" I ask. "There's no more root beer." She states. "What a shame. Oh, wait," I say while looking under the counter and pulling out a root beer. Jeb watches while he eats. "Yay." Ella says with a smile. "Thanks Mike! Am I going to see you after work?" She asks. "Maybe," I say playfully. "Ok, see you then." Ella waves to Jeb and leaves as I ignore Jeb's stare. "You know she won't fit in the microwave, D." Jeb comments, breaking the silence. "Leftovers or not." He adds and I slam the tip jar. "Alright!" I yell with a smirk. "They dated for like a week," I add, knowing full well Jeb and I would inevitably have this conversation. "It was a little longer than that, dude." Jeb states while eating. "What happened?" Jeb asks. "I don't know, man," I answer , "We just hit it off." Jeb nods. "Hey, she made the first move, dude," I say as if it mattered. "You tell Tim?" Jeb asks. "Yeah," I told him, "He said they were done anyway." "Hey, whatever makes you sleep better," Jeb adds while tossing his scraps in a doggy bag. "I'm just

258

playing, man. I'm sure you two will live happily ever after." Jeb says with a smirk. "Thanks," I joke. "Ok, Debo, I'll see ya Manana." Jeb slaps me hi-five and heads out the back screen door. *Tim and I have been fighting over the same girls ever since we met. In his defense, he usually came out on top. No pun intended. With all that said, Ella would be the last. He and Obee are both married now with children. Although we still keep in touch, I haven't seen my friend Tim in over a decade.*

As Jeb drives away, I finish cleaning up the shop and then head home. The next morning, I come downstairs, and my excitement is temporarily cut short. "Hey, Cock Sucker." Says Tic with his evil stare. "The fuck do you want!?" I shout in my empty house, "Shouldn't you be off somewhere killing helpless animals?". By now, I had enough of him and his comrades, to say the least. Some newfound confidence had given me the ability to ignore my shitty companions. For the most part, anyway. Tic tries to speak but instead coughs. It's something he has never done before. Something was off. He didn't look good. I mean, he never looked good but still. "What's wrong with you?" I ask as if I give a shit. "Nothing, I'm just peachy. Your girlfriend has nice tits. Think I like Amy's better, though." He adds. "What do you want, Tic?" I interrupt. "Get rid of her."

He says simply. I laugh and say, "We're giving advice now?" I add. "I don't like her." He yells with a second cough. "I gotta go," I say finally and leave the house.

I drive Ella in a blue four-door I bought off my folks. It's daytime, and Ella laughs about something I said. *You see, the thing about her was, well, there's actually not much to say about Ella. In fact, I wouldn't even have brought her up. Except for, well, something attached to her. An entity of sorts. Something so vial, it could only have come from the darkest corners of hell.*

THE MOTHER FROM HELL

A woman in her late 40's smokes a cigarette. She blows the smoke through a sliding back door in her living room. She was average size with brown hair to her shoulders and she wore small glasses. Ella and I come into a connected kitchen. "Hey, mom! This is Mike," Ella says, "I'll be right down, and then we can leave." She leaves the room, and I am stuck with her mother, who hasn't yet said a word. I smile and look around with a stupid look on my face. "So." I finally say, "This kitchen is sweet. Have you guys put it in recently?" Ella's mother, Ava, puffs her cig until finally speaking. "Ella's grandfather put that kitchen in forty-five years ago." She claims. "Ohh," I say aloud while nodding my head. "So," Ava says. "Ella tells me you're twenty years old." Caught off guard, I answer quickly. "Twenty years young," I reply. "And what year are you in?" Asks Ava. Knowing full well that I can't do simple math on a normal day, I can only now guess. "I…am, a sophomore," I say finally. Ava nods slowly while blowing out some smoke. "Hmm." She mumbles. After a year or two, Ella finally comes back down the stairs and into the kitchen, where Ava and I are now silent. "Ok, mom," Ella yells, "We're going to the movies." "Nice to meet you!" I say with a smile that only exists due to the fact that I was getting the fuck out of there. "Be home on time." Says Ava while continuing to puff her cigarette.

"A little heads up would have been nice," I tell Ella as we drive to the movies. "For what!?" She asks. "Um, I don't know that I'm twenty years old and go to college!" I say abruptly, "What's up with THAT?" Ella sighs before answering. "If my mother knows you can buy me alcohol, she won't let us date." I'm still a little confused with it all, but not wanting to make a big deal, I smile and say lightly, "Ok, well, next time, just let me know, is all."

A school bell rings through the hallways of a building that holds grades K through 8. Faith leaves a crowd of kids her age and runs towards me. Both in jackets, Faith and I walk down the paved bike path. The sun breaks through some clouds in the cold sky. Now home, Faith and I smash buttons on our controllers in the living room. Punches and kicks land in the game we play while Satch cheers on Faith from the couch. "Nice!" He says. "Aww, shoot," I yell as Faith counters. "Trunks is a badass!" Satch yells. "Yea, grab him! Do the fucking thing." I give Satch a look for cursing in front of Faith who is now around twelve years old. "My bad. Get it! Aw shit, look out!" Satch yells. "Gotcha!" Faith shouts. "Damn, Dude!" I say while dropping the controller. "If I had Final Blast, you would have been toast," I tell her. "But you didn't!" Satch interrupts, "She beat your ass, dude." "We'll see how you do," I say while doing a blow tic.

The gym. Satch and I put up a good two hundred pounds on the flat bench. "Aw, man," Satch mutters while looking across the gym. "What's up?" I ask. "That's Andy Mills." Satch whispers as I rack the bar and sit up to see who Satch is talking about. "So?" I say out loud while

262

Satch shakes his head. "I used to shove him in his locker with a mouth full of cookie dough." He states. I try to think of something more heartfelt to say, but all I come up with is. "Nice." Followed by a laugh. "Come on, man," Satch complains. "Sorry, man, I just got an image." I say while trying to bite my lip. *You see, over the years, Satch has developed a reputation of being, well, an asshole. For whatever reason, At the end of high school, Satch started doing a 360. Instead of tying random classmates to the flagpole, he would stick up for them. Even going hypocritical as throwing fists in their defense. I never asked him why he took this route, but I figured it was because he didn't really like himself all that much. I don't mean to put words in his mouth, but it's just something I always thought we had in common.*

It wasn't until the summer after I graduated high school that I hit the gym hard. A year later, I had gained twenty pounds of muscle and about fifty pounds of confidence. As shallow as that may be. "I gotta go say something to him," Satch adds. "What?" I reply quickly, "What are you going to say. Sorry, I stuck you in a locker with a mouthful of cookie dough?" "I'll be back," Satch says as he approaches the boy. Andy drops his weight and backs up with a concerned look. I watch as Satch tries to

263

reassure Andy that he just wants to talk. Satch says something and puts his hand out. Andy thinks for a moment before nodding and shaking Satch's hand. I shake my head with a smirk and lay down for my next set.

It's still early on a sunny day when I drop Satch off at his house. It's a neat-looking rancher with an old sports car in the driveway. Satch's Dad has the hood up and wipes a wrench off with a rag. Satch gets out of the car and walks past his Dad while I pull away. "Hey, Mr. D," I yell to Lou. "Hello, Michael." He says, waving with his wrench free hand. "Hey, Dad." "Hello, Satch, You two working out?" "Yup." Says Satch as he walks by. "That's good! How's Michael? Does he still do that twitchy thing?" Lou says seriously. "It's called Tourette's, Dad." Satch chuckles. "A Tourettee? Naa, he's probably just eating too many sweets. Have him run around the block. He'll feel better." Lou adds. "How's the car coming?" Satch asks. "It's good, It's good. I'm going to take it out for a joy ride later. You should come." "Yea, maybe." Satch walks up to his small porch with a nice-looking table and chairs. His brother Ray comes out. "Yo Satch." "Hey, Ray." Satch heads in the door as Ray heads towards the driveway.

Ella and I play a video game in her living room. "You're not bad," I say while dodging her attack. "No one beats me on rockets." She says while looking at her younger sister watching from the couch. "TUT!" I yell without thinking. The more comfortable I get with people, the more tics slip out. As I've probably mentioned, holding them in is easier said than done, and before the day is over, they will escape one way or another. With that said, there is one person I am far from comfortable with. I look in the kitchen from my seat on the floor, but no Ava. "What was that?!" Ava says, standing somehow right behind me. The question is ignored. "Hello!" Ava yells. "That's just Mike's tic's mom," Ella says as she pushes away a small yellow dog. I can feel Ava's cold stare in my direction. "Tics, huh.?" Ava mutters before turning her attention to Ella. "Ella! You better be good to that dog! Your uncle loved it more than us," Ava says with subtle sarcasm. *Don't worry, the dog will be fine, I promise.* A car horn beeps, and Ella and I head out the front door. The dog follows. Ava calls it back in the house while Ella and I get into a car. "Bye, Mom!" Yells Ella.

The car driven by Ella's girlfriend drops us off around the corner. We quickly hop into my car. "Remind me why this is necessary?" I ask. "If my mom thinks you're driving, she'll think we're leaving my friends to go…you know?" Ella says as she reaches into her bag. "You think she's really that dumb," I ask. Ella opens her root beer and pours in some rum, *which for the record, I did NOT even get her.* "It's better this way. Trust me." She tells me with a smile.

Later that night, in the woods of Shimmer Run. I look around the floor of my back seat. Ella chugs a root beer and wipes the sweat off her forehead. She is wearing a hoodie, and a blanket is wrapped around her lap. "What are you looking for?" She asks with a smile. "Evidence," I say while grabbing a condom wrapper and tossing it out an open window. "Hey, litterbug!" She yells. *Though out of character for me to trash the woods, these, my friend, were desperate times.* "We'll when your mom comes out with a fucking spotlight, I'll be ready," I tell her. "Mike!" She pleads. "It's better this way, trust me," I add as I hop in the front seat. I see a mean stare from Ella. "Fine," I say, finally giving in and opening my door. As I grab the wrapper, I see its companion lying in the dirt. Noticing something is off, I pick it up with a stick. Ella sees it and looks nervous. "Is that!?" We pause for a moment while looking at the broken condom that could now be used as a Chinese finger trap. "It was," I say with a disheveled face.

It's morning now, and Ella and I are parked at the pharmacy. Ella is crying in the passenger seat. "You know, you don't have to take it," I say as she looks at the pill. "Are you serious!?" She says. "Do you know what my mom would do if you got me pregnant!? Not to mention taking my virginity." I turn to Ella with a surprised look on my face. "You ain't a virgin!" I yell, knowing full well from Tim. "She doesn't know that! She made me promise I would wait for marriage." As Ella cry's, I slowly hand her a root beer. She grabs it and takes the pill.

I'M NOT TAKING YOU TO MISSISSIPPI

It's a fairly normal day at Phat's. Levi walks through the back with a box of steaks. He stops and looks up at a leak in the ceiling. He puts down the box and checks it out. Later, Clark answers the phone. "Phat's. A what!?" Clark looks over at the old pizza oven that to be honest I have never seen in use. "Are you sure? Ok, half hour." Clark goes over to the old pizza oven as Flynn walks in. "What are you doing bro?" Asks Flynn. "Someone wants a pizza." The two friends scratch their heads. They each take out a wad of dough from the fridge and stretch it out in awkward ways. Throwing it up and taking a side each and walking around to stretch it wide. They throw on some sauce and cheese and, voila. The pizza is now done, and it's shaped like Texas. Clark and Flynn are very happy with their creation.

It's almost dark now as I come into the empty Sub Shop. The phone is ringing. "Hello?" I say before answering the phone on the wall. "Phat's. Where too?" I make a cheese steak and bag it up. I look around again before grabbing a two liter of soda and walk out the back door. As I drive away the phone rings and Tepper walks in. "Hello?" He shouts. I pull up to a crummy house with the number *209*. I sigh and shake the two liter of soda while banging it around. *Now I'm not giving Phat's a bad name. In all seriousness, if you had ever eaten there I'm sure that your food was good and clean. Unless maybe you lived at 209. All of us had our own way of dealing with the stiff. I don't mean change or a dollar. I mean zip. Not one cent. And this wasn't once in a while, this was every time. I mean as much as you should tip a bartender, still we're not cracking a beer for you, we're making you dinner and driving it to your house, so if you stiff your driver every time, you get what you get. I think Clark's way was my favorite. His logic was "If you're too fucking stupid to not tip,*

268

your too fucking stupid to do math", and he'd just change the price to whatever tip he thought he deserved. He must have been right because they never figured it out.

I drop the sub and step on it before picking it up. I knock on the door and look into several teens watching TV. They call out for Hank. A teen comes out of his room and opens the front door. "Ten bucks," I mutter. The kid hands me a ten. I grab it, hand him the soda and sub, and walk away. "Yo man." Says Hank as he holds out four singles. I walk back and take the cash. "Damn it." I think to myself. "Thanks, man, hey watch that soda, it fell from a shelf. Hank nods and shuts the door.

I get back in my blue car that is parked under a now-lit streetlight. Before starting my car, I look in my rear-view mirror. In the back seat sit an old black lady. She is dressed in nice old fashion clothes with a hat and a bag in her lap. I turn around. "Can I help you?" I ask. "I'd like a ride please." Says the old passenger. I look around before answering. "This ain't a cab lady," I say calmly. "Oh." She says sadly with her head down. "Well," I ask. "Where are you going?" "Hanny Ave, Mississippi." She says. "I'm not taking you to Mississippi" I reply, quickly interrupting.

"Anywhere else?" "I guess I'd just like to drive around for a bit." She states. I turn back around and start the car. "Now we're talking," I say as I light up a smoke. I offer one to the old passenger but she kindly refuses. As I pull up to Phat's, Ted comes out with a bag of subs. "Gunther's." He says as I grab them and head back to my car. "Who the fuck is that?" Ted shouts after seeing the old passenger sitting politely in the backseat of my car. "I don't know," I say while shrugging my shoulders. Levi pulls up and walks by Ted who is still looking at the old lady in my backseat. Levi looks as well. "Who the fuck is that?" Levi asks as I back up my car. "He doesn't know." Answers Ted. The old traveler looks over at Ted and Levi as I pull forward and leave Phat's parking lot. "Crazy Mike." Levi says while shaking his head. He heads into the shop with a bag of hoagie rolls. Ted does a double-take and follows.

ALEX VS AVA

In my bedroom on my day off. As I look around the room, I notice something's off. I look under the bed and then in my closet. I throw clothes around on the floor but can't find what I'm looking for. A short while later I eat cereal with Faith and Mom in the kitchen. "Has anyone seen Alex by any chance?" I ask. Mom and Faith look at each other. "Where is he!?" I say loudly. After getting my answer I run out of my front door in a surfing hoodie, sneakers, and jeans. I jump in my car and peel away.

Now at Ella's house, I knock on the front door and crack it open. With no cars in the driveway, I assume no one is home. "Hellooo!" I say out loud. As I walk through the eerie silence, I notice the shades are pulled down and there are no signs of life. I walk upstairs and into Ella's room where I find Alex on her bed. She asked about my old friend a week ago and for whatever reason thought it would be cute to kidnap him. She was wrong. As I walk back down the stairs, I hear something in the kitchen and or living room. "Hello? It's just me." I say out loud. I walk into the kitchen and see a trash can pulled out from under a counter. "It is out farther than it should be," I think as I glance in. And there it was. The box of the morning-after pill. With it the receipt. "How could she be so stupid!" I yell in my head. As I stare in the trash the silhouette of a person behind me slowly rises out of a chair in the dark living room.

271

From outside the house, Ava is heard yelling. *Now I don't remember exactly what was said but I know it went something like this.* "So how fucking old ARE you?! Was that your plan all along? You might as well have grabbed some tools and done it yourself!" Ava says as I sit in a chair with my head down, as if I had any other option. Ava takes a breath and looks at Alex who is sitting on the kitchen table. "And what the hell is that!?" She yells. I pick my head up and finally speak. "He's my favorite stuffed animal," I say softly. "What!" She yells. "Every kid has one," I add. "Enough!" Ava yells before taking a deep breath and abandoning her rant. Ava sits in a chair at the table and puts her pack of smokes down as she tries to light a cigarette in her mouth. "Look, I'm not stupid ok, I know my daughter isn't a virgin. However, if you two are going to be sleeping together, you need to be a little more careful." At first, I was caught off guard by her comment. "Was she being cool?" I thought but then she said this, "At least until this little fling is over." As the words left her mouth my demeanor changed. I turn and look at Ava before getting up. I pick up my chair and drop it back down facing Ava who is still trying to light her cigarette. *Now, you have to understand something here. At the time I thought that I was in love with this girl. Ella and I were no fling. That meant no one was getting in the way of my*

newfound happiness.

Ava looks up at me while I pull out a lighter from my pocket and light it in front of Ava's face. Still with a scowl she leans forward and lights her cig. I sit and grab a smoke from her pack. She looks surprised as I light up. After blowing the smoke away from Ava I speak, "Listen Ava, I think me, and you got off on the wrong foot. Now I apologize for that." I say when pointing to the trash can. "I'll take full responsibility, and I assure you it won't happen again. But this little, *fling* isn't going anywhere. With that said, I think it'd be better if me and you just, got along." I put out my cigarette in a tray and stand up. Ava says nothing. She just stares. "Keep the lighter," I add before leaving the house. I jump in my car with a confident smile and turn on the stereo to rock guitars cranking out. As I look over the back seat, I reverse to perform a K-turn and that's when I hear it. The sound of something bouncing around under the car is heard with a yelp. It was Ella's yellow dog. "He's alive." I hope quickly while coming to a stop. He seemed to have missed the tires. I slowly turn to the front and turn off the stereo. Ella's yellow dog lays in the street. "Get up," I say out loud for fear the dog was hurt. After a moment that felt like fucking forever, the dog jumps up and takes off for the house without even a scratch. I sigh with relief and drop my shoulders. I'm guessing that was the last car my little friend ever chased. I look slowly over to the porch where Ava stands. Without moving anything but her arm she opens the door and lets the dog inside while staring directly into my soul. My confident smile was now a big pile of shit. I then do an awkward K-turn and drive away. Little did I know then that the worst was yet to come.

THE BOYFRIEND FROM HELL

The buds on the trees are finally sprouting and the first gust of warm air flows through Phat's as I make an Italian sub with the works. Clark, Ricky, Flynn, Obee, and Levi crowd a table by the grill. I wrap up a sub and go see what the commotion is. "What are you guys doing drugs?" I ask, "I want some!" "Get the hell out front!" Yells Ted as he comes from the back and blocks me. I go back out to the front and grab the mop. As I ring it, the guys come out with a birthday cake. The cake reads *HAPPY TUT-TUT 23*. "Happy TUT TUT twenty-three!" They all yell with laughter. "It was all Flynn man. Brilliant!" Ted says as I give Flynn a hi-five. "I laughed the whole way back." Says Flynn with a grin. "It's amazing," I yell back with a smile. I cut it up and dish it to my friends.

My cousin Matt and I rock out in a bedroom studio. Matt plays drums and sings with me while I jam on guitar. Afterward, we crack a beer and hang on a couch in his bedroom. "When are you heading back to Jersey?" Matt asks. "I got work Wednesday so I'll probably head back tomorrow, I say before chugging my beer. "Sucks you can't stay another day or two." He adds. "We got a gig tomorrow night. I'm sure we could get you up there to shred a song." Matt continues. "Hm." I say. "You know what, Obee owes me one." "Let me see your cell." Matt throws me his flip phone and I dial-up. "Yo man,...Is Obee working?...Obee!" I yell seconds later. "Yo man can you cover me on Wednesday?" I ask. "Yup, you're the man. Thanks, bro!" Matt points to the air. "You have to hit the button." He says as I finish my phone call with Obee. I press the end button and close the flip phone. "Awesome," I say with a grin, "Let me just call the old lady." "She going to be pissed?" Matt asks. "Naa, I'm sure they could both use a break from me," I say while dialing. "I'll call the house phone and put in some brownie points. Nice, I got the answering machine. Hey guys! It's your favorite person, ME!" I say. You're an asshole." Matt laughs while I cup the cell with my hand. "I'll be away for another day or two, but I'll see you guys when I get back. Alright bye!" I close the flip phone and toss it on the table while Matt eats some chips and chugs his beer. "So her mom's a real bitch huh?" He asks as he cracks a new can. I burp before answering. "Understatement of the year my friend."

My adventure in Connecticut comes to a close as I make my way home. The sun is going down as I park outside of Ella's house. I head into the house relieved that only Ella's car is parked in the driveway. "Hey, Ella?!" I yell as I barge in the house. "I'm baaaccck!" I say, now in the kitchen as Ava smokes a cigarette at the sink. "You gotta be fucking kidding me!" I think to myself, now back in the kitchen with Ava. "Oh hey," I say scratching the back of my head. "Sorry I saw her car," I say. "Ella's out with her sister and grandmother. They should be back in a bit." "Oh, ok well, I'll just come back a little later." "Actually." Ava interrupts. "I could use some help." "You could use a lot of fucking help," I say in

276

my head. "Ok, sure," I say out loud with a smile. Ava grabs her keys and heads out the door. "Ok." I think as I follow. Ava gets in Ella's car and starts it. "This is weird," I tell myself as I get in the passenger seat. "So, where are we going?" I ask. "Food shopping," Ava answers calmly, and just like that, we're off.

Night has fallen and after driving for a while, Ava pulls over on a side street. She lights up a cigarette and offers one to me. As I hesitate, Ava offers again. I finally take one and roll down the window before lighting up. She goes through her purse, "Can you open the glove box for me?" She asks. Now even more confused, I open the glove box, and guess what? I'm no longer confused.

THE TAPE

Now worried, I look over at Ava who has pulled a small tape from her purse. She puts it on the dash with her other hand out. I knew exactly what was going to happen next and why I didn't just get out and run, *I still don't quite understand.* I hand Ava the tape recorder that had been strategically placed in the glove box. She puts in the tape and hits play. "You gotta hit the button." Those words repeated in my head up until this point. *I thought about whether or not to put this part in but, fuck it.*

MIKE: "I'll be away for another day or two, but I'll see you guys when I get back. Alright bye!"

MATT: "So her mom's a real bitch huh?"

MIKE: "Understatement of the year my friend."

MATT: "What's her deal?"

MIKE: "Nothing. She's cool, she just needs a nice big floppy Cock is all!" MATT: "A little dried up down there?"

MIKE: "Remember when we broke into the water slides in November?"

The laughter from Matt and I's voice fills the car as I cringe with every comment. Ava hasn't flinched. "Is it over yet?" I think to myself. "No." No, it's not.

MATT: "Ouch, we'll from the looks of Ell it's worth it. She let you in the back door yet?"

MIKE: "No...But I'm GONNA!

BOTH: Laughter

MATT: Tear that ass up bro!

MIKE: She'll be pooping her pants for a week!

"CLICK." Ava turns off the recorder and puts it in her purse. She starts the car and drives off. After sitting in silence for a long time I finally speak. Apologies did not exist at this point, so I simply ask, "Where are we going?" Ava looks at me as if nothing had happened and says. "We're going food shopping." She couldn't be serious. After that? I turn back to the front and puff my cigarette. "Food Shopping." I think. It was brilliant.

Back at Ella's I carry two handfuls of bags in the house and drop them on the table in the kitchen. Ella gets off the couch and walks into the room. "Where the hell were you guys? You were gone for like two hours!"

Ava starts putting food away. My eyes are now as wide as Ella's. "Ella

didn't know." I think to myself as I watch Ava "Her mother hadn't told

her." I slowly look back at Ella before answering her. "We went food

shopping." Another win for Ava. *Not that it mattered much after that*

anyway. Ella and I, in total, only lasted about a year.

   Today I have no ill favor for either of them. I would happily drink

a beer with Ella and smoke a cig with Ava. At the time though, I took it

hard for some reason. I pace in my bedroom on the house phone. "You

said she was on vacation!" I yell through the phone at Ella. "So where

were you!" I hang up and toss the phone. I walk downstairs to the living

room where I stare at a lamp. We look at each other for a moment as I tilt

my head. The irrational thoughts in my mind are now gone as I see myself

grab the lamp and smash it to the floor. *What you have just witnessed or*

rather read, is what I call. The Snap. Through the course of my life I have

experienced the snap only a handful of times. Maybe two handfuls. Where

does it come from? Who knows? Holding in feelings, anger, tics or maybe

it's just life. Either way, most of the time it's directed towards inanimate

objects. Once in a while, a human has slipped in but in my defense, I can

assure you that they most probably deserve it, and on a more serious note
it has never and will never be a girl. I mean let's face it, only a douchebag
of a man would hit a woman. I'm not going to sit here and tell you all my
Snap stories, as entertaining as they may be. Instead, I will share one.

AMY AND MIKE VS THE WORLD

On my 21st birthday, I was hungover and barely alive. Amy said
my dad's car broke down and we needed to pick him up. While trying not
to puke I watched as Amy pulled into a grass lot that said *Sky Diving*
Adventures. Jeb, my fam, and Tim were there to join us. After jumping out
of a plane I landed, threw up, and enjoyed the rest of my birthday which
included Amy treating me to a movie. Tim and Tess accompanied us to
the zombie flick that Tim and I had been anticipating. After hitting up the
concession stand, we found our seats in the crowded theater. As the
coming attractions roll, we talk amongst ourselves. Two boys around my
age were doing the same thing in the row behind us, however, quite

loudly. I assumed they would quiet down when the movie started. I was wrong.

Knowing full well that Amy would not put up with this for long, I let her do her thing. Amy turns around and says something like, "Hey, shut the fuck up!" This subtle approach only worked for a few seconds before the two boys were at it again. "My boyfriend's right here!" Amy threatens as Tess and Tim slide lower in their seats. The four of us had just polished off a J in the parking lot and out of all the people I love, Tess holds the gold medal for getting high and not talking for three hours. Tim holds silver. I knew I would eventually have to turn around and say something. As I procrastinated, the boys started throwing candy. That's when I checked out. The last thing I remember was a single kernel of popcorn rolling down my shoulder in slow motion. When I came to, I was in the row behind us on top of one of the boys. He was somewhere in between a laugh or a cry as I repeatedly slammed him into the back of his seat by his collar. One by one, the boys' friends try to pull me off as I throw them aside. I did not know where this rage had come from for these guys were at least my size and in a group of seven or eight. As they tried to pull me off, Amy stood on her chair yelling something like, "What now bitch! I told you he was going to fuck you up!" She grabbed one of the guys by his hoodie and pushed him away from me to lighten the load. During the scuffle, an usher came in, took one look at us, and took off back up the ramp and out the door. I eventually realized the extreme measure I had taken in the crowded movie theater. I let go of the loud boy and climbed back in my seat where Tim and Tess were now on the floor. They were not happy. However, one person was, Amy. With a big smile, she put her head on my shoulder and we watched the rest of *28 Days Later* in complete silence. *Now believe it or not this trait was passed down to me by my dad. One of the nicest guy's I've ever met, but every once in a great while...*

It's the mid 70's and a young Mom and Dad sit in a bar. A beer bottle flies through the air and smashes into Dad's face and then their drinks, splashing up and getting them wet. A jock wearing the number 52 gets up next to them and heads to a group of other jocks in the bar wearing football jackets. They're all laughing. "Damn bro, you could have just called my name." Say 52. Dad hands Mom a napkin and she smiles and cleans up. "Are You ok?!" Mom asks. "I'm fine." Says Dad with a crazy look in his eye. My 5'8" thin Dad in his 20's gets up and walks toward the football crew. He stands next to them, but they don't acknowledge him. He

283

looks around and focuses on the biggest guy there. Dad grabs an empty

beer bottle and smashes it on a high table. With his right hand, he grabs

the biggest football player by the collar and slams him into a wall. With

his left, he puts the jagged end of the bottle to the football player's neck.

They now acknowledge him. The big football player puts his hands up.

"Whoa, man chillout!" The Jock says. "Who threw it?" Dad asks. "Threw

what man?" Asks the the football player. "The BOTTLE!" Dad says as the

player points. "It was him, man! It was him!" Still with a crazy look in his

eye, Dad looks over at the ball player holding a fresh beer who eventually

drops it and runs for the door. Mom softly puts her hand on Dad's

shoulder, "Mick, let's just head home, ok?" Dad's crazy look fades as he

lets go of the football player. He backs up and puts the broken bottle on a

table before putting his arm around Mom. They walk to the door as Dad

throws some cash on the bar. The big ball player rubs a small drop of

blood off his neck while saying to his friends, "That little guy was nuts."

THE LAST DAY AT PHAT'S

It's closing time at Phat's. Levi and Ted clean up. They hear a noise outside and look at each other. They walk out the back screen door and see me smashing a trash can on the dumpster. I yell loudly. Levi and Ted put their hands up and try to calm me down. "YO DUDE!" Ted yells. I hold the trash can which is now in pieces as I calm down and drop it. "You alright?" Asks Levi, "Give me your belt, I'll get you out of here." I hand him the money belt. Levi takes it and heads inside with a smile. "Crazy Mike." He mutters. "You alright man?" Ted asks. I mumble something unkind about Ella as Ted puts me in a headlock. "Ah." He says, now understanding my rage. "Fuck her," Ted says and walks me inside with a smile. Perhaps remembering a time in his life that today matters not.

The next day a man comes down from a ladder in the back of Phat's. He had just inspected the leak in the ceiling. He looks at Ted and Levi who wait with patient faces. The man shakes his head. "FUCK!" Yells Ted as he throws a rag. "Come on man!" Levi adds.

The entire Phat's' crew cracks a can of beer and chugs in down in the now, empty sub shop. The old pizza oven is all that remains. The laughter and stories echo through the shop as we take turns remembering our favorite stories that had gone on long before I even started working there. Later, we head out the front door and Levi puts up a sign that says, "We moved." The Phat's' crew continues to laugh in the hot sun as we say our goodbyes. Ted holds a golf club with a cover on it. The cover has a big picture of me making a stupid face with a big smile. "You still got that?" Obee asks. "Hell yea!" Ted answers. Surprisingly, Ted was a big fan of my Pollyanna gift. However, Ella's mom didn't find as much joy in her's. As Ted holds up the club, I have a flashback of Ava holding a coffee mug with the same picture of my stupid smile. As she lowers the mug, I'm there to greet her with that same smile. Still, outside of Phat's, I do my blow tic. "Are you working at the new place?" I ask. "Nah, time to move on bro," Clark says. "Besides, the location sucks. You?" I shake my head. "I don't know." Flynn slaps me a hi-five on his way passed. "Have fun in Cali bro!" Ted yells to Flynn. "Thanks, Ted!" Flynn waves and climbs into a small truck with Clark.

That was the last time I saw Flynn. He had pursued his passion for golf in California. A passion he excelled in. Before his return, Flynn was killed by a drunk driver. Obviously, he deserved much more in his young life, to say the least. We talk of Flynn often. He always brings a smile.

Jeb takes out some jumper cables and hooks them to the magic bus, that besides a few parades, has been parked at Phat's forever. I hop through Jeb's passenger window as he lights a cig and revs his engine. Levi sits in the driver seat of the VW bus and prepares to turn the key. The crew watches as they get in their cars. "Not going to happen," Ricky yells from his car. "Alright!" Says Levi turning the key. After some engine sounds the bus starts up and the Phat's' crew cheers as Jeb unhooks the cables. Levi waves as he drives off the lot, and one by one we all follow. A month later the Phat's building was bulldozed to the ground. As Clark guessed, the new location was a bust and about a year later, Phat's closed for good. However, I like to think the real last day of Phat's was this day. When the last car left that crummy lot and the old building stood alone.

A punk rock concert. Two girls duck under a crowd throwing their hands up. One is petite with jet black hair past her shoulders. The other is tall with long dirty blond hair. The black-haired girl goes in her bag and takes out a plastic water bottle filled with booze. She sips it and passes it to the other girl. The tall girl sips it and hands it back. A kid slams into them and the bottle falls to the ground and gets stepped on immediately. As the taller girl pushes away the drunk who slammed into them, the black-haired girl picks up the now empty, crushed plastic bottle. The tall girl speaks, "What the hell man." "Damn It!" Sophie shouts as she chucks the crushed plastic bottle, "Come on." Sophie and Jade make their way through the crowd and come out to a bar on the far wall. It's empty. They sigh with disappointment. Sophie looks to the far end of the bar, smacks Jade on the arm, and points.

Satch and I are the only two people at the long bar. We have on jeans, tight t-shirts, and skater shoes. We sip beer from our see-through plastic cups and nod our heads like douchebags as we fix are super cool armbands. I look over at the crowd and smack Satch on the arm. He looks in the direction I point to with my head. Sophie and Jade are seen from afar, smiling and waving in our direction. Now a foursome, Satch, Jade, Sophie and I bounce in the crowd. We each hold a see-through plastic cup of beer. Satch and I easily toss aside moshing eighteen- and nineteen-year-olds that get in our way. Now with beer and a comfortable view of the stage, Jade and Sophie are satisfied. As the lead guitar player solos on his ax, I look up. I am intrigued.

Jeb finishes packing his station wagon in the mid-summer heat. He closes his trunk as his girlfriend yells at him. *Jeb and I are far from saints and during the course of our lives have been yelled at quite a bit. Probably for good reason although on this day I know Jeb was not at fault. Usually, Jeb's girlfriends and I are close. His high school sweetheart and I were practically best friends. This one, not so much.* Jeb whistles softly for the dogs. They hop in the side door of the wagon. "I don't think so asshole! Here boys!" She calls and claps as the white and black dog jumps out and runs towards her. Jeb puts two fingers in his mouth and whistles as loud as humanly possible. The two dogs run back into the wagon and Jeb closes the door. He gets in and drives off the farm. He does not return.

CLARK AND THE DAY OF SHIT

The morning sun peaks through a dark shade in a messy bedroom. In the room are golf clubs, hockey gear, clothes, surfboards, and a picture of Clark and Flynn in high school wrestling gear. They're both putting up

289

their pointer finger. Clark sleeps in. A few hours later Clark walks past a bathroom and pounds on the door, "Sally!" "Yeah?" She yells. "I gotta shit." "Well, I'm in here." Sally states. "But I gotta go bad!" Clark shouts again. "You can't shit in here Clark!" Sally interrupts. Clark sighs and goes down the stairs. "Hey, mom," Clark says to his mother sitting at the kitchen table. "Hey, Clark." Says Mary while reading a paper. Clark goes to grab an egg sandwich on the counter. "That's your sisters," Mary says. Clark looks around the kitchen before asking, "Well, where the hell is mine!" "I asked you if you wanted one." Mary chuckles as she gathers her keys and purse. "I'd make you another, but I have work. What's your plans?" Mary adds. "Job," Clark states as he grabs a box of cereal. "Applying or interview?" She asks. Clark plops down at the table and pours a bowl. "Both." He mutters. "Well good luck." Says Mary as she leaves. "Thanks," Clark adds as he reaches for the carton of milk. Before grabbing it, he stops and puts out his pointer finger. After jabbing the empty milk carton, he gets up, walks to the egg sandwich, and takes the biggest bite possible before putting it back on the plate. He then heads into the living room and grabs a game controller.

Later in the day, Clark is still playing a video game on his couch. He looks at the clock that reads "4:14". He gets up and heads to his room. Now in a suit and tie, he runs a comb through his hair in his bedroom mirror. As he comes downstairs in his suit, his cell phone rings. He picks it up. "Hello, for real?" Clark walks out his front door now in a wetsuit. He locks the door and walks to his truck which has a short board sticking out the bed.

Clark drives as he puffs his cigarette. I grab one out of Clark's pack and light up. "How long have you been smoking?" Clark asks. "On and off, like ten years," I answer. "Sounds like a good time to start buying your own." He states. "Tomorrow," I say before lighting up. "So, head high huh?" I ask. "According to Chuck." Clark answers. We eventually pull up behind a white truck parked on the curb. "Oh no, it's Chuck!" Says Clark as we come to a stop. A tall skinny guy with short blond hair comes stumbling out from under the boardwalk. He hits his head on the way out and rubs it. He looks disoriented. "What the hell was he doing under there?" I say loudly. "Who knows," Clark says as if annoyed. "Probably fucking kids." I immediately laugh out loud at Clark's dark humor that matches his attitude of the day. Clark cracks his first smile, and we leave

291

the truck. The three of us in wet suits climb the stairs to the boardwalk and look at the waves. Before complaining, "Aww man. Damn it, Chuck!" They said head high!" Chuck yells back. "WHO!? Surf Gear!" Clark shouts. "It might pick up." Chuck adds. "AAH Come on," I say. The silhouettes of four surfers in the waves. Behind us is the setting sun.

Clark parks in a backyard filled with cars. Now dressed in board shorts, tank tops, and flip-flops, Clark and I watch as a brand-new sports car parks in front of us. Two attractive girls get out. "TUT!" I yell while putting out a bohg. "Ally Hendrix," I say while staring out the window. "She's so hot," I continue. "She's a fucking whore!" Clark interrupts. "You bang her?" I ask. "No." He answers, "I think Tepper did." As we walk to the back of the house, we pass the two girls who are still at their car. Clark gives me a look and I nod. "Hey, guys." Ally says as Clark and I walk by and blatantly snub her and her girlfriend Shay who she showed up with. The girls roll their eyes and follow behind. After a long quiet walk to the back deck of the house, Ally speaks again, "Oh, what Clark?" SHUT THE FUCK UP Ally!" Yells Clark with a smile. Shay and I crack up as Ally pushes Clark up the steps to the deck. "Asshole." She mutters. "What's up,

Devaney?" Shay says. She throws an arm around me, and we walk into the party.

There's a long line to the bathroom. Music is playing and the house party is in full effect. Clark walks up and sees the line. Ally is at the beginning of it and instantly blocks him from cutting the line. "Aw, what the fuck." Clark says. "What are you crying about?" Ally mocks, "You're a guy, just go outside." "I gotta take a shit!" Yells Clark. "Well, now you know how we feel!" She replies with a shit-eating grin. Clark walks away. Out in the corner of the yard, Clark does his business. He pulls his head away from the smell and grabs his underwear off the grass to wipe with. Walking with his underwear now rolled up, he heads to a trash can in the yard. Before reaching it, he stops and looks at the party where people are now playing beer pong on the back deck. Two friends sink the last cup and celebrate by holding one finger in the air, which instantly reminds him of Flynn. The cheers fill the large backyard as Clark stares at the lively party. His irritable face that he carried throughout the day, slowly fades to sadness. He turns away from the trash can and heads toward his truck. He passes Ally's car and with one flick of the wrist chucks his underwear.

Clark gets in his truck and drives away as his shitty boxer briefs colorfully slide down Ally's entire windshield.

SOPHIE'S OTHER SLEEVE

I sit on the fallen punching bag in what's left of my garage. I smoke a bowl of weed while looking out at the cedar trees that had held the mighty tree fort of my childhood. Only one of the three cedar trees remains intact. "Those were the days." Says Tic now sitting beside me. I exhale as he puts out his hand. I look him over before handing him the bowl. "Remember when Jeb jumped off and missed the hay bin?" I laugh as Tic smokes up. "You're fine," I told Jeb as he spits up blood. Tic chokes on smoke and coughs into his hand. "Speaking of." He says as he shows me his palm now covered in his own blood. "Fuck me." He mutters. "Ok man what the hell!? You haven't said anything rotten in months and now your Mr. fucking memory lane." Tic looks at me with his beady eyes. "The box." He says. "Don't open it," I remember the box but have no clue what's in it or why Tic has been acting so strange lately. I sigh, "You

294

were right about Ella." Tic laughs. "No shit jerkoff." I smile, get up, and head toward the house.

I sit on the wooden coffee table in my parent's living room on a cloudy day. I tune up and hit the fresh strings on my acoustic guitar. Heartbreak, anger, regret. All good ingredients for a rock song. Still, there seemed to be something missing. It's been three years since I have been alone. Time will heal, but patience was not one of my virtues. The simple fact was there is a hole in my core, and I wanted to fill it.

A white oblong pill with 10/325 printed on it. It sits on the small pink kitchen table. Satch enters the kitchen. "You're still looking at that thing. Gimie it!" Satch says. "I'm going to eat it!" I tell him, "I'm just thinking." "Satch shakes his head and grabs some beers out of the fridge. He walks out to the porch where Jade and Sophie sit. "What's Mike doing?" Jade asks as she takes a beer. "I don't know, he's crazy." I hear Satch say sarcastically as the screen door closes. I pop the pill and chug my beer. Satch drives his jeep down a back road that stretches into the night. The girls sit in the back while puffing a joint. Sophie is wearing a light white fur jacket and Jade has on a hoodie. Satch and I are in T-shirts.

"You guys want to hit the movies or the tape store?" Satch yells to the back. "Tape store." Says Sophie. "Yeah fuck the movies!" Jade adds, causing a laugh. "How Ya feeling?" Satch asks as he smokes his cigarette. "I'm cool, yeah I don't even feel it," I say referring to the pill I took in my kitchen. "Good." Says Satch as he flicks his cherry into the cool summer air that hours before was soaked in humidity.

Jade and Satch walk down a long aisle of VHS and DVDs while Sophie and I look at the massive horror section that has been my favorite aisle since I could walk. "What do we have here. Oh, shoot! The Gate. This movie used to scare the shit out of me!" I say. "Let's get it!" Sophie states and adds, "Oh, nice. We need a Jason for sure." "Which one should we get?" She asks. "I like them all," I mention as I grab the original. "This one's a bonus." Says Sophie as she reaches for *Sleep Away Camp*. "I knew I liked you." As the words leave my mouth, The sleeve of Sophie's fur jacket grazes my arm. My pupils shrink and the noise in the tape store changes to a light hum. My entire body is now completely covered in the white fur that had graced my arm. My head, hands, and feet are the only thing exposed to the air now as I look down at the tiles I'm no longer standing on. I look at Sophie. She smiles while lying horizontally in thin air. She slowly flicks a VHS of *The Evil Dead* with her finger. It spins through the air and stops in front of me. I smile and grab it. Satch and Jade walk to Sophie and me who are now holding four or five horror movies each. Satch laughs, "You guys are high as hell."

A week or two ago my dad and I replaced the 2x4s on the porch and painted it green. Since then, someone referred to it as *The Greenroom*. And that was that. Satch and I sit in two chairs and smoke cigarettes. A small table sits between us. The porch light is off as we chat through the faint screams of a horror movie. Inside, the TV flickers over the coffee table which is filled with empty snacks and beer bottles. Jade and Sophie spoon on the couch. They are both asleep.

"Hey, can I get another one of those?" I ask as I light another cigarette. Satch hesitates. "I don't know man." He says. "Oh, come on," I say sarcastically, "You think I'm going to get addicted?" "It creeps up man," Satch says as he goes into his pocket. "What do you get prescribed for anyway?" I ask. Satch stretches out his back. "My back man, sucks." Satch hands me a pill and I thank him. "I like these things. I haven't even thought about you know who." I state. "Ella!?" Satch interrupts, "She's trash, Mike." "Yea," I say, "But you know, feelings." "What, you think

you loved her, come on!" Satch yells through the darkness before lighting

his next smoke with his last. "What do you mean?" I ask, now confused.

"You don't love her!" He states while leaning out of his chair and turning

towards me to ask. "Remember Jill?" Satch asks. "Aw shit!" I yell. "Do I,

you were on suicide watch. Ya see!" Satch says, "I didn't love her." "Bull

shit!" I interrupt. "So, what was it then?" Before answering, Satch sits

back and puffs his smoke. "Nothing. She was just super-hot." He says.

"Get the fuck outta here!" I yell. "For real," Satch says before peeking

through a window at the girls. "What you should be doing is pushing up

on Sophie." "Yea no shit!" I yell quietly. "Doesn't she have a boyfriend

though?" "He's a fucking douche bag!" Satch says louder than a whisper.

"You've been hitting the gym dude, you're good." He adds as I rub my

face. "Yea but my face is like, pointy," I say while grabbing my nose.

"You're retarted." Satch laughs. "You're a regular-looking dude! "Na,

your face is normal looking," I state after chugging my beer. "What my fat

nose!?" Satch yells, "I look like Martin Short!" "You know who I always

thought you looked like?" I ask. "Robin Williams," Satch says quickly.

"Holy shit!" I yell. "How'd you guess that?" "Because that's who you fucking look like!" Satch ends with as our laughs ring out through my yard like a symphony in the night.

THE GREEN ROOM

It's late morning and Mom, Dad, Sis, and Faith pack up the blue station wagon in the driveway. Dad puts his hand out for a shake, "After we drop Sis at school we are going to Grandma and Pop's. You sure you don't want to come?" "Na, have fun though," I reply, and we say our I love yous. And they're off.

That night I strum my acoustic in The Green Room. Jade hits her bowl as Sophie has a sneeze attack. Satch lies lifeless on the living room couch. I sing. *Jade hits a bowl with weed from the city. Sophie sneezes hard though she's still pretty. Satch is out of pills, so he feels shitty. The only friends I've seen in a month. What a pity!*" The G chord rings out and Sophie and Jade pay me in laughs. Jade's phone rings and Satch finally gets up. "Ok, thanks anyway," Jade says as Satch hit the door. "Damn it!"

Satch shouts. "I'm sorry, I tried," Jade says as she hangs up. "Your good Jade," I say in her defense, "He'll be ok." "Try Jeb again Mike," Satch says with his face in a cushion. I pull out a flip phone and Jade and Sophie let me have it. "No fucking way! Wow! I'm impressed!" They shout and I shake it off. "Yeah yeah," I say as I dial on my first cell phone at age twenty-three. "Welcome to the club, Mike. How does it feel?" Jade asks. "It's dumb," I say as I wait for Jeb to pick up his phone. It's only been a month and these two know my battle with technology. "Yo man you got any things?" I ask Jeb over the phone. "Yea Satch won't get off the couch." "Yo Satch, he said you have to blow him. Hell yea!" Satch yells, with the energy he's gained from the knowledge of their arrival. "He's on his way," I call out as I close my phone. "Thanks, Mike!" Satch yells. "Is that him!?" Sure, enough Jeb was on his way here. Satch comes out on the porch as Jeb pulls up. "Lady's." He says, now in The Green Room. Satch yells. "You're the man Jeb."

Jeb, Satch, and I stand around the kitchen table as Jeb goes in his backpack. "Sophie huh? Let me guess, Mike likes her." Satch laughs out loud and punches my shoulder. "We're just friends," I admit. "Who's the other one?" "Jade," I answer. "That's Satch's girl?" "Na, we're just hooking up." He claims. "Yo, he's crazy," I shout. "She brings him pills, food, fucking shoes!" I add as I throw Satch's new pair of sneakers off the table. "She's cool man." Satch chimes in, "I'm just not trying to have a girl." "Well." I say, "You got one." "Aw man, what are they?" I ask as Jeb pulls out a bag of small blue pills. "These are the blue boys." Jeb hands over some to Satch and crushes another on the table. "You snort them?" I ask. "I do. It hits you faster. Hold up," Jeb asks, "Since when did you start taking pills D?" He adds. "I warned him!" Says Satch. "Yeah, yeah." I say as I wave away their concern, "How fast?" I ask. "A minute." Jeb states. "Damn! You snort them, Satch?" I ask. "Nah," he says. "I like the wait. It's like free happiness." "Fuck that," I yell as I take the rolled-up bill from Jeb.

A day or two later I cut through the old shortcut to Jeb's. He sits at the desk in his room. A small fan is in his window, blowing out the smoke from his cigarette. The shades on his windows are down and slowly tapping against the wood of the window frame. The sunlight shines through the side of each shade. The rays brightly light up whatever gets in its way. With light blue wall paint, it creates a blue tint in the dully lit room. I come up the steps and into Jeb's room. He pushes the door open

301

and greets me. "What's up, I got tics boya?" Jeb says with a grin. "Sup bro?" I greet back. I sit on the small couch and turn up the TV. A Sci-fi movie plays. "What are you up to tonight?" I ask. "Nothing guy, just chilling." Jeb replies. I see Jeb's abandoned, blue line of powder. "Let me get a tail? I ask. "No," Jeb answers sternly. "Come on dude!" I plead. He cuts a little piece of his line and bumps the bigger of the two. He hands the bill over to me and I finish the rest. Jeb's mom yells up the stairs, "Hey Jeb, does Mike want some dinner?" "Yes please!" I yell as Jeb spins around in his big desk chair and turns up the volume. The two of us laugh at a line in the movie we've heard a thousand times.

On a small stage, I hit the strings on my new Les Paul, hooked up to a medium amplifier. Jeb plays on a drum set behind me. On the floor are a distortion pedal, a Cry Baby Wa-Wa, and a loop pedal. After singing an upbeat chorus to an original *CITY GATE SOULMATE* I slam my foot on the loop pedal and then the wa-wa for a solo. The bar is half full. Satch sits at a high top with a random friend. Clark sits at the bar looking very drunk. A bartender named Kev comes over to talk to Clark. He's in his early to mid-20s, has black hair in a part, and a friendly face that always carries a smile. "Yo Clark, you want another?" Asks Kev. Clark nods. Kev

302

cracks a beer and puts it in front of Clark. "So, I heard through the grapevine that you're job searching?" Kev says as he wipes a glass. Clark nods again. "Well, I could probably get you a job here if you wanted," Kev adds. Again, Clark only nods. "Cool man, Kev says with a smile. "When can you start?" Clark looks around and points his finger downwards, implying "Right now." "How about tomorrow. Kev laughs. Clark smiles and gives the thumbs up.

The song ends and low cheers and claps echo through the bar. Jeb and I put down our gear. And head to the bar. Kev cracks two beers and plops them in front of us. Sounds good guys! Kev walks away to tend to another customer as Jeb and I sip our beers. I take a notepad out of my back pocket and scratch out *CITYGATE SOULMATE*. The Names below it read *LITTLE PIECE OF LEXAPRO, SOPHIES OTHER SLEEVE, SAID TO ME*, and *MANNEQUIN*. Three guys in their early 20s sit at the bar a couple of seats down. They look like a cross breed of hippie and a hillbilly. "Who are these douchebags?" I ask as Kev makes a drink. "Those guys are sharing your Tuesday spot," Kev tells me. "WHAT!?" I yell. "Sorry man." Says Kev. "I've been meaning to tell you, Randy said you guys don't play enough covers." He adds. "We're not a cover band!" I

303

complain. "Yea I told him that man, sorry." "These guys call themselves the "STUMP JUMPERS." "The what!?" I ask. "Are they fucking each other?" Jeb says chiming in. Kev laughs, "I don't know man, maybe. They sound pretty good though." As Kev walks away Jeb remembers something and makes a face that I know all too well. "What!?" I yell, now frustrated. "I'm starting a steady DJ gig on Tuesdays," Jeb says reluctantly. "So, get rid of it!" I yell again. "Can't dude, it's my money maker, I'm sorry D." "Yeah whatever." I interrupt. "It's cool." As Jeb heads to the bathroom one of the Stump Jumpers walks up to me. I'm not happy. The guy was my age with light brown hair to his shoulders. "Hey man, I'm Will." He says politely as he holds out his hand. I shake it with a straight face. "I'm Mike," I say. "Looks like we'll be sharing a spot." He adds. "Not anymore," I say before chugging my beer, "I lost my drummer." "Aw, that sucks!" Will says as he looks to his bandmates before adding, "Damn, well we can't fill the whole spot yet. Hm, I'll tell you what man, play with us." "With you!" I ask, now confused. Will grabs his drink off the bar and explains. "Yeah, dude! At least for a set. Then on our break, you go singer-songwriter on their ass! I'll even learn a couple of your songs. I mean, I don't know about punk rock but your ability to shred that ax is on point! What do ya say, man?" I think it over while Kev pours two shots and slides them towards us to seal the deal. "We take long breaks," Will adds with a smile. I eventually match his smile and the two of us shake hands before cheers-ing the shots and tossing them down with Kev and Clark.

A TEN-YEAR-OLD PROMISE

A few Tuesdays later, the bar is packed. The Stump Jumpers play *Simple Man* while I solo on my guitar. Cheers and claps are heard as the song ends and I rack my guitar. "Esteban Junior everyone." Says Jack, the lead singer. The claps continue as I walk off stage. I light a cigarette and head outside with Satch.

Jhonny party enters the front doors and walks through the bar. He spots a pretty girl and makes his move, "Hello, I'm Johnny. Can I buy you a beer?" "Sorry." Says the girl. I don't drink." As she walks away Johnny turns to another couple of girls and asks them the same question. They smile and walk away. Johnny looks around the bar until seeing Tess. She's in mid-laugh as her long blond hair is tossed to the side. Tess turns to watch the band as Johnny approaches. "Hey Tess, can I buy you a beer?"

He asks. "Hey, Johnny!" Tess greets with sincerity, "Sure man!" "Ok," Johnny says before turning to Clark, "Hey Clark, can I have a beer please?" Clark cleans a mug behind the busy bar and answers. "You have a beer, Johnny." Tess gives Clark a dirty look. "No, it's for Tess," Johnny says quickly. Clark cracks a beer and slams it down in front of Johnny. "Fifty bucks," says Clark with a straight face. "Fifty bucks! For a beer?" Johnny yells. "He's fucking with you, Johnny." Says Tess. Somewhat relieved that Clark is joking, Johnny joins in, "Oh, well, how much than Clark?" "For you, Johnny, Nothing," Clark says while cleaning his hands. "Oh wow, thanks, Clark!" Johnny responds as he hands Tess the beer and she say, "Thanks, Johnny Party!" I come back in and over to Tess and Johnny. "Hey!" I yell through the live music as Tess greets me. Haley jumps out of nowhere for a hug, "Devaney!" "Hey, stranger! How ya been?" I ask. "I'm good dude," Haley says while handing me a bottle of Mexican beer. "Gracias," I say as we take a seat at the bar and catch up. After a few, Satch goes out for another smoke. Tess and Haley head to the bathroom with some other girlfriends. Now alone, waiting for some cheese fries I see a girl my age sitting across the bar. After quickly recognizing her, I call Clark over while the girl texts on her phone.

306

Clark and Kev move her beer and put down two placemats, plates, silverware, a bottle of champagne, two glasses, and a candle that they found randomly. As Clark walks away with her beer she turns and calls out as Kev lights the candle. "I wasn't done Clark." Says the girl as her confused look slowly turns to a smirk while hearing champagne being poured. She turns to me as I hold up a glass and say. "Hello Lilly, would you care to join me?" Still smirking, a now fully grown and still beautiful Lilly takes the glass. I quickly grab my own glass and cheers my old friend as Clark and Kev put out two extravagant plates of cheese fries. "You know Mike, I could have been on a real date," Lilly says with a smile after sipping her champagne. A song or two later, The Stump Jumpers finish. Ok we're going to take a quick break but for your entertainment, we have singer-songwriter, Mike Devaney. Friends and the crowd cheer as I grab my guitar. The lead singer hops off while the other two stay on for the first song of my set. I hit the strings and lean into the mic, "This one's RELENTLESS."

It's now the end of August. I find myself in the downstairs bathroom of my parent's house after dark. I look at cigarette cellophane as my board shorts drip on the unfinished floor. Inside the cellophane are four pieces of the blue pill. As I crush one on the sink, a chain saw is heard loudly outside, followed by a scream. I look up at the side of my garage which holds the projection of *The Texas Chainsaw Massacre*. A group of friends watch the horror movie from floating rafts in the pool. I bump the blue line and stick the wrapper under some old newspapers on the back porch. Hours later I nod out in the living room. Satch, Sophie, and Jade are asleep on the couch. The TV lights the dark room as I reach in my pocket to get out the cellophane. It's empty. "Damn," I say out loud. One pill is usually more than enough I think to myself. I see Satch's pill bottle on the far end of the wooden coffee table. "No need to wake him. I'll just throw him some cash tomorrow. I slowly move Sophie's legs and reach over the coffee table to grab the bottle. As I reach for it, a song plays. The song is *IT'S SO EASY*. It's been a while since I've heard or seen the music video, however pieces of it race through my mind as I pop off the lid and take out one of my little new friends.

Some nights later Jade pulls up with a friend that Satch and I had not yet met. "Where's Sophie?" Satch asks considering we have never seen them apart. "She's hanging with Barry." Says Jade. "This is Victoria." She adds. We say hello and she joins The Green Room. Random friends stop by that night for an acoustic jam session. With air conditioners blasting, my parents and the rest of the neighborhood sleep soundly. Around two in the morning, Victoria heads to her car. Satch gives me an elbow as Victoria waves goodbye. "A cute girl flirts with you all night and you just let her walk away." He pauses as I put down my head. The crickets take over the conversation until finally, Satch puts his forearm on my shoulder, "She's gone, dude." Satch says referring to my ex. Victoria drops her keys. "She shouldn't be driving Mike." Jade chimes in with a smirk. I chug my beer and jump off the porch. As Victoria and I leave the driveway, Jade and Satch wave with a smile. "Be back in time for breakfast!" Jade yells. "Yeah, your moms making pancakes!" Satch adds. He puts his arm around Jade, and they head back inside.

The next several months or so were somewhat of a blur. I moved in with Will, his girlfriend, and this dude named Frances. Our close-by neighbors consisted of Clark, Mason Tepper, and whoever else called dibs

309

on the couch. Will and *The Stump Jumpers* had a colorful crew as well. One of them as mentioned was Frances who is, Hum. Well, if you didn't know Frances you would assume he was a douche bag. He would do things like, go to the tanning salon, gel his hair before bed, and would avoid any weightlifting on Fridays. I asked Frances why he wouldn't lift on Fridays and his answer was, "Because Fridays are for the BAR, and I don't want my biceps worn out for a fight night." With all that said, it didn't take long before Frances and I were good friends.

The Oxy's hit the bar scene hard at that time alongside another drug that has been at the bars forever. Cocaine. I fucking hate Cocaine. You feel great for a half-hour and then you're fucked. Some people like the chase but I don't. The first time I tried the white stuff was because I was out of the blue boys. I was at a random bar and some guy said, "Hey try this. It's kinda like the blues." Since that night, every time a white line is put out, I say to myself. "I hate that shit. I'll just do one." Today, however, I do none. But I digress.

Long Story short, *The Rug* barely lasted a year. The bar's personal financial reasons on top of us taking it over with loud music and colorful characters quickly took its toll. *In fact, I can remember the last night I was at The Rug.* Jeb's hippy jam band played while Tepper slapped craft singles on Maverick's tits. Why Maverick had his shirt off with cheese nipples I can't remember. I've played music with Jeb's bandmates throughout high school and on occasion would join them for a set. On this night we jammed out to a *Dead* song while other members of the dance floor would perform unnatural acts with the pile of cheese that was stacked on the bar floor. I think we did this to scare off shoobies and other unwanted guests but who the hell knows. Around three in the morning, I stumbled out back to find a ride home. To my surprise, Sis was still at *The Rug* with one of her girlfriends. "Nice." I think as I puff my cig. They were talking to some would-be friends, so I planned on finishing my smoke before approaching. As I stood there, I saw some random guy reach around and pinch my sister's side. The guy looked about thirty years old and was about 6'2 and thin. Sis smacks his hand away and the guy starts to walk away. It would have ended there except he made a mistake. "Whatever cunts!" He yells. Now I'm not a big fan of sneaking someone with a punch so instead, I approach him and flick my still-lit cigarette at his face.

It hits his chest and now at least he knows it's coming. "You mother fucker!" he says as he walks towards me. With fists up, I take one more step with my left foot and throw a right cross. "CRACK!" I connect and the guy falls back and clips his arm on a broken fence that surrounds the dumpsters. The guy grabs his arm as blood sprays out like a faucet. Before I can think, Sis grabs me and throws me in the car with two random friends we grew up with. She yells for Vicky to call in that a random guy at *The Rug* needs help. The cops showed up immediately and the medics took away the guy bleeding at the dumpster. Sis told the cops that the guy I hit was injured while getting out of a moving car and they must have believed her because that was that.

After *The Rug*, *The Stump Jumper*s and I played some gigs in Atlantic City. During a gig, I met a brunette who just got out of a seven-year relationship and liked guitar players, *so that worked out*. After the last AC gig, *The Stump Jumpers* and I parted ways. I see them and Frances from time to time over a beer but that's about it. Our shared days of sex, drugs, and Rock 'n Roll have come to an end.

ITALIAN MUSTARD AND THE HAPPY STRANGER

Food never tastes better than on the beach. After a surf session, I make my way to a sub shop on the shore. The shop was called Lenny's. It was nothing fancy. They wouldn't even chop up the meat, just cook it, and throw it in the sub roll, but man is it good. Lenny is an old Italian guy that didn't put up with shit. If some stuck-up mom or prick from the city complained or got picky, they went to the wrong place. Satch worked there in the summer and fit right in. "Yellow mustard!" Yells Lou. "On an Italian, what are you fucking sick!" Oh, and I forgot to mention. Satch's dad works there too. "Get outta here!" Lou yells at the unhappy customer. "Hey, Michael!" Lou says with a new attitude. "What can I get ya!" He asks. "Italian," I say quickly, "Extra yellow mustard." "Hey!" Lou says, with a half-smile. "I got him!" Satch yells from the grill. "Ok." See ya, Michael." Says Lou as he disappears into the small crowded sub-shop. Satch brings me to the back bathroom and hands me a wrapped cheesesteak before walking into a tiny bathroom with a toilet and a sink. "Come on." He says as we squeeze in. Satch dumps out some white powder on top of the toilet. He takes a bump and hands me a bill. "You have any blues on ya?" I ask. "Sorry man," Satch says. "I'm getting more after work. I'll hit you up. That should help you get through," he says as I take the bump. A few months back I gave Satch a bump of the white stuff for his first time. *That was a bad idea.* We slap hands and I walk out the back door of Lenny's with a cheesesteak. The noon sun hits my face and now high as shit, I make my way back to the beach while saying hi to every stranger I pass.

That night Satch wakes up in his car. Confused about where he is, he looks around. As sirens approach, he notices that he's in the middle of some stranger's yard and puts two and two together. "Shit." He says as he picks up pills off the floor of his Jeep. One by one he throws them into an un-sealable plastic bag. He looks up and sees a cop running towards him and past the smashed-up parked car he slammed into prior. "Oh SHIT!" He says again as he picks up the last pill with seconds to spare. A cop taps on his window. Satch freezes with the pill bag clenched in his hand. The yard owner yells at the cop about what's going on. As the cop turns Satch sticks the bag of pills in a 20oz bottle of chocolate milk with a scratch on the label. He twists on the lid. The Cop sees nothing.

314

It's a cloudy windy day outside of *The Rug*. A sign says *CLOSED*. Clark and Kev walk out with a heated debate about sports. After closing up Kev remembers something. He unlocks the door and pulls out a big standing sign that says, *OUT OF BUSINESS*. They stand it up and walk away from *The Rug* still as they continue their debate.

THE V CARD

A shade taps the wooden window in Jeb's childhood bedroom. The light shines through onto my shoulder as I crush up a pill. Jeb sits at his desk and types. Nothing is said. The front door is heard opening and we freeze. "Jeb!?" We unfreeze after hearing the recognizable voice that could only have come from one person on earth.

Still with nothing said, Jeb hands me a book. I shrug it off, but Jeb shakes the book and I finally grab it and put it in front of the crushed pill. Johnny Party walks into the room. "Hey Mikey, hey Jeb." He says. Jeb doesn't flinch. I smile at Johnny and bend over the book to bump my blue.

"I had sex," Johnny says with a smile. Jeb and I freeze once more. Jeb

closes his laptop as I put down my rolled dollar and abandon my rail. We

slowly turn to our boy Johnny Party. After a moment Jeb and I jump up

yelling and screaming while grabbing Johnny for a shake.

Our celebration takes us to a local bar. With a car bomb in front,

we drop the shot and chug the beer. I beat Jeb by a hair. "Damn D," Jeb

yells as he throws up some cash on the bar. As Johnny struggles with his

car bomb Jeb and I interrogate him repeatedly. "So, Johnny, who was she?

What positions did you do? Yea, what'd it feel like!?" Jeb and I ask as if

we had never had sex in our lives. Johnny thinks for a moment, "It felt

good." "Nice!" Jeb says cutting in, "So, what else is new Johnny?" "I got

a job," Johnny adds, "It's just stocking shelves for now." "Nothing wrong

with that," I add. "My girlfriend and I moved in together," Johnny

mentions before Jeb interrupts, "Whoa, hold up. You made this girl your

girlfriend?" "Yeah, we met at my Job." He replies. "Damn Johnny. Good

for you man." Jeb states as we sip our beer. "Yea good work dude," I add

as Jeb orders another round. Johnny thanks us and drinks the rest of his

now curdled car bomb.

That night Jeb and I sit around his bedroom once again. Now just the two of us Jeb crushes a pill with a cigarette in his mouth. "Damn dude," I say out loud, "So let me get this straight. Johnny party has a job, his own place, and a girlfriend." Jeb thinks shortly of what I said and nods. "We don't have any of those things," I state. "Nope," Jeb says while shaking his head. I had recently moved back in with my parents and had been living off unemployment. "That's it, man, I'm done. No more rocks for me." I say. "Sounds good man," Jeb says as he holds up what's left in our bag of Oxy's. "Hank was asking for some so I'll just…" Jeb starts. "Woah, hold up!" I yell. "Not my share!" Jeb turns, "I thought." "Well yeah." I interrupt and add, "But I just decided a second ago." "So how many do you want?" Jeb asks. "Five," I tell him, "Actually. Make it twenty."

BANDIT

A tow truck pulls up to Satch's house with his Jeep. Lou gives the driver some cash and he leaves. Lou goes into the Jeep and looks around.

After twenty years of Satch opening his cabinets to sugarless snacks, what does his dad do? What's the one thing he grabs? Yup. The chocolate milk.

Meanwhile. I lay on my bed and look out the window. My eyes are bloodshot and I'm somewhat in pain. The twenty pills I said would last forever are gone. Now at this point, I was only averaging two or three, thirty-milligram oxy's a day. So around forty or sixty bucks. *This meant I wasn't blowing old dudes, stealing, or selling all my shit. Now some people were taking ten a day and some even twenty. At twenty dollars a pill that's like four hundred bucks a day. Satch had a script for most of his but the other people taking ten to twenty a day well, I have no idea how they keep that up. I could sell all my stuff, steal, blow old dudes, work, and still not make enough for that shit.*

I lay on a small couch in my room but can't get comfortable. I walk around the room; I try to play a video game but drop the paddle and turn it off. *However, much you take, one thing is for sure, when you stop, it sucks ass.* I lay on my bedroom floor in board shorts. *I've heard some people compare it to the flu but that's bullshit. The flu comes in waves. You feel like shit, then you get a break. With the Oxy withdrawal or the WD's as we called it, there is no such compassion. Even if you're not puking, one thing is for sure, you will shit your brains out.* I sit naked on the toilet. Later I look out the downstairs window in the living room, I grab some OJ and head back up to my room, and lay on my bed. *Your body feels like Joe Pesci's at the end of Casino and forget about feeling any type of comfort or happiness. At least for a while. Not to mention exhaustion, dyssomnia, and depression, and that lasts for weeks, even months maybe, and I'm still on the first day.* I took my last bump seven hours ago! "Ah Fuck this!" I say after sitting up in my bed. I pick up my flip phone and make a call.

As I walk down the bike path, I see a mut sniffing through some trash. He has no collar and has the look of a tramp. I get down on one knee and whistle. He runs up to me and licks my hand. After seeing I have no food he runs off. A few minutes later I walk to an old beat-up house. Inside, the place is gutted. No walls, just beams, and brick. Some jagged pipes stick out of the floor. In the would-be kitchen are a fridge, a microwave, and several surfboards. A possum climbs out of a hole in the wall and eats some potato chips on the floor. It dodges a beer can and scurries away. "GET!" Yells Mason Tepper. Tepper sits at a small table that has an open laptop. Next to him are a TV and a couch. Mason grabs a

319

PlayStation paddle and plays an army game as I come through the front door. "Hey, dude. It's on the table." He says. "Aw thanks, man, I was hurting," I say while grabbing the pill bag off the table. I open it and chew one up. As I plop on the couch, a rat runs out from under it. "What the...," I say with a leg up. "Aah, He won't hurt ya," Tepper assures me as he tosses a paddle and says, "You're up next." "Yo man you know who I thought I saw for a minute," I ask. Masson looks at me with curiosity. "Who." He replies. "Bandit," I say as Tepper smiles and remembers he and Liam's first pup. Bandit lived off neighborhood trash and table scraps until he was twenty human years old. From what I remember he hated dog food." "Yeah, man," Tepper says. "He was an old soul."

As I wait for the game to end, I put a cigarette in my mouth and pull out a lighter. "Hey!" Tepper says, pointing to a sign that reads "No smoking." It's the only thing hanging on the brick wall. I put my cig in my ear. "How'd I forget?" I say, sitting back on the couch, a pigeon flies down from a rafter and lands on the arm of the couch. Not bothered, Mason and I mash buttons on our controller. *Years later, Mason and Liam Tepper started their own house flipping company. Despite Mason's current living arrangements, I hear their company is quite successful. I haven't talked to*

320

either of them in years but I'm sure that our paths will cross someday once again.

It's night now and I am finally comfortable. I walk home and head up to my room where Dad sits on the small couch watching TV. He gets up, "Hey, bud." "Hey, you can hang." I offer. "Nah I'm meeting up with Manning." He says as I look over and see a comic book behind the TV with a credit card on top of it next a blue line. "Nice, how's he doing?" I ask. "He's good." Dad laughs and adds, "He's Manning. I'll see ya later." "Ok, see ya." The door shuts and I check the comic book. My parents aren't dumb. Although it's extremely easy to get away with a pill habit, one simple fuck up like that and my parent's keen eye would be on me 24/7.

Days later 1 lay on Jeb's bed while Jeb sits on his small couch. The light shines through the window on his shoulder as he flicks through some channels with his remote. Jeb's cell phone rings and I sit up. "Is it him!?" I ask anxiously. Jeb finishes the call quickly and hangs up. "You ask him about the rocks?" I ask. "It wasn't him, relax!" Jeb shouts. "Oh, and by the way, rocks mean crack so you might want to start calling them something else." He adds. "Whatever man who cares!" I shout. It's been

321

two days since either of us had any blues. I get off the bed and start to look around on the floor. "What the hell are you doing!?" Asks Jeb. "I don't know," I answer and add, "The way you handle them there's gotta be something down here." "There's nothing there, D!" Jeb says as he answers his cell. Again, the call is short. "What'd he say?" I ask. "He won't have them for a week." Answers Jeb as he tosses his phone on the bed. "A week!? Might as well be a year." I say while leaving the room. "Where are you going?" Jeb asks. "To check your car," I say as Jeb shakes his head and opens his laptop.

A week later Jeb and I sit in an empty parking lot in Jeb's wagon. *This was the worst part. This. Right here. After waiting a week, sitting in a parking lot to meet some unreliable asshole who might not even show.* We scored a couple of pills during the week but nowhere close to enough. Jeb and I look up at a car that drives by. After seeing it was not who we were waiting for we melt back into our seats. A car rolls up next to us. We sit up and look out Jeb's driver's seat window at a man who shakes his head with disappointment. As our stomachs sink with rage, the man holds up a bag of blue pills. "Nah, I'm just kidding." He says as Jeb and I rejoice. If I wasn't so happy, I'd smash his face in.

GOODBYE FOR NOW

It's the middle of the night and I lay awake during a thunderstorm. A sheet covers my lower half and some of Amy who lays next to me. She is asleep. I watch her breath for a moment before calmly moving her arm off my bare chest. I get up and put on board shorts before leaving the room. As I walk through a dining room, lightning strikes and lights up a thousand little eyes that stare back at me. The walls are covered with shelves and glass cases displaying hundreds of porcelain animals. I find my way to a familiar couch in Amy's mother's living room. Lighting once again flashes through the window as I sit. Thunder follows. I grab a straw and card off the coffee table and scratch whatever white powder is left and finish it up. I light a cigarette as a gust of wind showers the window with rain. I blow out the smoke while staring at my quiet friends that hide in the shadows.

A night later I sit in a local bar. Bars have come and gone over the years but this one I'm sure will be there until the end of time. To my right is a pyramid of used napkins covered in buffalo sauce. Across is Haley who is helping me attack a plate of wings. Tess and her boyfriend Clyde sit with us. "Hey, Devaney." Says Haley, "Me and Jay are opening a coffee shop on the island, you have to come jam out your songs." "I'm already there," I reply. "Sweet! The coffee girl is super cute." She adds, "I think you two might get along." I look to Tess for approval of this coffee girl Haley speaks of. Tess holds a big handful of pretend boobs in front of her own. "Ya know Haley, I'm no psychic but something tells me we're going to get along just fine."I tell her. "I thought you only like dudes Devaney?" Clyde says chiming in. "Only in drag," I answer and get a laugh as we sip our beers. Clyde and Tess have been dating for a while now. *I never know what to expect when the girls get new boyfriends. "Oh, hey and this is MIKE. Some fucking dude that hangs around." With that said though it has never been a problem and honestly Clyde is usually the first one to hit me up.*

Amy comes in the back door. Haley sees her and gives Tess a look. "We're up for drinks," Tess says as she and Haley leave the booth. "What do you want Mike?" Tess asks. "Whatever," I tell her. "Can you come help out, Clyde?" Tess says. "Na I'll just chill here with Mike." He says

324

before getting a look from her. "Oh yea, I guess." He says after noticing Amy. As the three walk away, Amy sits across from me. "There she is," I say with a smile. "Here I am," Amy says. "You're just in time," I say, peeking out at the others ordering drinks. "They saw me," Amy says before I wave them down. "You can help me finish this," I say sliding her my beer. Amy thanks me and takes a sip. She then holds the beer with two hands and taps it with her pointer finger. Amy is unusually quiet. "So," I say breaking the silence. "I was thinking we'll cut out of here a little later and meet at your mom's again," I say as Amy smirks. "I don't know Mike, we've been down that road." Amy admits. "Well, I'm not saying we go to fucking prom or anything," I say sarcastically, getting a smile from Amy as she tilts her head. "I…" Amy pauses and looks down at the beer. I put my hands up and wait for her to talk. "Met someone." She says finally. "Oh," I say while sitting back in my chair. Amy and I have stayed friends and had met up on occasion, but she didn't really didn't need to give me an explanation at all. Still, I admire her sincerity. She could hate my guts for all I know and also throw it in my face that she met someone, but she didn't. "Really," I say as if I didn't care. I grab a french fry and put it through my pinched fingers. "So did you guys…?" I ask. "No." Amy interrupts with a bashful smile that is rarely seen on her now more than ever pretty face. "I met him yesterday." She says. "Yesterday!" I yell playfully. "Damn Am, throw a stake through my heart!" Amy's last laugh fills the crowded bar. She of course would have many more but none that belong to me. "I like him." She says referring to the man she met a day ago. I wipe my mouth with a napkin and toss it to the pyramid. "OK," I say simply. "Oh really!?" Amy says smirking to my passive remark. "I mean, what am I going to say? NO?!" I say as my smile fades and the table is now quiet. *Wish You Were Here* is heard as the jukebox plays its first song of the night. Amy reaches out with two hands. Missing mine she places hers on my forearm before looking directly into my eyes. "Thanks, Mike." She says softly. Amy's not thanking me for anything at all. What she's doing is finally saying goodbye. I can tell this time it's for good. "You love birds coming or what!?" Yells Haley. "Yea!" Tess adds, "These drinks are getting, cold." As our three friends laugh at the bar, I ask Amy one last thing, "Well can we at least get fucked up!?" "Hell yea!" Shouts Amy. We get out of the booth and join the others at the crowded bar.

Some years later, Amy got married. She has two boys and a girl that could pass as her little twin. Amy and I don't keep in touch, but I

326

always wish her well. Tess and Clyde got hitched as well and the three of

us are still good friends to this day. They have two baby boys and live up

by the Finger Lakes. I've been called a bum numerous times by Tess for

not visiting but I have recently promised a trip up and I don't plan on

breaking it. And of course, Haley, with her pretty smile and that classic

laugh. A little ways down the road, Haley had a baby girl with her long-

term boyfriend Jay. A few years later, Haley was taken from the earth. We

think about her all the time. Needless to say, Haley is very missed.

SPOILED MILK

Satch walks into a motel room where a guy named Paul is sitting at

a table smoking a cig. "Hey man, I'm sorry but it fell through." Says Paul

as Satch sits at the table with a now disappointed face. "I got the other

stuff though if you want it." He says. "I don't want that shit!" Says Satch,

"You said you had pills!" "It's not even strong, I'll just give you a little."

Offers Paul. Satch thinks while he rubs his neck. "Whatever, just get it."

Satch looks around the crummy motel as Paul goes to the bathroom. He

327

comes back and sits back at the table with a syringe, a bag, and a large rubber band. Satch eventually turns and sees what Paul has brought to the table. "YO! What the FUCK!" Yells Satch as he jumps to his feet. "You said you wanted some!" Says Paul now confused. "Not to shoot up!" Satch yells as he backs away from the needle. "This is what I got!" Yells Paul. "Fuck you!" Screams Satch, "Fucking scumbag!" "Get the fuck out bitch!" Yells Paul as Satch leaves the Motel. "Fuck you!" Satch yells again. He slams his car door and drives away.

Satch Wakes in his bedroom hours later. He looks sick. In a t-shirt and shorts, he walks to the bathroom and takes a pee. Ray comes in through the garage. He walks into his laundry room which leads to the kitchen where a dim light hangs above the sink. Ray opens the fridge and looks around until he sees the chocolate milk with a scratch on the label. He grabs it and closes the fridge.

Satch leans into a bedroom doorway where his thirteen-year-old brother plays a video game with a friend. "Hey, guys. What you up to?" Satch asks. "Hey, Satch. We're trying to get past these stupid rats." Says Lou Jr. as he mashes buttons on the controller. "Try the staff." Suggests

Satch. "I told you!" Yells Lou Jr.'s friend as the two boys bicker. "You

didn't tell me that!" Yells Lou Jr. Satch smiles and walks away. Satch rubs

his back as he walks into the kitchen. "Hey man." Says Ray as he eats a

chicken wing over the sink. What's up Ray. How you doing?" Asks Satch

as he turns on the stove. Satch puts his hands on the handle of a teapot

with his back to Ray. "Good, how about you? Ya don't look so good."

Adds Ray. "I'll be alright." Says Satch. "If you know who saw ya sleeping

at seven o'clock he'd be shitting bricks." Says Ray with a smile. Ray grabs

the chocolate milk off the counter and brings it to his mouth to take a

swing. As he tilts it back, Satch turns his head and sees the tear in the

label. He quickly turns around and smacks the bottle out of Ray's hand. As

the milk hit the floor Ray runs to the sink and spits the sip out before

rinsing his mouth with water. "Damn Satch! A little overkill for some sour

milk." Ray looks at Satch who has a straight face before looking over to

see their dad in the doorway. Ray looks down and sees a bag with blue

mush hanging out of the milk bottle that drips into a puddle on the floor.

Lou sees it as well. "Dad," Ray says before getting interrupted. "Leave us,

Ray." Says Lou. Reluctantly, Ray walks out of the kitchen. He stops and

looks at Satch before leaving. Satch stares straight ahead at his dad. After

Ray is gone Satch and Lou sit in silence before Lou finally speaks, "Tomorrow, pack your bags. I want you out by noon." "Dad, I was…" Satch starts to say. "Tomorrow at noon Satch. I want you gone." Lou says, interrupting once again. Lou walks past Satch and out of the kitchen. Satch is left alone with the puddle of spoiled milk.

7,800 BOTTLES OF APPLE ALE ON THE WALL

I walk up to my parent's house on a sunny day. The buds in the trees are starting to bloom. Faith sits on the porch with a friend as Mom tells them the end of a story. "That was a good one! Thanks, Mom!" Faith says as the girls run off the porch as I walk up and sit with Mom. "Hey, poopy heads," I say to the girls who laugh and run away. "Hey Hun, how have you been?" Asks Mom. "Good, which one did you tell them?" I respond. "Oh, just a new one I've been working on. You know it wasn't that long ago when you guys were sitting in the grass listening to a story." Mom mentions, "You were a little younger though." "The good old days," I add. Mom and I chuckle together as we sit in the warm day with blue skies.

To get off the blues for good, I needed a plan. So, I made one. It was a list, a list of Four rules that I couldn't break under any circumstance. I don't advise this for anyone else, however, it did work, so on the off chance it can help someone else I'll say it out loud. Rule #1 is routine. Whatever reminders you have throughout the day, you'll want to avoid as best as possible. Change your ringtone, change your text tone, the things you eat, the places you go, the things you do, the way you take to work, and the way you take back from work. Whatever you do now, do the opposite.

Rule # 2. Contacts. This might be the most important rule of all. Whoever has had anything to do with your addiction, delete them. Lucky for me, when it comes to remembering numbers, I'm dumb and can't remember a single one. Either way, delete them. Don't block them because then you still have them in your contacts, and you can still call them with the push of a button. If you think they're your friends, guess what, they're probably not. Now we come to the next part of rule #2 which is close friends and family. You might think this is difficult, but it's not. Simply call them and say "Hey, I'll talk to you again in a couple months, bye." If they can handle it, great. If not, fuck 'em.

Rule #3. A hobby. Whatever keeps your mind busy and pumps that happy juice back into your brain. That includes exercise and diet as well. Lift weights, ride a bike, play the fucking xylophone! Whatever you can enjoy, do it.

And the final rule. Rule #4. The crutch. Now as I said before I don't recommend this, it's just something that helped me. Now maybe not at first but eventually, you might want to indulge in other ways to abuse your body. I for one like to drink beer and alcohol and I didn't want some stupid addiction in my early 20s to fuck that up for the rest of my life so, I'd get a six-pack after work, sit on my porch and drink them while chain-smoking cigarettes. Then it was time for bed. Instead of my old friend *Beer*, I went for something different to make up for the sweet blue nectar that no longer dripped down my throat. It was an apple ale that tastes like well, apple juice. I drank a six on the weekdays and twelve on Friday, Saturday, and Sunday. That equaled Sixty a week. I did this for two in a half year, which equals about 7,800 bottles of apple ale, which also means that quite possibly I have drunk more apple ales than anyone on the fucking planet. But hey, I'm off pills.

THE CRYING BLUES

I sit on the small table in my kitchen and eat ham and cheese. Dad comes in and goes through the fridge as *Monster Vision* is heard coming from the living room TV. *Now you can have as many rules as you want but bottom line is, without a reason, you'll never quit. It doesn't have to be a big one. I know mine wasn't. You'd think the love of family, friends or a significant other alone would be enough but, it wasn't. My reason came one night in the kitchen with my dad.* "Man, I know there was one left." He says while searching the fridge. "What's that?" I ask. "A beer." He says simply. "There's some wine," I add. "With a sandwich!?" States Dad, "Ehw, nothing washes a sandwich down like a nice cold brew." "Grab that soda," I suggest. "It's just not the same," Dad says as he grabs the soda a beer can is now visible in the back of the fridge. "There she is!" Dad yells. "Nice!" I say with a mouth full of ham. "You know Mike, It's the little things in life," Dad says while smacking my shoulder. He walks to the living room. As I sat there on the table, I remembered all the little things in life that wouldn't bring happiness to an addict in a million years. And guess what. I wanted them back. I join Dad in the living room. We eat chips and laugh at an old Abbot and Costello black and white movie. The next day I quit the blues for good.

I sit on the small couch in my bedroom. It's nighttime and a dim lamp lights the corner of the room. The light from the TV shines on my bloodshot eyes. With help from my rule book, I would come back from the blues. *Today I am truly happy to be clean. I once again can enjoy the little things life has to offer and more. With all that said, one fact remains. When you dance with a devil, you never fully, come back.* I look through a long text on my phone. The tail end reads "I'll talk to you then bro." I hit send and go to *Jeb* in my contacts. I hit delete. I look at the screen which now reads *You have ten contacts.* As I put the phone on my bed it rings. I hit the FU button and put it back down. Thinking for a moment I then look at the number. Grabbing a nearby pen and paper I write the number down. Under it, I write the name *Holly* with a question mark before executing rule two. I toss the phone which bounces off the bed and lands in between the wall. Mom is heard yelling up the stairs. "Dinners ready!" I look up at the blue screen on my TV and get up. As I leave the room, I can hear a song playing ever so faint. The song is called *SON OF A GUN*. I stop and listen to the chorus. *The sun shines in the bedroom when we play. The rain always starts when you go away.* I recognize the song but have no idea where it's coming from. "Who knows?" I think to myself as I walk down the stairs. Maybe it's all just in my head.

CHAPTER 7 — THE PARANORMAL, TRUE LOVE, AND A KID NAMED BOOGER

The Q-Ball breaks the others on a pool table. Eightball is underway, and it's midnight at a dive bar. Two bikers play Satch and me in a game of pool. The men are in their mid-30s and both a little bigger than Satch. A taller lean biker with a cowboy hat stands at the bar. I sink two balls and miss the next. "I hand the pool stick to Satch as the bikers set up their shot. I walk up to the bar and order two beers next to the cowboy. "Yo guys, you good?" I ask Clark, who sits at a high-top table with Jade and Sophie. They nod. "Hey, move!" The cowboy yells. "Huh?"

336

I say, confused. "You're in my spot." I pay and grab the beers before walking away. "It's all yours," I tell him. The Cowboy gives me a dirty look. "Yo Bill, you still mad about your old lady?" Says one of the bikers we play pool with. The cowboy doesn't acknowledge them. Instead, he drinks his shot of whiskey. "Don't worry, buddy, she'll come around." The second biker jokes.

As the game of Eightball continues, Satch and I drink our beers and laugh with the two bikers. The rest of the bar was on the empty side. A handful of other men in their mid to late 30s sit around drinking in the dingy bar. They all had somewhat of a grimy look to them. Clark chugs his beer and says, "Damn, I guess I did need one." "We'll get them," says Sophie and Jade. I watch the Cowboy talk to the girls while they order. "Hey, like I told your fucking friend over there, that's my spot." Says the Douchebag Cowboy. They apologize and head back to the table with a full pint. "I'm ready for that, *J* Sophie. You want to smoke, Clark?" Jade says. "Nah, I'll puke." Replies Clark. As Sophie and Jade walk outside, I stare at The Cowboy. *In the movies, when two guys get in a bar fight, the entire place jumps up and starts beating the shit out of each other. As a kid, I thought it was awesome. Later in life, I figured it was just added to the*

scene for effect. It turns out "I" was both wrong.

BAR BRAWL

I walk over to The Cowboy and stand in his spot. "Hey! You can say what you want to me, but don't be talking like that to the girls, got it!?" The Cowboy grabs me by the throat with his right hand and squeezes. I quickly turn my left shoulder inwards and hit his forearm with my own in one upward thrust, causing him to let go. With his face wide open, I throw a right cross and hit the bridge of his nose. As the sound of a punch rings out through the bar, tables are flipped over by random men who literally start beating the shit out of each other. As Satch laughs with the two other bikers, they see The Cowboy and me, each with our left hand grasping the other's collar as we take turns punching each other in the face with our rights. Satch and The Bikers drop their pool sticks. Satch punches one of the bikers in the face with a straight right as the other man cranks back his fist. Satch throws a quick left and hits him in the face causing him to fall back and onto the pool table. I throw my left elbow up, causing one of the Cowboy's punches to slide off my forearm and miss.

Aiming for his face, I counter with a right-left combo that sends him flying back and into a high top. As I look to my left, a random guy runs toward me. Clark comes out of nowhere and checks the guy with his shoulder, sending him slamming into some chairs. Clark and I meet eyes for a quick second before a flying bottle smashes over Clark's head. He falls to the ground. As I look his way, The Cowboy leaps back and punches me in the face. I fly back and into some chairs at the bar. Satch gets slammed on the pool table, and Biker One picks him up while Biker two punches him in the stomach. The two bikers grab Satch and throw him across the bar. His shoes fly off his feet.

Outside, Sophie and Jade pass the joint as they giggle. Behind them, in a big window, random men swing at each other as bottles and chairs fly through the air. I don't know what song was playing, but I do remember it was loud. I shake off the last punch to the face and look for The Cowboy, who is now taking turns punching a random guy with one of his biker buddies. As I run towards him, a big bouncer reaches out to grab me in a bear hug. I duck it, and when I come up, I'm face to face with The

Cowboy. We both swing but mine is quicker. I hit him once more in the face and send him flying into a table, where he falls to the ground. I stand over the unconscious Cowboy and stupidly waste time insulting him before turning back to the fight. The Bouncer takes advantage of my stupidity and grabs me from behind. As he picks me up in a bear hug, I kick backward, hitting his knees. He moves forward, trips over my legs, and we both go flying. My face slams into the corner of a brick wall.

I wake seconds later on my hands and knees. I look to my left and see The Cowboy coming toward me with a kick. I shield my face with my left arm as he kicks me in the shoulder. I stand up for round three but am temporarily blinded by blood that pours into my eyes. The Cowboy and his associate still stand. On my right, a random, last-standing fighter steps in and stands by my side. The Cowboy and his friend slowly walk off with a black eye and busted lip. I wipe the blood from my eyes and look over at the last standing fighter. The guy was an old friend of mine. We had a falling out years before. We look at each other for a second before shaking hands. He nods and leaves the now empty bar.

Outside, Clark, Jade, Satch, and Sophie stand in the parking lot. The Bikers peel away from the back of the bar. Satch holds one of his shoes in his hand. "There he is!" Clark says. "What happened to you?" I ask Satch with a shoe in his hand. "I got thrown across the bar. My fucking shoes flew off!" "Oh shit, Mike, your face!" Says Sophie, interrupting Satch. I wipe the blood from some cuts that the brick wall caused. "Yea, my nose broke my fall." I say while giving the sign of the cross. "That thing is broken," Clark states. "I knew this place was a bad idea! I'm done with the bar scene, man," Satch claims. "Yea, bars are dumb," I add, half kidding. The five of us walk out of the parking lot and away from the dive bar.

SATCH AND THE NEST OF TERROR

Sophie, Jade, Satch, and I sit at a booth. The dinner was open 24/7, and the food was always delicious. We finished the plates that lay in front of us. A butterfly bandage falls from my face. Sophie grabs a new one from my hand and puts it on my upper lip. "I knew these wouldn't hold." She complains, "I think you're gonna need stitches." "I got super glue," Jade adds. The girls and I laugh as Satch wipes his mouth and gets up. He grabs his cigs. "I got to poop." "Your gonna smoke in there!?" Asks

341

Sophie. "Best cig of the day!" Says Satch as he walks away. Jade helps Sophie with my bandage as I do my blow tic. "Hold them in, man!" Jade yells. "He can't hold them in. Can you?" Asks Sophie. *What happens next has been debated for over a decade. If you choose not to believe it, you're not alone. Some friends and even family question its integrity due to the bizarre story I tell you now. All Satch and I can tell you is, it happened.*

Satch makes his toilet paper nest in the stall. He sits down and lights the cig that has been in his mouth. He takes out a folded newspaper from his back pocket and reads the sports page. The man in the stall next to him starts to moan. Satch ignores it at first, but after the next louder moan, he speaks. "Just breathe, bro. It'll happen." Satch says as blood pours onto the floor and into his stall. Satch comes flying out of the bathroom and into a wall. As he stands up, he pulls his pants the rest of the way up and walks fast down the aisle with a frightened look on his face. A random spoon drops and Satch turns around fast looking back at the bathroom as he buckles his belt. By now, we are laughing at him. He lights a fresh cigarette and heads outside. "Don't go back there!" He shouts as he exits. He goes outside to suck down his cigarette as the three of us look at each other and then at the bathroom.

Inside the bathroom. I squeak open the door and stand inside as it creaks shut. I stand in eerie silence and look over at the two stalls. The first was open halfway, and the far one was closed. Without looking further, I smile and shake my head. As I turn to walk out, a man screams and barges out of the closed stall. From the nose down, his face and clothes are covered in blood. The man appears to be slightly older than me. He had regular-looking clothes on, short, clean-cut hair, and all-around looked very normal, minus being covered in his own blood. In his hand was a sheet of toilet paper. He fell towards the sink and put the paper down on it. I slowly back away. "They got us, man, they fucking got us." He screams. "I just pulled that thing out of my fucking nose!" The man starts to cry as I carefully look at what he had put down. On the bloody toilet paper was what looked like a raw piece of a red fish, shaped like a worm. "They put that shit inside us, FUCK!" the man screams. "Who?" I ask, now intrigued. "I don't know." He tells me. "Me and my wife meet these people. We thought they might be swingers or something. They seemed nice and all, so, one night, they asked us to come to some party in the Pine Barrens, and when we got there, it was some kind of cult! They tied us up and put these fucking things INSIDE US! They must have put a tracking device in my truck! I think they're following me." I get closer and lean in towards the worm to get a better look. It moves. As I jump back, Satch opens the bathroom door and sticks his head in. "What the fuck are you doing, Mike? Let's GO!" Satch yells. "You see that!" I ask as I point to the sink. "This guy's fucking CRAZY!" Satch shouts from the doorway, "Talking about pulling worms out of his dick, let's GO!" Satch and I leave the bathroom and make our way back to the booth. "That was the craziest fucking thing I've ever seen. We need to go, now!" Satch mutters. "What the hell were you guys doing?" Jade asks. At this moment, Worm-man comes out of the bathroom and heads down an aisle. Random people look as he passes. My friends and I freeze as he walks to the door. He stops and looks out the window at a car pulling up in the side ally. His eyes get wide, and he runs out to his truck, hops in, and peels away. Sophie and Jade look at each other and crack up laughing. Satch and I look at each other, but there is no laughter. There's something I could never understand about Satch. He'd fist fight anyone, big or small, win or lose, but he was scared to death when it came to weird shit like the paranormal or small defenseless animals.

Several months later, I walk into an apartment building. I'm wearing jeans, sneakers, and a hoodie over my shirt. During the cold seasons, this is pretty much all I wear. Up some stairs, Satch opens his door in full hockey goalie gear. "What took so long? Get up here!" He yells. "What is it?" I ask. "I don't know, man, but it's flying around like a fucking gargoyle!" On hand and knees, Satch and I creep up to a turned-over couch that blocks an open doorway to the living room. We peak over, and Satch puts up his hockey mask and points at the door to his bedroom, where the creature is perched. "There it is!"

A small flying squirrel glides down and into the living room. Satch yells and jumps up to run into the kitchen. "Did you see it! Where is it!" He shouts. "It's a flying squirrel! I didn't know we had them here. Maybe it's a pet." I calmly add. "Just catch IT!" Satch interrupts as he hides behind an open fridge. I walk over to the squirrel and look at an old baseball cap with a picture of a cardinal. I grab the hat off a shelf, drop it on top of Satch's monster and call it a day.

Sophie, Jade, Satch, and I sit in a crowded movie theater. Satch is in a bad mood. Two girls talk in a row below us as Sophie, Jade, and I trade candy. *Satch got off the pain pills as well. Not that he had much of a*

345

choice, his doctor got popped by the Feds for writing shady scripts. It got

so out of hand that Satch had to go out of state to fill a prescription. He

also stayed clean from being an asshole, but every so often he would have

a relapse. "Yo!" "Shut the fuck up!" He yells at a row of talking people in

the theater. Satch calms down and joins in on the candy trade.

Sophie and Jade hung around for another year while they finished

up at a local college. We lost touch with them after they moved away to

finish their education. I never heard from Jade again, but I wish her well

wherever she is. Sophie became a teacher in the area. I ran into her about a

month ago at a bar. I bought her and her boyfriend a drink and ranted

about the crazy worm guy. After finishing the story, Sophie smiled and

said, "Sorry, Mike, I don't remember that but, in your defense, I smoked a

lot of pot at the time." She laughs. This did not help Satch and I's debate,

but it's all good.

THE SHORE MALL

Clark and I walk through an old beat-up mall. In this world, there

are only a few places that match no other. A place so magical that words refuse to do it justice. The place I speak of is none other than the Shore Mall. Some people say it's a dump. But they're so wrong. I thought it was great as a kid, but as an adult, it was even better! An arcade, a comic book and video game store, an Asian massage parlor, and the best pizza on the planet. Clark too shared this love for the dying mall. We sit outside a furniture store in two recliners with a small cooler on the floor. We reach in, and each crack a can of beer. Clark never got into the Oxy's, so he was always a good shoulder to lean on.

"You fucking asshole!" He shouts at me as I wipe my nose, "Are you still taking pills?" "No man just got the sniffles," I tell him. "Oh, well, that's good." He says. "You ever have to suck anyone's dick?" He asks. "I never HAD to," I answer. Clark laughs. "Nice, well, I bet George had to," Clark says. "Really?" I ask as I chug my beer. "You have to eventually, right? "Clark adds. "Yea, I never got that." I interrupt. "Yea, I think it's a rule," Clark says. "A rule!? What like they just keep blowing each other until someone hands over a bag of dope?" I ask. "Yup," Clark answers casually. A mall worker walks by, and I point to a row of lights on the ceiling. One out of fifty were actually lit. "Hey, you guys have a light out," I mention. The worker looks confused and walks away. "Yea, how are we supposed to see around here?" Clark laughs as he cracks another cold can, "Hey, what are you doing tomorrow? "Nothing," I answer. Clark nods. "Maverick has his girlfriend's hot pink convertible. He wants to drive around and whistle at construction men. You in?" Clark asks. "You had me at pink convertible," I say with a smirk. "Remind me to wear shoes." Clark agrees as Sis walks up with her boyfriend, Fred. Fred gives us hi-fives. "Hey!" Says Sis as they join us in recliners, and we hand them each a beer. Fred and Sis have been dating for a while now. Some of Fred's hobbies include drinking beer, shooting guns, and heavy metal. "They got a light out," Fred says as he cracks his beer. We get along just fine.

The depression of winter ends, and summer is here once again. The Devaney family drives through some mountains in Pennsylvania in a packed station wagon. As kids, Sis and I had many vacations throughout the years with Mom and Dad. When Faith was born, the vacations came to a stop. When Faith asked us why she never got one, we told her it was because she was an accident, and now we are broke. The half-true joke never got old. However, one year, Faith had enough and demanded a family vacation that would fit in all she had missed. So, we emptied the vacay coin jug, and besides skiing, of course, we did the best we could to grant her wish.

Dad checks into an old hotel in the mountains as the rest of us look at old pictures that hang on the wall. I point to a picture of the old hotel we were staying at. "Holy poop, top ten haunted places in America." I read out loud. "No way. Are you serious?" My sisters yell. "Don't worry, Faith, there's no such thing as ghosts." Mom chimes in. Mom knew that we knew she didn't believe in ghosts, but she still has to say it every time. "Where's the bathroom in this place," Faith asks. "It's right there, Hun," Mom tells Faith. Faith comes out of the bathroom shortly after and starts to walk back to the main lobby. She stops next to a door and looks out at a deer that sits across the road. A man comes out of the men's room and heads towards the door. Faith sees him coming and opens the door for him. The man had long black hair and dark clothing. "Thank you, young lady, and a great day to you." He says." You too!" Faith replies. "That guy looked creepy, Faith," Mom says as Faith catches up. "Who?" I ask. "Just some guy. She answers. A hotel worker adds a signed picture of Alice Cooper to the wall. Faith looks at the picture and points at it. "Hey, that's him." Sis and I laugh. "You held the door for Alice Cooper?" I ask. "I don't know what his name is, but that was him. The counter girl then agreed with Faith's statement and smiled. We stop laughing and fast walk to the door and open it up. Outside, a big black bus pulls away. "Aw, man!" Sis yells as I shake my head and state, "We weren't worthy."

I DO BELIEVE IN SPOOKS I DO I DO I DO

Mom, Dad, and Faith paddle a canoe while Sis and I paddle kayaks down some light rapids in the sun. We get back to the hotel around seven o'clock and sit at a small bar for the rest of the night. We sleep in conjoining rooms. Mom and Dad have their own. I have my own bed, and Sis and Faith share the other. A loud banging sound is heard. Sis wakes up. "Faith! Do you hear that?" Sis asks. "What is that?" Faith says as the loud bang is heard repeatedly as if someone had a sledgehammer to the walls. The door handle starts to shake. Sis and Faith are now scared. They call my name, but I show no signs of waking up.

The next day we get ready in our summer gear. Mom comes out of the bathroom, in her and Dad's room, and walks towards the door. As Mom passes the TV, it turns on. She stops and walks over to the old box

TV. Mom looks at the knob that turns the TV off and on. We hit the lake to ride some horses through the mountain before returning to the hotel. Storm clouds roll in as night falls.

Dad brushes his teeth next to a closed shower curtain. He peeks his head out of the bathroom door. "Hun, have you seen my glasses?" He asks. "Their right here." Mom answers. "That's great, Hun," Dad says as he walks back to the sink. Dad looks over at the shower curtain that is now open. He looks back in the mirror with a casual smile as if nothing happened and spits out the toothpaste. *My dad is the kind of person that could actually see a ghost and go back to whatever he was doing as if nothing happened.* Sis and Faith lay wide awake. The loud banging starts again from all sides of the room. The closet door slowly creeks open. Sis and Faith are scared once again. Mom lays awake in her room while Dad sleeps before looking at the TV and getting up. I wake this time to the banging sound.

"What the freak is that?" I shout. "We told you!" Says my sisters. Mom examines the dial to the TV in her room. She turns the knob, and it clicks on. In the kid's room, the doorknob shakes. The girls yell, and I jump out of bed and to the door. I grab the jiggling handle, quickly unlock

351

the door, and pull it open. There's no one there. I look out into the empty hallway that stretches out in both directions. Meanwhile, Mom turns the TV knob, and it clicks off. As she walks away, the TV knob clicks back on by itself. Mom turns around with wide eyes.

That morning we pack our bags. "This place is awesome. I don't know why we have to leave MOM." I say. *With another person around, I have fun with the whole "ghost" thing, but if I was there alone, I'd be shaking like a little bitch.* "I think maybe she saw a ghost." Says Faith. We all laugh except Mom. "There's no ghosts. I just don't think we need to sleep here with all that banging." Mom answers. "Right," I mutter as I stuff my backpack. "Ok, we got a new place. Let's go." Dad says from the hallway. As we leave, I look around the room once more with a look of disappointment before leaving the room and closing the door. *Now there are only two things that can explain the events that took place here. One, the place is rigged for ghost, happy guests. Or two, well, you know. If there is a 3rd reason, just maybe, it exists somewhere in the very back of our imagination.* With the room now empty of the living, the closet door opens, and footsteps are heard walking toward the TV. It turns on by itself, and seconds later, a thud is heard plopping on the bed.

The sound of wedding bells rings out through Bakersfield as Sis, Fred, and the rest of us come popping out the doors to a church. In a wedding dress, Sis holds her fist up in the air and celebrates. A club song starts to play loudly in the parking lot. Me, Fred, Dad, and Sis pass a flask around as we stand outside the church. Jeb is parked out front with his DJ speakers set up in his wagon as he pumps the tunes. "Just a little sample, Mr. D," Jeb yells. "Sounds good, Jeb!" Dad yells back with a grin. Fred and Sis get into a limo, wave, and drive away.

It's morning time in the fall. I stand at the living room window and look out with no expression as I watch the neighborhood critters prepare for the future. There's a knock at my front door. In sweats and a t-shirt, I walk to the door, open it and look out the screen door at a man who looks my age. He stands with his back to the door. He is dressed casually and has short brown hair. I open the screen door as the man turns around. "Holy shit," I mutter loudly. A clean-shaven Leo looks up and smiles. "What's up, Mike?"

Later, Leo and I sit at a bar inside of a strip club. Two dancers are on stage. I drink a beer and Leo an old fashion. "Damn Leo, good to see ya! So what's new, man? You're all cleaned up, I see." "Yeah, dude, I'm a counselor now." He tells me. "No shit, so you can drink?" "That's cool," I say as we sip our drinks. "Yea, not at first, but I've earned it by now," Leo says. "So dude, I heard your album Adolescence." "It's good shit, man." "You did?" I ask as I do my blow tic, "Thanks, dude." "You playing out or what?" He asks. "I was, but now I'm just chillin," I answer. "Well, if you're still serious about it, Cali's a good place to get it out there," Leo says. "Yea, but I heard it's expensive as shit." "My couch ain't." Leo interrupts with a grin. "For real!?" I shout. "Yeah, man, least till you get on your feet," Leo explains. "Me and my bro started a small label out there. I could use another songwriter in the studio, and I'm sure you have some new stuff yourself. Think about it." He tells me. "Damn, dude," I say. "Yea, I definitely will. For now, though, let's get drunk," Leo says as I buy us a round. "Lap dances on me." He adds. We cheers and chug down our drinks.

Leo drops me back off at my house late that night. I eat a ham and cheese sandwich and stand alone once again in my parents' quiet house. As I walk to the living room, I see him. Tic sits in the corner of the living room. "Hey, buddy." He says as I stand quietly. Tics' eyes are bloodshot, and he looks very pale. He's thin now and coughing with no hand over his

354

mouth. He is dying. He spits out a wad of blood. "I told you not to open the box." He mutters. "And why on god's green earth would I ever listen to you," I reply. "Do you know what was in it?" Tic asks with a wheeze. I see the open box in my mind. It was on the counter the night I took my first painkiller. "We tortured you every day. We hated you so much, but still. Still, you stayed the course. Even through all the fucking bullshit." "What does that have to do with it?" I interrupt. Tic chuckles, "The doctors always said you'd outgrow me, do you remember?" "That date has come and gone a long time ago," I say as I turn my head. "Maybe," Tic says with a cough and adds, "Or perhaps they only were referring to your hardship. You ever think of that?" I shake my head. "After all those years of suffering, why open another box." Says Tic. "I'm done with that blue shit!" I tell him. Tic nods. "Everything takes time to heal. How many more scars." Tic asks. "Fuck you." I interrupt once more before putting my head down. I take a breath and look back up, but Tic is gone. I didn't feel any different, but I knew. I knew that I would never see him again. I walk over and look out the same window where I started my day. The full moon shines bright on the side yard. I wear the same expression on my face that

I woke with. The critters are no longer busy. Instead, they rest for the long journey that lies ahead.

SEVEN YEARS LATER

A girl in her mid-20s drives a car. She's thin with long wavy blond hair and blue eyes. She sips her morning drink from a straw. Her cell phone rings, and she gets upset. She ignores the phone for a moment before picking it up. "Son of a- WHAT! I fucking knew it. Where's your car? I'm like halfway. Alright." She hangs up the phone and turns the car around in a dirt driveway before heading back the way she came. The hot sun shines on me as I sit on some steps to a one-story, lime green house with a finished attic. The steps and porch are cement. Jazz pulls up, and I get in the passenger seat. I'm wearing a t-shirt, jeans and hiking shoes. We pull away.

It's been seven years since that day at my window. Now in my early 30s, I have a goatee and short brown hair with a hint of gray. Besides a little bit of age, I look the same. "What took so long? I was sweating my ass off." "So, put on some shorts!" Jazz Interrupts. "That's not professional, Jasmine." I kid. "Ya got some mustard on your lip." She tells

me. "What were you eating? Wait, was that my Chinese!?" She yells. "It

was old," I argue as I wipe my lip. "I got it yesterday!" "So, what'd we

miss? I ask, changing the subject. "Um, let's see, Tina got stabbed in the

leg with scissors, Vic cracked his face open, and Yen threw up in the VHS

bin again." She rants. "Damn, man, it's not even nine o'clock." "Wait a

sec." Jazz hides her smirk as I pause. "That's why you picked me up!" I

shout as Jazz starts laughing. "I'm not dealing with that shit myself." She

states. I turn up the air. "Wake me when we get there," I tell her as we turn

off the main street and head down a long county road.

Late afternoon. A trailer in a wooded trailer park. A death metal

song plays through the open windows. In a bedroom of the trailer are a

half-stack amplifier, gothic statues, medieval daggers, and axes. A street

sign hangs on the wall that reads *HOLLY ST*. A tattooed hand makes a

power cord on the neck of a flying V guitar as he plays along with the

death metal song blaring from the amp. Jazz drops me off in front of the

trailer and drives away. I hold a six-pack of light beer before putting it on

top of my car in the driveway. It's a small sports car with a spoiler. Holly's

green Jeep Cherokee from the '90s is parked next to me with a landscaping equipment trailer. I open the sports car and grab some board shorts, a tank top, and flips. I open the front door to the trailer and walk in as a metal song is heard from the back room. "Holly!" I look to the back before opening the fridge. As I make room for my beer, a hand comes down from the top of the refrigerator and pokes me on the ear.

"Got ya last, till tomorrow," Holly shouts. "Aw man, I knew something was up with that freaking blanket," I say. Holly lays on top of the fridge under a blanket. He jumps down, laughing. We sit on the trailer's porch on two plastic chairs with a small table between us. The porch has random bikes and kid toys lying about. Now in my summer attire, I crack a beer and sip it. Holly has a shaved head and is covered in tattoos from the shoulders down. He has on a sleeveless t-shirt, black cargo shorts, and black work boots. "You want one?" "Not yet," Holly says, waving his hand. "Did your guy come this month?" I ask. "He was supposed to come today." Holly answers. A black car pulls up and parks in front of the trailer. "Speak of the Dick Head." Says Holly getting up. As he walks over to the car, I hide my beer. *Let me back up for a moment.*

Back when I was messing with the Blues, Holly developed his own addiction. Holly sits at a wooden table in the middle of a campsite. A girl kisses him and walks away. *Ever since I met him, Holly had one kryptonite that reigned supreme.* "Damn, dude, good work," I say as the pretty girl walks away from the picnic table. "What's that?" Holly pulls out a small black box and opens it. Inside is an engagement ring. "I love her." He says as I freak. "OH, MY freaking…" I shout with frustration. "She's the one man. I know it!" Holly says. "You met her three DAYS AGO!" I yell. *That was just like Holly. He could fall in love with a new toothbrush.* A few years after Holly's one-day engagement, I visit his mom's house. Kids in their mid and late teens hang in a finished basement of a long rancher. I come down the stairs and give Holly's younger brothers and cousins hi-fives. I then walk into a room where Holly watches the homemade movie we made some years earlier. "Yo man, what's up?" I ask. "Hey Mike, I'm just showing off our action flick. "Your parkour is awesome!" Says a girl in her teens. I laugh. "I didn't know it had a name but thanks."

Annie kisses Holly leaves the room and smiles at me on the way out. I smile back and close the door behind her. I turn around and look at Holly, who at the time was in his early twenties. Holly finally looks up. "I'm in love with her." He says simply. "OH, MY freaking," I yell as

Holly interrupts. "It just happened, man! Her parents know. Everything is cool." "Wow, parents of the fucking year!" I yell, "Do you know what they do to sex offenders in prison?!" "What!?" Holly interrupts. I slowly look at him as if he didn't know. "They FUCK THEM!" I scream. "You were hanging with those emo chicks." He implies. "Oh, you mean the girls who were over eighteen years old." I point out. "How old is this one, Holly, sixteen!?" I ask. "It's not like she's twelve, dude." He adds. "Yea, no shit, I'd be kicking your face in!" I say before calming down and taking a seat. "Look, man, I know you, ok. I know that you're harmless and just really fucking stupid." I tell him. "I told you never to call me that!" Holly yells. "Yeah, well, just don't drop the soap," I mutter with nothing better to say. "I'm telling you, Mike, it's all good. I got to take a piss. You want a beer?" I don't answer. "Oh, what? You're not going to hang out now." Holly asks. "Pft, I'm not fucking her," I mutter, "Why would I leave?" "Good, I'll get you a beer," Holly says as he leaves the room. I grab the controller as a random girl comes in and sits next to me with a plastic cup. I look over as she smiles and sips from a pink straw. Seconds later, Holly holds a beer and smokes a cig with one of his brothers on their front porch. I run out the front door and straight to my car. "Where are you going? I got you a beer!?" Holly yells. "I'm outta here!" I jump in my car and peel away.

Back outside Holly's trailer. Holly says goodbye to the man in the black car and walks away. The car drives off. Holly sits back down, and I hand him a beer from a small ice bucket. Turns out the parents of Holly's ex-jailbait girlfriend changed their minds. Big surprise. Holly spent a year in prison. Parole, though, that shit lasts forever.

That night I walk in the front door of Jazz's lime-colored house. Jazz sits on the couch and works on her laptop. "Yo." I nod. "Hey." Jazz says and I go to the fridge and grab a beer. "You want a beer?" I ask. "No, I have to finish this paper." I get her a beer anyway, walk to the living room and hand it to her. "Here, you need a break." Jazz takes the beer, and I turn up the TV.

Several empty beer bottles later, I look at the clock. "Alright, time for bed," I say out loud. Jazz puts her beer down and opens up her laptop. "What are you doing? It's like 1:30." "I told you, I have to finish this paper." Jazz sighs, "It's due tomorrow." "Damn, that sucks. Alright, well, see ya," I say as I walk upstairs. Jazz rubs her eyes and continues to work on her paper.

DANI AND THE TRIPLE DOG DARE

The following day, I drive down a back stretch of road surrounded by woods. I punch some numbers into my flip phone. "Your available balance is two dollars and..." I hang up the phone. A man named Jack eats from a bag of chips. His long hair hangs as he looks through a small glass window in a classroom. A small boy holds a plastic square in front of a lightbox. A husky boy named Yen sits next to me and colors as I give him a thumbs up. A tall kid named Lou sits at a desk while having a snack. Lastly, a small girl named Tia sits on a chair and lets out a loud scream. Jazz sits at the teacher's desk on her laptop. She looks tired. "Yo Mike, come here." Yells Jack. I walk over to a small padded room with a square window. I look in with Jack. A thirteen-year-old boy is wrapped up like a pretzel as he looks at some game cards. "Can you bend like that?" Jack asks. "I'd never leave the house," I say jokingly as I shake my head. "Um, it doesn't take two people to watch Vic." Yells Jazz. "Can one of you find something to do?" Jack and I look at Jazz and then at each other. We both laugh and ignore Jazz by looking back in the window. "Worthless." Jazz says while the small boy smacks the square on his lightbox. "You need help, Teak?" Jazz asks. "Yes, please." He says politely.

Teak's sixteen years old and about three feet tall. He is always dressed nice from head to toe and has big glasses that make his eyes look gigantic. He has gelled black hair combed in a part, and he speaks with a strong Indian accent that completes his incomparable personality. Jazz helps Teak with his shapes. "I gotta get out of here, man, "I say. "Later." Says Jack while Jazz interrupts. "Well, take your kid! "She shouts. "Hey Yen, you want to come," I ask. "NO!" He answers me while he grabs a crown. "Well, take one of them." Jazz says with a hand up. "Come on, Teak." Teak hops off his seat and walks to me with a slight limp. "OK." He says simply. Jazz drops the plastic shape and puts her head in her hands.

Teak and I walk down the hall. I take out a pack of gum and offer some to Teak, who is stimming by putting his thumb on his chin and smacking it into the other hand. "No, thank you, Michael." He says. "Hey, Teak!" Says an attractive lady who is walking out of the bathroom. "How are you?" Teak answers without stopping what he is doing. I pop some gum in my mouth. "Hey Teak, can I have a hug?" The woman bends down and hugs Teak. "Watch out, he bites," I warn. "Oh, he does not!" She

yells, "Do you bite Teak?" "No." He lies as he gives the lady a hug.

"Your way too sweet, bye Teak." The young woman walks away, and I

look back as she does so. "Why didn't you bite her, dude?" I ask. "I don't

know, Michael." "Well, good job," I say as I hand my friend a piece of

gum. This time he takes it and pops it in his mouth.

I walk into a room where I see my large friend Terry sitting behind

his desk. Terry's a black man with army tattoos covering his left arm. He

sits behind a desk as his students in the room eat lunch. "You do your

picks?" I ask with a handshake. "No man, you?" I take out my football

pick sheet, and we talk them over. Teak looks over at a kid eating

popcorn. The boy sees Teak and bites his own hand. Teak walks over to

him. "What is this, Mike!?" Terry asks. "My picks, man." As Terry

laughs, a smack is heard. Teak lands hard on the ground, and his glasses

fall off. "You alright, Teak?" I ask. "I'm ok." He answers. He then grabs

his glasses and puts them back on. "Stay away from Sal, man. You know

he likes his space." I remind him. "How old is that guy?" Asks Terry.

"Teak? He's like sixteen, I think." "No shit," Terry replies. "Alright, man,

I'll be back," I say aloud.

Teak and I walk into the nurse's office, and I pour a cup of water from the cooler. I hand it to Teak, who has now jumped up on a seat. As Teak drinks it, I pour one for myself. Jack and Vic walk in the door. Vic is a skinny boy with a baseball cap that he has never taken off. He is around fifteen years old. "You leave Jazz by herself?" I ask. "Yup." Says Jack as he hits up the water cooler. A lady named Dani talks to the nurse. She is in her mid-forties, has brown hair to her shoulders, and is thin and attractive. "You think they're real." Asks Jack as we stare at Dani. "Who cares," I state blatantly. "I'll give you twenty bucks if you find out." He adds. "Ha, what's that in jail money?" I ask. "A twinkie." Jack jokes. I laugh as I think about his request. "You got it on you?" Jack holds up a twenty-dollar bill. I walk towards Dani. As I do so, I give a head nod to a kid in a chair holding a football. He smiles and hands me the small ball. I spin and crouch down as I walk toward Dani. The football kid jumps up and chases me. I drop the ball before picking up Dani to move her out of the way. "Look out!" I shout. "Oh wow, I didn't even see him. Thanks, Mike." She says as I put her down. The football kid picks up the ball and sits back down with a smile as Jack hands me the twenty. "Not bad." "Their firm." I interrupt.

Dani eats her lunch in a quiet break room that afternoon. I slap the twenty-dollar bill in front of her. "Change, please." Dani goes through her purse and hands me two tens. I grab one of them. "The other is yours," I tell her. "What, why?" She asks with confusion. "Someone paid me twenty bucks to grab your boob." Dani breaks out into laughter. "Oh, my god, just take it." She offers as I wave it off. "Nope," I say. "Why." She asks. "Because then it's sexual harassment," I answer. "Then what's this?" Asks Dani while she finishes her tuna sub. "Just prostitution." Dani laughs at my comment as I leave the breakroom. "He's so funny." She says out loud to a lady sitting across from her. The lady looks at Dani with a face full of disapproval as she eats her salad. I felt bad taking Jack's money, for he didn't know the close relationship Dani and I had, but he's taken my money for less. That afternoon at a liquor store, I put down the ten-dollar bill on the counter with a six-pack of beer. The clerk takes the ten and gives me two dollars which I dump in a jar, thank her, and walk away.

Holly and I sit on his trailer's porch. I crack a beer and toss the cap in a trash can. "I'm so poor," I admit. "Yea, I have lot-rent, and then I'm right there with ya," Holly adds while playing an acoustic guitar with a self-rolled cigarette in his mouth. He plays a part of a verse to our original song *Clean Slate*. "Turning of the tides." Holly sings, guessing the lyrics.

"No, not Turning. Damn it." I reply. "What's the chorus again?" Holly

interrupts. "A minor to C. Wait, shit, give it to me," I ask. Holly hands me

the guitar, and I sing and play the beginning of the chorus. "She don't

wanna make any mistakes." I sing as Holly grabs his own acoustic and

jumps in.

Holly and I walk down a cedar stream in the woods. We are

surrounded by thick brush, green overgrowth, and large fallen trees with

earth pulled up at their roots. Holly cracks at some bushes with a machete.

"Here's one." He shouts. An hour later, we pull up to a back road sub

shop in the woods. Holly's Jeep and our clothes are completely covered in

mud. We get out and walk in. We are both wearing boardshorts, tank tops,

and surfing booties. "Is that it?" Asked the counter girl as I hear a familiar

voice yelling from the back. I look towards the grill. "Hold up! Scratch

that. We'll take a whole Barnyard." I tell her, "He'll know." "What are you

doing?" Holly asks. "Trust me," I answer. "Hey, Ted! You know what a

Barnyard is?" Ted turns around at the grill. "FUCK YEAH, I KNOW

WHAT A BARNYARD IS!" He screams through the crowded sub shop. I

crack a smile and wave. "Yo, buddy!" Turns out Ted was just helping for the day, but it was good to see him in a familiar setting. We catch up for a while before Holly, and I leave the shop.

Holly and I eat the Barnyard in his Jeep with the windows down. "Aw, man!" Holly shouts with his mouth full. I just smile and nod as I savor every bite. A landscaper's truck pulls up next to us, and Holly hops out. "You need help?" I ask. "Na." He answers. Holly opens his trunk to the four big pieces of muddy driftwood that we pulled from the stream. He takes two out and gives them to the landscapers. He gets back in the Jeep and hands me forty bucks as he lights up a cig. "What's this?" I ask with a cigarette in my mouth. "Forty dollars. You said a buck fifty." I interrupt with a shout. "Maybe If we sold them online!" Holly says. "You want to do that!?" I shake my head, "Nope." "Hit the store?" Holly asks. "Yup." We drive away from the sunny green parking lot and head to the liquor store.

Holly works on the sander in his shed. "That drummer ever get back to you?" I ask. "Nope. So, what do you wanna do tonight?" He asks, "I'm sick of being here. I got the kids tomorrow, so let's do something." "Like what?" I ask, knowing we have no money. "You want to go ghost hunting at the old nudist colony?" I laugh at Holly's comment and sip my beer bottle. "Why not?" He asks. "Because it's not ghost hunting anymore, Holly. It's just breaking and entering." "You are such a pussy!" Holly states in his best Marty McFly impression. "What happened to you?" Holly asks, using his final trump card. "What'd you just call me," I say. "A gigantic hairy ass pussy." He replies. "Really?" He shakes his head. "Huge." "Oh, yea?" "Yup."

THE OLD PINE BARREN NUDIST COLONY

The dark woods. An abandoned row of eerie cabins. Holly and I walk down a dark path and place a tape recorder down on a chopped log by an inground pool. The pool has been unwillingly transformed into a small pond that now harbors swamp trees and wildlife. The rain drizzles softly as we open our packs and crack a beer. The cherry of our smokes lights up randomly while we sit in the silence of the pines. That night I walk upstairs to my bedroom in the finished attic of Jazz's house. The silence of the house quickly helps me fall asleep. The sound of static. My eyes open, but I can't move. I make a humming sound but can't talk.

The next day Teak holds on tight as I push him through the halls on a flatbed at school. We walk back into our class with the flatbed parked outside in the hall. "You guys get the orders done." Jazz asks as she looks up from working with a student. "Damn, Mike, you look like ass." She adds before we can answer. "I couldn't sleep last night. I keep getting stuck." I tell her. "You get stuck?" She says. "Yea," I answer. "It hasn't happened in years, but last night I couldn't shake it." Yen runs towards the door. I block him by leaning into him. He screams in a unique way as he squeezes and scratches my arm. "Aw, come on, dude, not today," I say as Jazz laughs. "It's like he knows, man!" Jazz adds.

That night I head up to my room. I lay asleep. The sound of static. I am once again stuck. I squint my eyes open and stare at my bedroom. I can't move. This time, at all. I hear men talking and walking around downstairs. I can hear their conversation crystal clear. They discuss why there are so many people living under one roof. "Who are they?" I think to myself. I then hear dishes crashing to the floor. I snap out of it and sit up. I grab my black pocket knife out of a drawer in the nightstand and run downstairs in nothing but shorts. After turning on the light, I look around the kitchen, but it's empty. "Jazz!" I shout as I come down her bedroom hallway. Her bedroom light is on, and her door is open, but she is asleep. I shake my head with confusion and go back to bed.

The sound of static. I am stuck once again. This time I see something waving in the moonlight that shines through my window. I struggle to turn my head to see what it is. My eyes open wide, and I start to make that same humming sound as I try to scream. Nothing comes out. At the window is an old lady in a white flowing gown. She is looking out into the distance. She slowly turns and glides across the floor towards a closet. She passes through the moonlight that only shows part of her long white hair. She then glides behind the open closet door. I snap out of it and jump up. With the light switch too far away, I dig in my drawer and grab a flashlight. I get up, and with fright in my eyes, I slowly walk to the closet door shining the flashlight around the room. As I get to the door, I swing it closed and shine the light on a coat that hangs behind the door. There was no one. "What the fuck was that!"

"You got an incubus." Says Holly as he plops down a book in front of me. "That's not good," I reply. It's morning time, and the sun beams through a dirty window in the kitchen of Holly's trailer. I look at the cover of the book and see it's a book of demons. "Oh, come on, dude," I yell,

"We need a real book. Like a med dictionary or something." "Actually, my ex might have left one. Check by the TV." Holly replies. I head over, find the dictionary and bring it to the table. "You believe that shit?" Holly blurts. "Finally, she's gonna be making big money, and we split." Says Holly, referring to his ex. Actually, Holly, that makes perfect sense." I tell him. "Aw, here it is!" I say as I read through the dictionary. "Sleep paralysis! Yup, I think I like this book better." I say as Holly cooks some bacon. "Oh, please! You see a lady floating around in your fucking bedroom! That ain't normal." Holly says. "I don't know, man, maybe it fucks with your dreams and makes you see shit," I add. "You're gullible," Holly mutters. "Oh, I'm gullible?" "Coming from the guy that puts super into his 1990 Jeep Cherokee because some guy pumping his gas told him to," I say. "It makes it last!" Holly yells, "Well, whatever it is, I'll sleep a lot better believing this book!" I interrupt, pointing to his ex's dictionary. "You remember the recorder from the ghost hunt?" "I forgot," I answer. "There's probably nothing on it anyway."

Now back at work. I walk past a doorway where a girl in her late 20's sits on a desk talking to a co-worker. I back up and peek my head in before walking away. The same girl sitting on the desk is now in an empty sensory room. She sits at a table and watches her student swing away on a therapy swing. The girl is about 5'2" with wavy light brown hair that reaches the center of her back. She's pretty with squinty eyes and built like a gymnast. The girl can hear voices from outside in the hallway. "Come on, man, I'll get you a sub for lunch." I plead. "No, Michael." Teak states. "Don't you want to swing? It's fun!" "NO swing!" "Yes, you do! Come on, you owe me for Jazz's cupcakes!" "You ate them too, Michael" The door cracks open, and Teak stumbles into the room. He catches his balance and swats his hand towards the door with anger. He fixes his glasses and walks over to the girl. "Hey, little guy!" Says the young lady. "How are you?" "My name is Rose." She says with a smile, not understanding Teak's accent. "You ok?" She asks. "NO." Teak mutters. "Aw, what's wrong?" Asks Rose. "Michael." States Teak. "TEAAAk! TEAAAk!" I yell as I come into the room. "Oh, there you are!" I shout politely. "Man, I was looking all over for you." I take a seat near Rose. "Hey, how ya doing?" "Hey, good, I'm Rose." She answers. She puts her hand out, and I shake it. "Hey Rose, I'm Mike. I see you've already met my friend here." Teak looks at me with an angry face. "Yes, I have. He is very polite." Says Rose. "That he is. I see you have Fin. He loves that swing." I tell her. Fin laughs and claps his hands as he swings. "I know, right? It's all he ever picks." She tells me. "He seems awfully happy about it so..." "I do the same thing when I get on it," I tell her. "Really!?" Rose says with a smile. "Yea, I sneak in after work sometimes and go to town," I add. Rose laughs out loud as Fin jumps off and runs out the door. "I better get him. It was nice to meet you." "You too," I say with a half-wave. "Bye, Teak." Rose leaves the room, and I turn back to Teak, who is still mad. I drop my smile, take my badge off my neck, and squat in front of Teak, "Alright, man, you get one."

Jazz drives her car. I sit in the passenger seat and look at my fat lip in the mirror. "Damn, you said Teak did that? He must have been maaaad." Jazz says with a grin and asks, "What happened?" "My man's got a mean hook," I answer as I light up a cig and crack a window. "Aw, hello!" Jazz shouts. "It goes right out the window," I argue as she yells again, "Put it out!" "It's almost done," I say as Jazz turns the wheel, and I bump into the door as my lit cigarette falls on my lap. "Shit!" I say, slapping my legs. "That's what you get." Jazz says, now satisfied.

SLEEP PARALYSIS

Midnight. I plug a night light into the wall next to my bed. Jazz comes up the stairs, and I quickly pull out the night light as she comes into the room holding a smartphone. "Have you seen my phone charger?" She asks. "Nope," I say, holding up my flip phone. "Oh yea, I forgot you're like fucking ninety. Alright, Night." She heads downstairs as I plug in the night light. The house is Quiet. My hand starts to shake. The sound of static. I look around the room. In the corner stands a figure. I see it and my eyes widen. The dim night light shines on the figure, which looks to be someone with an old blanket drenched over them. I close my eyes and try to break free but can't. When I open my eyes, I see the blanket man standing next to the bed. With all my might, I put my hand out to try and grab the blanket. The figure leans over me with a deep growl. As I snap out of it and sit up, the tail end of the growl is heard, but blanket man is gone. I wake up on the couch in the morning.

Jazz is cooking eggs. "Yo Mikey, you want some." "Mikey!?" I shout. Jazz laughs at the name she has never called me. As she does so, a small handful of people who have dubbed me Mikey run through my mind. "Sure," I say, sitting up and turning on the TV. I see the hand recorder on the TV stand. I grab it and sit back on the couch as I turn it on. It's only the sound of air, then Holly says something, then more air. I stop and rewind it and listen again. After Holly speaks, there's five seconds of silence and then a man strumming a guitar and saying, "Anytime." After that, a girl says, "No." With a shocked look on my face, I hit rewind. "Damn," I say out loud. "What!" Jazz asks with some curiosity. "Holly's going to shit his pants!" I yell over the sizzling pork roll. "Oh, that reminds me. I'm shitting my pants all next week." Jazz says. "No, you're not!" I shout. "Yup, me and Tina are going to Vermont, so if anyone asks at work." "You're shitting your pants," I interrupt. Jazz drops a big plate of breakfast and hands me a fork. "Are you and Tina going to make out?" Jazz shakes her head, "Na, I need a man." "Men are disgusting!" I shout, "We piss and shit, got hair everywhere." I flex my bicep. "I didn't say a boy." Jazz interrupts while handing me some hot sauce.

I look at my newly shaved face in the window of the padded room. "What happened to the goat Mike?" Jazz asks. "I just got sick of it," I answer. "Really, it wouldn't happen to do with that new girl, would it?" Jazz asks. Jack looks up from working with the tall kid and nods at Jazz. "Why'd they give you that kid anyway, Jack?" I ask. "Yea, you know, while we're changing the subject, I should take care of that." Jazz says. "You better not!" Yells Jack. "He's not even aggressive." Jazz claims as she makes some notes at her desk. Rose and Fin enter the classroom. Fin holds a box of tissues. "Hey guys, we're here for a delivery." Rose says. "Go ahead, Fin, give them their delivery," Rose says softly. Fin chucks the box of tissues, and it flies past Teak's head and hits Jazz's classroom computer. "Whoops! Sorry!" Rose says sweetly. "It's ok. Old Mr. K delivers it the same way." I kid. Rose laughs, "Aw, I like old Mr. K., except he always smells like cigarettes, ew!" "Yeah, cigarettes are gross." Jazz says while smiling at me. I give Jazz the middle finger by scratching my nose.

Later that day, the tall kid gets upset in the classroom. I duck a chair thrown at me and help Jack put the tall boy in a safety hold. The tall kid elbows Jack in the nose and kicks me in the groin. I fall back and knock into Teak's lightbox. We manage to get the tall kid to the ground and slide him safely into the padded room. Jazz slams the door as we run out. She hits the lock button, and the three of us lean on the door and wall. Jack wipes his bloody nose, and I rub my stomach. Jack turns to Jazz, "Not aggressive, huh?"

377

AN UNEXPECTED VISIT

After work, I drive down an old familiar street and park at Jeb's house. It's around three o'clock in the afternoon. It's been several weeks since I've seen Jeb, so we made plans to make up for lost time. I turn off my car and look at other cars parked out front. A man I don't recognize comes out smoking a cigarette. I can see other men sitting at the kitchen table with Jeb. The man outside flicks his cigarette and goes back in. I take a breath and think for a moment. I then turn my car back on and drive away. I sit at a counter in my kitchen and drink a beer. Jazz comes in with a suitcase. "Where the hell are you going?" I ask. "Um, Vermont. I told you like twelve times. I'll be back in a couple days." "Oh, alright. See ya." I say as Jazz walks out the front door. "Ok, have fun with Blanket Man." Jazz cracks up laughing as I throw some pretzels at the closing door.

I plug in my little bitch night light and lay in bed. On my nightstand is a flashlight, a holy cross, and my black pocket knife. I fall asleep. Sure enough, I wake, stuck in motion. I open my eyes but hear no static. I look around with only my eyes. Across the room is a girl. She seems to be looking at a picture on a shelf with some of my belongings. The girl had short blond hair to her shoulders. She was in her mid-twenties, wearing jeans and a yellow hoodie with light blue writing. She turns and looks at me with a pretty smile that I recognize immediately. "Hey, Devaney." She says as she walks over and sits on a small couch next to my bed. She looks me up and down. "Paralysis, huh? That sucks, man." She says. I tried to speak but was unable. I had a lot to say but could only smile to the best of my abilities. "I miss you guys." Is the last thing I heard her say before a classic laugh that echoed till morning. That was the only night I've ever had in paralysis that I did not force myself awake.

I open my eyes to the sound of robins and sunlight. I walk over and pick up the picture frame viewed the night before by my unexpected visitor. Looking at it, I remember something I hadn't in fourteen years. I quickly undo the small hatches on the picture frame and slide off the back. Sure enough, what I had remembered was inside. I stare at a picture of Haley as if I had just put it there yesterday. The picture had no obvious reason to be hidden and to be honest I'm not entirely sure why it was at all. I replace the photograph on display with the one I had just found. *I know my unexpected visitor wasn't really Haley. I like to think that wherever we go after here is far away from this place. With that said, maybe a little*

piece of energy is left behind. Not a lot; I mean, it's not YOU, more like a

projection, perhaps. I put down the picture frame and head downstairs

with a grin.

Daytime in the woods. Holly drives through narrow dirt paths as

Beast and the Harlot pumps through his stereo. I ride as his passenger.

Holly rides up some sugar sand and flies down a ravine into a cedar

stream. Water covers the inside of the Jeep. I move my lit cigarette from

the water. My cousin Matt sits in the back seat, holding on to the *oh shit*

handle with two hands as he bounces around. Now parked on the far side

of Shimmer Run Lake, Holly has the hood popped and works on the

engine. I get out of the lake and look up at Matt. I light a cigarette by the

Jeep.

CRANE IN THE QUARRY

Matt moved away when we were about thirteen years old. One

morning on a visit, Matt woke me up early and said we had someplace to

go. We hopped on our bikes and rode for three hours through the hills of

Connecticut. We came to a quarry with a fifty-foot jump to the black water below. The quarry had swallowed up a crane that still sits at the bottom of the eerie black water. A fat cable ran from the top of the cliff to the crane below. This served as the only way back up and out of the giant fishbowl surrounded by rock. Without looking off the edge, Matt sprinted, jumped through the air, and fell into the 50-foot hole without knowing his fate. I quickly follow Matt to the water below. On the way home, we scavenged some smokes, accidentally burnt down a quarter acre of marshland, and were home in time for supper. It was spaghetti and meatballs.

"Come on, man, Sis, jumped off that thing." "It's really high," Matt yells from the top of a pine tree at Shimmer Run. Holly watches with a cigarette in his mouth as he works on his Jeep. "He's joking." I laugh. I turn back to Matt, who is now climbing down from his abandoned tree jump. My smile turns into shock as my cigarette falls out of my open mouth. Apparently, if you live in New England long enough, they castrate you. Matt jumps to the ground and runs over to me and my opened mouth. He looks down at my bunning cigarette. "Uh-Oh," Matt says before picking up the cig and putting it out in the dirt. He blows on it and puts the butt in his pocket. I'm speechless. "What's up?" Matt asks. "What did they do to you?" I say finally with a straight face. "It was high, man!" Matt

laughs as he hops into the Jeep. "Unbelievable," I say out loud. Holly

slams the hood and climbs into the driver's seat. "This guy was the craziest

fucking kid!" I tell Holly. "This one time, we found this tractor." I open

two beers from my backpack and hand one to Matt. He thanks me with a

smile as I continue the story. My memory stays at the clearing as Holly

takes us back through the woods of Shimer Run.

After many years of school, Matt became something that I can't

even pronounce. He basically works on saving nature. I guess he's making

up for how much of it he destroyed as a kid. It's not a bad thing to finally

grow up, I guess. Today Matt still visits, and we always have a good time.

On that day though I had to say goodbye to my oldest partner in crime.

Night has fallen, and I find myself watching TV. My bedroom

pillow and blanket are with me on the couch. I hoped there would be less

paralysis activity in the living room. I was wrong. The night visitors lasted

precisely one month after visiting the old nudist colony. I'm not saying it's

connected, but still, it's pretty fucking weird. The sleep timer turns off the

TV. The sound of static. I open my eyes. A man with an open flannel

stands in the corner of the living room as a pair of bare legs are dragged into the darkness. A man with short black hair is only a foot away on his hands and knees. He wears a tan, tucked-in, button-down collared shirt with brown stitching. He rants a prayer in another language while looking directly at me. For some reason, I was not afraid of this man. What frightened me was the man in the corner with the flannel shirt who was fixated on me as well. I snap out of paralysis. "Fuck this!" I grab my sheets and head up to my room. The static starts again as I sleep in my bed. I open my eyes and see Blanket Man. The ends of the blanket lay on top of me. Blanket Man slowly begins to rise. He floats in the air and starts to growl. I felt nothing under me as well. As if I was a foot off the bed. As the growls reach their loudest point, a bright white light shines from the wall next to the bed. White butterflies fly out of the light, and Blanket Man disappears. I snap out of it and sit up. I look around the room, realizing there is no Blanket Man, only butterflies. I can see them. I stare directly at them until they fade away into my wall. The blanket that covered the growling entity was no longer in my room. However, it did exist. It was a blanket that Grandma D made the family many years ago. My loving Grandma D, also known as Nan, had passed away in my mid-twenties.

A visit from an old friend whose laugh stayed with me until morning. A blanket from my grandma, covering a growling entity and random butterflies. I understand this all sounds insane, but with that said, there are only two outcomes that I have come up with. One, paralysis works strongly with my dreams, and I had, in fact, imagined the entire experience. Or two, I had visitors. Some of them were there for good reasons, and the others, well, I simply don't know.

Sitting at the table in my parent's dining room. Dad cooks crab cakes, and Mom works on her special potatoes. Me, Sis, Faith, and Fred sit at the table, each of us with a beer. Faith listens to the recording of the guitar-playing man. "Shut up! Where were you!?" Faith asks. "Some old nudist colony Holly found," I tell her. "He would." Sis laughs. "And you don't think it's ghosts!?" asks Faith. "What in paralysis? I mean, it's not like I'm brushing my teeth or something," I tell her, "I'm half asleep." A three-year-old boy runs up and jumps in Sis's lap. She hugs him. "Hey, Freddy!" We shout. "Yea, like, if you saw it wide awake, you'd believe." Mentions Sis. "Doesn't your dad say some guy comes in and sits on his face?" Fred shouts. "It's my chest Fred," Dad yells from the kitchen as we laugh. "And he leaves me five bucks, so I don't complain." Faith waves her hand in front of her face, "Aww, Fred, was that you?" "Sorry." He lies. "Oh, come on, Fred, not at dinner!" Mom yells as she and Dad put food out on the table and sit down. Oh, and the other thing on my death row plate is my dad's crab cakes with a little wasabi and soy sauce. Holy shit.

After moving around a bit in my mid-twenties, I moved back in with my parents once again. By the time I turned thirty, living with my parents had gotten pretty stale. In this flashback, a pretty brunette is naked and kneeling in front of me as I stand at my closed bedroom door. "Dinners ready, guys!" My mom yells from the hallway with a knock. "Be right down," I shout. Fortunately, my girlfriend at the time was used to this type of interruption and finished what she was doing without hesitation.

A year later, I moved in with Jazz. She sits on the couch in her living room as her girlfriend tries on bikini tops. Jazz broke up with a boyfriend and needed a roommate. I could forget about saving any money, but it wasn't all that bad. I walk down the stairs and into the living room. "Ask Mike." Jazz suggests. "Mike, which looks better, this one or..." Her friend turns away and switches tops before turning back around. "This one?" I think about it and rub my chin. "Hum...?"

Satch and I sit in Satch's new car in an empty parking lot. Satch is now in his early 30s as well. He looks the same but has put on a few LBs as age will do. Satch chews on a toothpick as I eat some jerky. "Where is this guy?" Satch say annoyed. "He ain't going to show, man," I answer. "Give me your cash." I hand over a bundle of twenties, and Satch puts it with his own money. A junky car pulls up, and a shady-looking guy gets out, looks around, and opens his trunk. "Here he is." We walk to meet him. "What's up, man." Says Satch. "I didn't have any blue ones." Says the shady man as he digs through a bag in his trunk. The man pulls out two hacked PlayStation Portable video game consoles. "I got some in black." He says. "YEAH!" We shout. Satch hits me on the shoulder. "Yo, it's got every game ever!"

A while later, we pull up to Pine Park and walk up to a football field where a Pee-wee soccer game is underway. It's late afternoon with an overcast. Parents cheer in the stands as a six-year-old boy scores a goal. We clap and cheer as we reach the bleachers. "Where's Will," I ask. "He's at his mom's." Satch answers. "Yo, I told him about you climbing the Pine

Park Tower when you were younger. He now talks about it every time we're here." "Nice." I laugh. "His friends don't believe him. "They're like. You can't do that. You'd die." Satch snickers. "Probably better that they don't believe," I add. "For real," Satch adds as we approach Ray and their dad, Lou. Lou stands and cheers as Satch's son scores. "He's getting big, man," I tell Satch. "I know it's crazy." "Hey, guys," Ray says. Lou stares forward at the game. Ray and I look at each other and walk towards the bleachers leaving Satch and his dad alone. They both stare out at the game until Sachet's dad finally speaks. "Hi, Satch." "Hey, dad." They look at each other, and Satch gives his dad a nod. "How have you been?" Asks his father. "I'm ok," Satch Answers as his dad nods with a grin. "Good." Satch's son steals the ball and heads downfield. Satch and his dad cheer and clap as Zack scores once more.

Satch recently moved in with his new girlfriend and became a special education teacher for students with disabilities. He shares custody of his two sons, Will and Zack, with his ex-wife Nora. Like my nephew Freddy, Zack is also my godson. I stopped by Satch's house a week ago, and for the first time in our long friendship, I heard him say that he was happy, and that life was good. I nodded, and we continued our conversation about girls, movies, and video games while eating hoagies in his kitchen.

HANDLE ME WITH CARE

Rose and I play poker at a small table in the sensory room at school. Rose's kid swings and Yen goes through a box of old VHS tapes. "What you got?" I ask as Ross scrunches her face. "Can I draw again?" "Sure," I reply. Rose Draws again. As she picks her cards, I look over at Jazz, smiling and waving through the door's window. I give her a dirty look. Rose throws her cards on the table. "Three jacks!" She yells. "Damn, you win," I tell her. Jazz comes in with the rest of our class, and they spread out in the room. "Hey, guys. Who's winning?" Jazz asks. "Well, I was," I say as Rose smiles and waves to the class. Her cell phone rings, and she takes out a flip phone. Jazz quickly raises her eyebrows and tries to nod to get my attention. I see the flip phone and smirk. "Who's that your boyfriend?" Jazz asks. "Nah, it's my sister." Rose replies, "No boyfriend for me." "So should we put on a movie?" I ask, "Yen, what we got?" At that moment, Yen throws up in the box full of VHS tapes. "Whoops!"

Shouts Jazz. "He sometimes gets too excited," I tell Rose with a laugh. We all look back at Yen, who is still shaking a VHS in each hand. "I guess we're watching one of them," I add.

Jazz and Rose eat lunch together in the break room. They laugh about something as Jack, and I look through the window and nod. "So, how do you like it here?" Jazz asks. "It's nice." Answers Rose, "People here are cool, well, most of them." "Minus Mike and fucking Jack," Jazz mutters, getting a laugh from Rose. "You and Mike seem to be getting along." Jazz says with a smile. "Yea, he's really funny," Rose mentions. "Yea. I have to admit he is in pretty good shape for an old man." Jazz says as she looks over at us through the door's window and smirks. I shake my fists as Jack laughs. "Yea, he is cute. How old is he anyway?" Rose asks. "Early 30's, How old are you? I don't think you ever told me." Jazz responds. "Twenty-eight," Rose says as she eats her sandwich. I quickly count with my fingers outside in the hallway. "Really, wow, I thought you were my age." Jazz says with a mouth full of chips. "Thanks!" Rose says with delight.

After work, I walk Rose out to her car. "I heard it was good. You like scary movies?" I ask. "Yea, but they give me nightmares." Says Rose with a fake shiver. "I hear ya on that. Well, I was thinking of going tomorrow at like four. You want to come with me?" I ask. "Yea, that sounds fun! Maybe we can get some drinks after." Rose says. "You read my mind," I add. "Text me your address, and I'll pick you up." "Ok, see ya!" Rose shouts. She then gets in her car, but it won't start. The headlights are dimming. I see and walk over. "You alright?" I ask. "My car won't start. That's so weird. I never leave my lights on." Rose says as she scratches her head. "I got some jumpers. Hold on." I say while popping my trunk. Empty beer bottles fall out of the trunk filled with camping supplies. I close it fast and pick up the bottles while I look around. I see Jazz's car next to mine and sneak the bottles through a crack in her window. "Sorry, I must have lost them," I tell Rose. "It's ok. I must have done the same." "Yea, It's cool." I interrupt. "We'll jump your car tomorrow after the movie." "Thanks, Mike!" She says with a smile. "No prob."

I drive Rose down a back road with farmland and thick woods on each side. "I've been there for like three years, I think." "Aw, that's cool." Rose interrupts politely as her phone rings. "Hello, hey! Yea, Mikes driving me, I must have left my lights on. Sure, hold on. Jazz asked if we want to go to happy hour with her and Jack. It's totally up to you. I feel bad that you have to drive me." Rose says. "Naa, don't feel bad. It's right around the corner." I say as I point.

The four of us sit at the dive bar drinking beer. Jazz and Rose get up and go to the bathroom. "Hey man, I appreciate the help with inviting us to happy hour, but it ain't my first rodeo," I tell Jack as he chugs his brew. "Just a little fail-safe is all," Jack mutters. "Right," I add and chug as well. After mingling at the bar with Rose, I drive her down an old country road. It's around sunset, and the late summer sky bleeds red and blue. The windows are open, and I get a smile from Rose, whose wavy hair dances in the wind. We pull up to a big old house on a large property surrounded by woods. "You want to come in? I think I have some beers left in the fridge." She asks. "Sure," I tell Rose while parking. It's night now, and Rose and I sit by the fireplace in the den. "I moved away to Connecticut for a bit, but I've mostly lived in Jersey." She tells me. "That's cool. My cousins live there. It's pretty." I say over the crackles of chard wood. "What'd you do up there?" I ask. "I worked at a nature school. It was kinda like a sleep-away camp for adolescence." Rose adds. "Wow, that sounds awesome," I say with a grin. "What about you?" She asks. "I lived in California for like a year," I answer. But mostly NJ." "That's so cool," Rose shouts. "Do you have any pics?" "I have a couple, I think." I take out my phone and look through my pictures before handing it over. "Here's some of the Redwoods." "Whoa, you rock climb?" She interrupts. "I did that day," I say with a chuckle. "Holy shit, no ropes, that's high!" She says as I move closer to her and point to the tiny flip phone screen. "I was making my way to a cave, see that little dot." "You had a band?" Rose asks as she continues to scroll. "It was just me most of the time," I say, leaning in. "Can I have a CD?" "It's on iTunes." I brag nonchalantly. "But CDs were so much better." "Definitely!" Rose agrees. "We sit in silence for a moment as the fire lights up the room. Someone is heard walking around, and I look to the next room. "It's just one of my sisters." "Cool, well, I better get going," I say while standing up and catching my balance. "Are you ok to drive?" "Sure, I think." "Lay down. I'll get you a blanket." "Are you sure?" I ask. "Yup, my parents are cool." She explains. "I'll be right back." "Ok, thanks," I tell her.

The next morning. I wake on the couch and hear people eating breakfast. I get up and quietly walk to the front door. I turn the nob, and it slowly opens with a squeak. Rose's two Border Collies bark and run to the door. I sigh, close the door and pet them. Rose comes into the foyer. "Hey, how'd you sleep?" "Hey, not bad," I say. "Good, you hungry?" We walk into the dining room, where Rose's mom, dad, and two sisters sit at a big table. One of their boyfriends sits next to her brown-haired sister. The other sister has black hair, and both look like they're in their early twenties. The mom and sisters resembled Rose, and her dad is tall and had the look of a drill sergeant. "Hey everyone, this is Mike," Rose says with a smile. I get a nod from her dad and a friendly hello from the rest of the family. "Hey, guys, how ya doing?" "Have a seat, Mike. I'll make you a plate." Says Rose's mom. "Thank you, do you mind if I use the bathroom first?" I had to piss like a racehorse and planned on stopping in the trees on the way home. "Sure, it's past the kitchen." Says her mom. "He's got to poop," Whispers the sister's boyfriend. The girls laugh, and her sister smacks the boyfriend on the arm. After breakfast, Rose and I walk out to a sunny day. We head towards my car, parked in their dirt and stone horseshoe driveway. "This place is sweet," I say as I look around the yard. "You want a tour!?" "Definitely," I answer. We walk to the sound of summer bugs and birds as we pass a big garden and some old chicken pens. We come to a path cut out through the woods. "On Halloween, my

393

dad would use this as a haunted hayride." "Damn." I interrupt. "And I thought my yard was cool." Rose smiles. "He and his friends would dress up and scare the shit out of my sisters and me." "That's awesome!" I tell her as we turn a bend. "Here we are." We come to an opening in the woods. I look up and stop in my tracks as Rose keeps walking. I have a wondrous look on my face. In front of me is a tree fort with a tire swing in a big oak. The sun shines down on it through the trees. Only parts of the old fort remain, but I can easily see its awesomeness. "The ladder is broken, so we'll have to climb," Rose tells me. I look from the tree to Rose as she hops up and grabs a branch. As she does so, a song plays loudly as if by a hidden boombox. The song is *Handle Me with Care*. I'm not sure why it started playing in my head on that hot day in June, but soon after, it would play in the car randomly for the rest of summer. The first summer where Rose and I would be inseparable.

AC AND THE SAINT PATTY'S DAY PARADE

It's the middle of the day at the Atlantic City Boardwalk. Music plays as the Saint Patty's Day Parade passes us by. With beers in hand,

Clark, Maverick, our friend Gary, and I lean on the part of the boardwalk that goes out to the beach. We are all in hoodies except for Gary and his girlfriend Pam, who are dressed nicely. A girl with cherry blond hair and a tall blond talk with Rose and Pam. "Yo, look!" Maverick points at a shed on the beach. Gary and I laugh. "Oh shit." Says Clark, "That dude's getting a blowjob." "HEY!" Yells Maverick. "YOU'RE GETTING A BLOWJOB!" The guy waves us away. "I think he knows Mav," Says Clark with a chuckle. "His nuts are bigger than Devaney's," shouts Gary. "How do you know?" Asks Pam with a smile. "Amy used to pull them out during beer pong," Gary adds, getting a memorable laugh from the crowd. Maverick, Clark, and I all pee down by the sheds. As we zip up and walk back, Maverick darts through us with his hood pulled over his head tight. He crouches down and runs back up to the boardwalk. "What's that about?" I ask. "He's afraid of the seagulls," Clark responds. "Oh yeah." "Why is that again?" "I don't know." Answers Clark. "I think his uncle buried him in the sand as a kid and poured a bag of chips on his head." "That'll do it," I add. As we walk back up, a row of ten college girls pees in the sand a few feet away. They don't seem to care who sees. Clark and I glance over as we walk back up. "You see that?" I ask out loud. "I see it."

Answers Clark. "You got to love Saint Patty's Day in AC." Clark nods, and we head up the stairs. Now back up with the girls, Clark puts his arm around his girlfriend Rachel with the cherry blond hair. I come up behind Rose and do the same. She puts her head on my shoulder, and the eight of us stop and watch the parade. Levi and his wife and son are on a party truck. "Yo Clark, it's Levi," I shout. Clark and I call out to him and wave. Levi puts his hand on his son's shoulder while he waves. "Hey, look, it's Clark and crazy Mike." He says with a smile.

The last ride goes by, and our group walks down the boardwalk. "Who's Levi?" Rachel asks. "Our old boss from Phat's." I answer. "What is Phat's?" Asks Pam. Clark smiles. "It's where me and Devaney went to college." The rest of us laugh as the parade comes to an end. "Where we going, guys?" says one of the girls. "I got to eat!" says Gary, "You guys hungry?" "Always!" Answers the group as we walk down the boardwalk. "What are you guys doing tomorrow?" Clark shouts. "Nothing." I answer quickly. "Want to drink?" Clark nods. "Definitely." That night we all dance like poetic assholes on a dance floor at a random bar. Rose does a handstand while I land a backflip and show off some fancy footwork.

Maverick moved to California a year later. He got a job in a college as, get this, a librarian. Clark and I never understood it, but he makes a good living and is happily married to his girlfriend Lynn, who towers a foot over him at all times. Clark and Rachel married as well and still live in the area. Clark sells slot machines and, in his spare time, continues to surf, golf, and drink beers with me.

Teak and I walk into a random classroom at school. "Delivery!" I shout. "Thanks, Mike, and Teak. You can just put them in the cabinet." I nod to the teacher as I load the cabinet. Teak pulls some glasses off a kid sitting on the floor. The kid is asleep with his back against the wall. "Teak, leave him alone," I yell. Teak sighs, takes off his own glasses, and puts them on the boy before patting him on the head. He puts on the new glasses, and a big smile spreads across his face. He looks around the new world as if seeing it for the first time. Teak and I walk out and down the hallway.

Later, Teak puts the final shape on his light board in Jazz's class. "All done." Teak says simply. "Teak, you did it!" Yells Jazz. "Good job, dude," I tell him. "Wow, I knew you could." Jazz stops and looks at Teak's new glasses, "Where'd he get them!?" "They're his." I lie. No, they're not. "Teak, where'd you get those glasses?" Jazz asks. "Jamie." He

says. "Alright, come on." Jazz adds. "What are you doing? He can see

now!" I shout. "Their Jamie's. He needs them!" Jazz answers. I stand up

and grab scissors from Yen. "Needs them for what, eating string cheese!?"

I say. "Let's go, Teak." Says Jazz. "Ok." He answers Jazz as she leaves the

room. "Sorry, bud," I tell him. "Say bye to Mike!" Jazz says from the

hallway. "No, Mike," he says. "Pencil." Teak shouts. Jazz cracks up and

sticks her head back into the room. "Pencil?" I ask with an attitude. "Yea,

Pencil!" Teak says again. "What did you just call me?" I yell, half kidding.

Jazz continues to laugh as Teak says the name once more. "Oh, yea!" I

shout. "Well, then, now you're Booger!"I say. "No, Booger." Teak says as

he taps his chin. "Say bye to Pencil!" Yells Jazz. Teak waves. "Bye,

Pencil!" "See ya later, Booger!" I wave back.

Later, I eat a cheeseburger at Jazz's desk. I drip mustard and

ketchup everywhere. "Whoops," I say sarcastically. Jack gets up from

working with his kid. "Alright, man, I got to go." He pulls a suit out of the

closet and heads to the door. Jazz comes in with some of the kids and says,

"You going to make that money!" "Yup!" answers Jack. "Mike, how

come you don't get on that gravy train? Half the school got hired, I'm sure you would." Jazz adds. "I never went to college," I tell her with a mouthful of burger. "You don't have to! You just need experience!" Jazz says again. "I keep telling him that," Jack adds, "Alright, peace." "You know Mike, you'd like double your pay." Jazz says as she helps a small girl with a puzzle and adds, "You really want to work here forever." "Jack's working like twelve-hour days!" I interrupt. "Yea, but he's making bank!" Jazz says while she comes to her desk and looks at the mustard and ketchup. "What the hell is this shit!" "Wasn't me," I answer with a burger in hand. "Move over!" Jazz pushes me over and squeezes in the chair while stealing a fry. She turns on the computer. "Let's get you a real job." A week or two later, I sit in a chair wearing a suit and tie. How did Jazz talk me into this, I think? I guess she was just looking out for my best interests. Asshole. "Mr. Devaney, they'll see you now." Says a secretary. Looking unhappy, I get up and walk into the office.

NO MORE DRIFTWOOD

The next day in the woods. The hot summer sun shines down on me as I stand on a branch. I'm wearing a tank top, boardshorts, and my surfing booties. Holly bear hugs the trunk of a thick tree next to mine. He yells as he starts to slide lower on the tree. "Hold on, dude!" I shout as two German Shepherds bark up Holly's tree. "Help me out, man!" He yells. "With what!?" I ask while looking for a loose branch to throw. "I don't know, something!" "Well, what the hell you pick that tree for, man? There are no branches!" I yell back. As Holly slides lower, the dogs nip within inches of him. A rifle shot rings out of nowhere, and the dogs run away. Holly and I hop to the ground as a hunter comes out of the brush. "Do you guys know whose property this is? Those dogs would tear you apart." The hunter says. "No, but thanks, man," I tell him, "We're outta here." "Stick to the path." He says before disappearing through the trees.

"I think it's this way." I turn around to Holly, who is picking up a big piece of driftwood. "What the fuck are you doing? Let's GO!" I shout. Disappointed, Holly drops the driftwood and covers it with sticks and leaves as if it needed help blending into the woods. "I hope no one takes it." He complains. We come out to a path that leads to the bay. A two-man motorboat floats in the water. "Finally," I say, clipping my pocket knife back to my shorts. "My dad knows the guy who owns this property. We would have been fine." Holly claims. "Is that what you were gonna tell the fucking K9s as they ate your face!?" I ask as I drag in the anchor. Holly starts the engine as a plastic box hits the floor of the boat. I pick it up. "Is Uncle Joe a diabetic?" I ask, holding the insulin. Holly and I look around the small boat, and Holly scratches his head as he realizes his honest mistake. "Whose boat is this, Holly?" I ask with a straight face. Holly shrugs his shoulders, and I shake my head while cracking open a cold beer in the hot sun. "No more driftwood. I state. "I know," Holly answers with disappointment. He sits down, and we pull away.

Holly's trailer. In Holly's bedroom, we jam on our electric guitars. Our amps are turned up, and the trailer is shaking. We work on a transition to the chorus of our rock song. Now nighttime, in a garage with a bass player and a drummer, we play the chorus to our original song, *STAIRS*. A small fan gathering sits outside the open garage around a bonfire and cooler full of ice-cold Yinglings. Cigarettes are lit as we take a break and join the small gathering of friends that finish a story. "Yo, that's nuts," says Holly's cousin Steve. "Hey Devaney, tell us a story!" He shouts." "Na." "Oh, come on, says a random girl sitting with Holly's brothers. "A real one!" Says Steve. The crowd cheers me on, and I give in. "Ok." "Um." "Dildo Boy!" Holly shouts from the cooler. I shake my head, but it's too late. The crowd has spoken. I chug my beer and grab a handful of dirt from the ground below my beach chair. "In honor of the midnight society, I call this The Tale of Dildo Boy." I throw the dirt over the fire and tell the short story I tell you now.

I was nineteen and bored on a random summer eve. My mom and Aunt Lynn sit in the dining room as I lay on the couch wearing nothing but shorts. "Let's go!" Shouts Dad, who enters the house. "Where?" I ask. Uncle Pete's having a bonfire for your cousin Heather." "I'm good," I state. "Oh, come on, bud, you know those Pineys know how to party," Dad says as he heads out the door. "Up to you." He adds. "He makes a good point." I think as Aunt Lynn throws a picture of the invitation made by Pete's wife, my Aunt Sue. Aunt Sue loves making birthday cards more than any person alive. "That's Heather?" I ask, not recognizing the cousin I haven't seen in ten years. The picture included Heather and her girlfriends in daisy dukes and bikini tops. "Her and her girlfriends are having guy problems." Aunt Lynn says politely. "WAIT UP, DAD!" I shout. "That's NOT FUNNY, MIKE!" Mom yells as I jump off the porch. I grab a tank top out of my station wagon, and off we go.

Later that night, Dad, Tim, and I drink at the bonfire. We saw Tim at Wawa. I asked if he wanted to get drunk in the Pine Barrens, and here he is. "Pete, we're out of firewood!" Shouts a random kid drinking with us now at the party. "Grab the kitchen table!" Says Pete as he flips some burgers. At first, I thought he was kidding, but sure enough, seconds later, the boy and some friends began ripping apart the table they pulled from Pete's kitchen. "I'll never doubt Pete again." I thought to myself as they chucked it in the fire. While mingling with Heather and her girlfriends, I heard something from the woods. A loud dirt bike. The boy on it pulled up in front of the party and hit the kickstand.

Tim and I look at each other and then back at the bike. On it are pornographic air fresheners and a giant rubber dildo shaped like a penis, no less. It flopped up and down as the bike came to a stop. "Aw shit." Says one of the girlfriends, "It's Greg." "Is he gay?" Asks Tim as he looks at the still bouncing rubber dick. "Nope, just insane." Answers Heather. "I want nothing to do with that guy." I think to myself as he drags an innocent bystander headfirst into his dildo cycle. The kid was my age, had messy brown hair, and wore jeans and a dirty t-shirt with a pair of work boots on his feet. We continue to party, and eventually, Dad looks at his watch. "Ok, have fun, guys." He says as he walks to his car. "Oh, and

don't pass out," Dad adds as he points to Dildo Boy rubbing his bare ass

on a kid passed out by the chicken coop. Tim and I laugh and wave

goodbye. Pete had work in a few hours at the casino, so he hit the hay,

leaving my cousin, her girlfriend, me, Tim, and of course, Greg. "Ok, it's

time to leave, Greg." Says Heather. "Oh, yea, who's gonna make me?" He

says as he smacks the ass of Heather's girlfriend. *I've only known the girl*

for a couple of hours, but as a dumb kid, that's all it took. "Me," I shout as

I toss my beer.

The two of us walk out to a clearing by the small barn. We stand

eye to eye as I put up my beer gloves. He puts his fists up as well, and we

start. Dildo boy lunges forward and dives for a tackle. I grab him around

the neck in mid-air and slam his face into the dirt while landing on my

back. We jump to our feet, and he dives at me again. I'd rather be on my

feet in a fight, but I guess he was more of a wrestler. Now on my back, I

put up my fists and forearms to cover the blows. I somehow get the upper

hand and flip him on his back. I throw a hard right hook and clobber him

on the side of the face. I hold my fist up for another punch but refrain.

"You all done," I ask. "Yea, I'm done." He says simply. We stand up, and he walks to his dirt bike. He turns it on and peels off in my direction. "Oh

Shit." I think as I move out of the way. Dildo Boy does the same and only

spits in my direction. He probably missed, but it pissed me off, and I

grabbed a broken 2x4 and chucked it at the bike. It bounces off a tree, and

he rode off into the woods.

As I walk back to the girls, I feel a sting in my back, followed by

something wet. "You dumb ass," I call myself while wiping the blood.

The 2x4 had a nail in it and must have connected during the throw, slicing

a nice gash in my back and side. "Come on, I'll stitch you up, says

Heather's girlfriend. "Are you a nurse?" I ask. "No." She says with a

smile. "My dad's a drunk. I stitch him up all the time." Laughter is heard

as I end the story of Dildo boy.

Years later, I ran into Dildo Boy at a random party. I figured it was

round two when we stood face to face, but instead, he put out his hand

with a grin and said, "That was a good fight, dude." I shook his hand, and

for the rest of the party, we ran the beer pong table.

Last May, Uncle Pete passed away while having sex with his wife.

Although very sad, I still like to think that's how he'd want to leave. One

of the last times I saw Pete, he was at the inspection station. His truck had just failed inspection for a broken taillight in his back window. He asked

the man inspecting his truck if that light was needed at all. The man

answered "no," and sure enough, Pete reached into the truck and ripped

out the light with his bare hands. "There," Pete tells the inspection person.

"I passed." He waved goodbye and drove off with his new pup and a shiny

new inspection sticker.

SINGER SONGWRITER

Holly sits on the porch of his trailer. I pull up and get out of my car

with my Les Paul in its case. "I hope you're done landscaping," I shout.

Holly nods. "Good, we got time for a beer?" I ask. "We got all the time in

the world." He answers sadly. "What do you mean?" "The drummer

bailed," Holly tells me as he tosses his beer cap. "For today?" I ask with

anticipation. Holly shakes his head, and I kick over a box of kid toys.

"FUCK! Fucking drummers, what'd he say?" I ask. "Something about

taking care of his kid," Holly tells me as I sit at the porch table and shake

my head. "What an asshole," I add, "So, what now?" Holly asks. "We

finish the album, that's what." I interrupt. "At Telly's? It'll cost us for seven songs." Holly mutters. It looks like he has been drinking for a while. He stares off in the distance. I looked at Holly closely. "Is that you?" I ask. "YEA!" He shouts. "Oh, cool. I'm just checking since you started drinking early," I add. "Well, it's me." He says as I head inside the trailer.

Something I forgot to mention about Holly; usually, he can drink all day and be perfectly fine. However, a light switch goes off every once in a while, and he isn't himself anymore. Later that day, I walk outside after taking a piss and see Holly is face to face with the outside freezer. He draws a smiley face in the dust and points at it. "I want you to say that to my FACE!" He shouts. I slip away quietly and drive off, knowing what's to come. As I do so, I hear Holly yelling at his freezer. "I told you, your teacher wasn't there, DIDN'T I? I didn't FUCK her!" he rants randomly at the inanimate object. *I'm not really sure who this other guy is. All I know is that I don't like him.*

Sometimes, Holly was calm. For example, I place a hot dog in the microwave as Holly sits on the couch watching TV with a beer in his hand. "You want one?" "I'm good." He answers. I remove the hot dog from the microwave and turn around to see Holly sitting on the floor, Indian Style, in a state of meditation. I take my hot dog to go. Other times he wasn't as calm. I sit on the porch at night. Holly is inside. "Stupid fucking CHAAAIIRRR!" He yells. The legs of the chair come through the trailer window, so I leave. It didn't matter what happened during his blackouts; I knew he wouldn't be Holly again until the next day.

The next morning, I walk onto the porch and sit next to Holly. He pulls out a stack of hundred-dollar bills. "I got some cash for recording." He tells me. "Where the hell did you get that?!" I ask. He shakes his head as he answers. "I don't know." Drummer or not, we jam out on the porch that day with our guitars. Holly and I eventually finished the album. We procrastinated like usual on getting it out to the public but had it at the top of our to-do list. Sometime later, Holly had another blackout. It was to be the last one he ever had. Holly walks outside, waving at no one. He gets in his Jeep and drives away.

I drive in my car in a collared shirt and black tie as I pull up to Holly's trailer. I don't look happy. I walk inside, where a four-year-old boy plays with a handgun. "Hey buddy, can I see that?" The boy hands me the gun and runs outside. I check the empty chamber and put it in the waist of my pants. I walk to the back of the trailer. "Hello?" I stand in front of the open bathroom door and look into the bedroom. No one is there. I sniff and make a face. I look over and see Holly sitting on the toilet, waving. "HEY!" Holly says with a smile. "Aw, man," I shout, "Close the door. You stink!" Holly laughs as I walk away. With Holly's right arm hanging by his side, he grabs the toilet paper and unravels it with his teeth. I sit in the shed now in a tank top and shorts. Holly opens the outside door with his left hand from inside. He closes the door with a bag of tobacco in his mouth and a water bottle tucked in his left arm. I blow on a freshly handmade green shiny cherry burl pipe as Holly walks over.

After Holly lost the use of his right arm in his near-fatal accident, he quit drinking. He was told that he would never play the guitar again. He still has some surgeries scheduled, so we stay optimistic. "Your kid found your gun," I tell him as I pull it from the waist of the back of my pants. Holly's son leans in the doorway of the shed. "Yea, it's ok. There are no bullets anywhere." Says Holly. "You sure?" Holly nods, and I unwillingly hand the unloaded gun back to his son, who runs off with it. "Play with it inside!" Holly yells. "Is that for Rose?" He asks as I sand the pipe. "Yup." I answer. "How's the Hanky Panky?" He asks. I chuckle before answering, "It's frequent with extended duration." Holly smiles, "Nice."

"You allowed to have that thing?" I ask, referring to the gun. "It's old as shit." He replies. "I didn't think so," I say with a grin. "The end is coming, man. We're going to need it. You still have the one your pop gave you and your dad." Holly continues his insane rant. "Yea," I answer, "It'll probably blow up in my hand before the world's end, though." Later that day, Holly holds a baby in his kitchen as we laugh about a story we both remembered from childhood. Holly's ex-wife curls her hair in the back bedroom. "MICHAEL! Where's the hairdryer?" She asks him. Holly rubs his bald head and replies, "I don't know! You think I dry my balls with it!?" Holly shouts as I crack up. "You guys getting back together?" I ask. "Nah," he says with an unlit cigarette in his mouth.

With no job, cable, or the ability to play guitar, Holly went into a deep depression and started talking about this "End of the World" shit. He would sit and dwell on the only time in his life when he claimed he was truly happy. He refers to the time when he was with a girl named Annie. AKA Julie Jailbait. The law forbade contact between the two, and though I thought he wouldn't last a week without seeing her, he actually went TEN years without a word from her or himself. One day recently, he ran into her at the market.

Holly holds a bag with his teeth and puts some fruit in with his left hand. He sees Annie from across the store, and the two smile. Now outside in the parking lot, they sit in a parked car and talk. It turned out that she had felt the same for him as he had for her. The only problem was, on paper, Holly was still married to his ex. Holly and Annie begin to make out in the car as she climbs on top of him and takes off her shirt. So now, all Holly had to do was get a divorce, lift the restraining order, kick Annie's deadbeat boyfriend out, get married, have kids, and live happily ever after. All of this should take him a week. My friend Mike Holly, to this day, is able to surprise me with his acute ability to make wise decisions. He's slowly growing up to adulthood. I can admit I'm not quite there myself, but the day Holly grows up will be the day the earth stands still.

A sunny morning on the bay. September is here once again, and my father and I fish each in our own kayaks. As Dad unhooks a flounder, I start to reel one in myself. Dad puts his own fish in his kayak and paddles over to help me net my own. As my fish flops to the bottom of the plastic kayak, we rejoice with a smile.

I wake up next to Rose in my bed. I hit the alarm clock that reads *5:00 am* and get up. Rose turns over, "Don't I get a cuddle?" "I'll be late," I say out loud. "Aww, ok." As she turns around, I jump back into bed with a laugh that is shortly matched by her own. "Yay!" eventually, I shower, get dressed, and leave for work. I get back home at 7:00 pm. I get out of the car and walk up the front steps. A few hours later, I wake up and hit the alarm clock that reads *5:00 am*. I shower, dress, and drive to work. That night I get home at 7:00 pm and walk into the house. Rinse and repeat. I knew someday this was a possibility. I was finally living the mundane and boring career that funds life.

I leave school in a shirt and tie. It's around 3:00 pm. I pull my car up to a random house and get out for a home case, which is similar to the work I do at school. I knock on the door, and someone lets me in. I put it off for so long, promising myself that I would make it in life doing, well, not this. The career I have pays well and can definitely be rewarding at times, but it's never enough. What do I do? Well, I help kids with disabilities work on their behavior. Lucky for me, they hire off experience. With all that said, the long hours and focus take their toll on my shitty companions. It's fall now and getting dark. I do my blow tic and walk up the porch steps. Whether it was what I had planned in life or not didn't matter at the end of the day. I think to myself, "At least I have Rose."

ROSE

If I compare all my favorite hobbies in life, one reigns supreme. Rose laughs in the kitchen of her parent's house. Making Rose laugh. I add an impression to my comedic comment, and Rose leans on the counter as she belly laughs. I grab the salmon she has knocked over, and with my other hand, I catch her as she jumps on me with a hug. Making her laugh, I will admit, is a skill I excel at, from morning through night. The love for summer is something we have very much in common. We make the best of cold weather either way, but it's not our first choice.

This next memory is of a snow day as we sit at a table filled with beer bottles, board games, and cards. The stereo plays *Have You Ever Seen the Rain*. The song echoes through the house. Rose technically lived with her parents but slept over at my house three or four nights a week. Rose takes the salmon we dropped and puts it on the counter after giving me a kiss. I season some asparagus as she turns up *All Along the Watch*

Tower on the stereo. In summer, we wake up, do our thing, and before noon we're out the door and on the road, whether a destination was set or not. On those days, Rose would ask where I wanted to go, and I would simply say, "To water." If we weren't doing our own thing, we always had family and friends to visit. Rose has a rare hobby of exploring abandoned houses to see if they're worth fixing up. Once in a while, the homes weren't actually abandoned, and the family would kindly ask us to leave. Either way, it was a satisfying summer day. Tent camping, the lodge, lake, beach, or the docks by the bay. Neither of us is too picky.

As the asparagus cooks, Rose puts in the lobsters and requests a dance-off. At this point, we're both a little tipsy, but I promise not to drop her, and I don't. Dinner time is always an adventure in itself. Her parents' house, my parent's house, friends' homes, or the pub. These were the obvious options, but my favorite by far was when we had a house all to ourselves. Lobsters are ready, and the table is set for a smorgasbord of whatever we grabbed at the market. I pull out Rose's chair, and she thanks me with a smile as I wrap her up and bring her in for a kiss. Rose knows I'm more of a morning guy, but date night is a different story. With that said, the rest of the night is for my memory only.

Springtime's here once again. I pull up to my parent's house. As I get out of the car, a truck goes by and the man driving calls out, "Mikey!" "Yo Brian! Cabin trips set, bro." I say. "Fuck yeah," he shouts. "Say hi to everyone!" I tell him, referring to the wife and kids with whom I've shared many dinners in the past. Years earlier, I met Brian as I cut through my old shortcut to Jeb's. Instead of yelling at the new stranger in his yard, Brain greeted me with a can of beer. We've been friends ever since.

Brian pulls into a nearby driveway and throws up the peace sign. I walk up the porch to where Mom reads a book. Mom puts it down. "Hey Hunny, how are you?" She asks. "Hey, Mom, I'm ok." "You've been working a lot. How's that going?" "Sucks." "Yeah, it's no fun sometimes." She adds. How are you guys?" I ask. "We're good," she replies. "I'm working with the little guys at school now, and Dad's getting ready for his backpacking hike with his buddies." "You going with him?" Mom asks, "You guys had a lot of fun the last time you went with him." "Yeah, it was great, but I can't make it this time. I suck." I state. "No, he understands. So, how's Rose?" Mom asks. "Ok, I guess." We had an augment about something." "What about?" "Stuff," I answer. "Aw, well, I'm sure you guys will figure it out," Mom says with a grin.

With everything said and done, nothing's perfect in anyone. There are always things to improve. The goal, in my opinion, is to keep those things small. I don't consider myself naive. Every relationship experiences arguments and unapproved characteristics. To me, however, Rose is the sunshine. She glows wherever she goes. She also always has a smile. Except when she doesn't. On a blue moon, Rose hits a wall of sadness. It only lasts a day or two until, like the wave from a monarch's wing, it's gone. During this blue moon, I do my very best to show her nothing but kindness. I do this because I love her but also because when Rose isn't happy, I'm not happy. I guess this could be a selfish reason, but either way, when Rose is unhappy, I wish nothing but to be the monarch. I pull up and head into my house. I walk upstairs to my room. I take my tie off and throw it on the bed where there is now only one pillow. Unfortunately, it wasn't enough. Rose is gone.

AN OLD FRIEND

The next day I sit alone at a local bar. I check my smartphone for the time and look at the door as the bartender fills my drink. Today I'm meeting a friend. He is late. *Years ago, I was having a bad day. I had spent my last dollar on a round of drinks for Jeb and me. Jeb noticed I was off and asked if there was anything he could do. Kidding around, I said something about never swimming in tropical water. After leaving the bar that day, Jeb emptied his bank account, filled his station wagon to the brim, and we were on the road. A day and a half later, we were swimming through a reef in the Florida Keys.* I take a sip of beer and put the glass down on a coaster that reads *Valley Pub*. Scribbled on the coaster is an amount of cash that Jeb owes me. *It's unfortunate how sometimes we forget.*

"Yo, DEBO!" Yells a familiar voice. I see my old friend, and my annoyed face turns to a smile as I wave him down. Jeb and I sit out in the sun at a high top. It's around two in the afternoon. Jeb lights a cigarette as we each drink a beer. "So, what's up, man!? I haven't seen you in forever. You avoiding me or something," Jeb asks, half kidding. "Na dude, I just work too much," I tell him. "Yea, you said they pay pretty good, though, huh?" Jeb adds as he puffs his smoke. "Yea, it's good," I answer with a nod. "How's your DJ stuff going?" I ask. "It's wedding season now, but I was hurting for a while. Hey, I'm sorry, Mike, but I don't have that cash I owe ya." Jeb states. "It's all good," I say out loud. "You hurting?" He interrupts. "I'm just backed up on some shit," I reply. "I hear that. So, how's your girl?" Jeb asks. "I don't know, man, "I tell him. "Yeah," Jeb says loudly and adds, "They're a pain in the ass sometimes, but you know what they say..." "That we're a pain in the ass sometimes," I answer with a grin. Jeb laughs out loud and grabs his beer. "How's Trish?" I ask. "We're good." Jeb pauses for a moment. "We're moving to Florida together." He mentions. "Really!?" I ask as I look up at Jeb with a concerned look. "Yea, there's nothing left for me here, D," He answers with a straight face that catches me off guard. "No, I mean...Yea, dude! I think that would be really good for you guys!" I say with my chin up. "There are lots of opportunities," Jeb adds, "My mom said we can stay at her snowbird house until we find a place." "That's awesome, man," I tell him as he downs his beer. "You ready, bro?" He asks, "I got the next one." "Let's do it," I answer swiftly, downing my own. Hours later, Jeb and I pull out of the bar parking lot. Jeb goes right, and I go left. He beeps the horn repeatedly as I wave my arm out the window.

A few nights later, I walk out of a bar and head to my car with only the street lights to guide me. I'm drunk. I get in my car and drive away.

While driving, I see the lights of a cop car in my rearview. "Fuck." I pull

over and wait for the cop to walk to my window. "License and

registration." He says. I hand them over and try to look sober but fail.

"Where are we going tonight?" the officer says. "Home," I answer. "Says

here... you live on East Field." He says. "It's my parent's house. I never

changed it." The cop studies my license as his demeanor changes.

"Mikey?" "Huh?" I ask, caught off guard. "You go by Mikey?" Asks the

cop. "Sometimes." I shrug. "Did you live behind a girl named Annabelle?"

His question puts an instant smile on my face. "Yeah, man," I tell him.

"Holy shit, dude! She tells me all these crazy stories about you guys." He

tells me. "Really!?" I interrupt. "Yeah, man, I'm her husband, Nick. It's

good to meet you, man!" He says with his hand out. "Didn't you fall into a

well or some shit?" He asks as we shake. "I still got the scar. You call her

Annabelle?" I ask. "Damn straight, I do." He says with a grin. "Did you

ever?" He asks I shake my head. "Only once." Nick laughs out loud and

leans on my hood. "How is she?" I ask. "Yea, she's good. You live close?"

He asks. "Like half a mile," I answer. "Cool, I'll follow ya, you fucking

reek." "Thanks!" I laugh. "Hey, tell Hill I said hi!" I shout as he walks to

his cruiser. He nods. "Absolutely." The smile that I needed that night stayed on my face for the ride home as I remembered random shit that Hill had gotten us into at a young age. My old friend Hill had gotten me OUT of trouble for the first time ever, and she didn't even know it.

I jump through the door of Jazz's classroom. "What's up?!" I yell. "What are you doing here!?" She asks. "Just saying hi," I answer while approaching her desk and eating some of her lunch. "We share the same house, dumb ass." She says. "I haven't seen you in a week." I interrupt, "You're off at lover boy's." "It's better than our shit hole." She points out as she grabs her sandwich back. "True dat. Well, I really came to see Teak. Where are they?" I say as I look at the empty class. "They're at gym, but I don't know about Teak. They moved him." Jazz says. "Why?" "I don't know, man, but I heard he's not doing great." Jazz says with a look of worry. "He'll be alright," I say as I wave from the doorway. What to say about Jazz? Well, her and lover boy are no doubt getting married. His name is Cory, and thankfully one of his favorite hobbies is breaking Jazz's balls. This works out for me because, eventually, doing it myself would have gotten boring. I'd never say this to Jazz's face, but to be honest, she's a good-looking girl that's fun to be around. She has a great sense of humor, and her lunch is always on point. Most of all, she's a good friend, for I owe her more favors than I have to offer. Someday though, I plan on paying them back. Just not today.

In a different classroom, Teak looks around as I knock on the door window. I point at him with a smile. I enter the class and wave to the teacher, who is reading to the rest of the class. "Teak! What's up, buddy?" Teak looks at me with a blank stare. "Hello?" I shout, bending down and getting in his face. "Booger! It's Pencil!" I tell him. Teak looks at me but says nothing. "What's wrong with him!?" I ask. "I don't know, Mike." Says the teacher. "I know he had a couple of bad seizures, or maybe the meds." I bend down and try one more time. "Teak, who am I?" Teak looks at me and studies my face. "I don't know." He answers. I stand up with disappointment, and Teak walks away.

I sit now in the sensory room with Dani. Her kid swings. "I love my job!" She says. "Everyone's always bitching here but not me. I don't think those ladies like me," Dani adds. "Yea, because you're hot with big fake tits," I state with half sarcasm. Dani laughs as I get up. "Ok, I got to go. I'll see ya." I tell her. "Ok, say hi to Rose for me." She says. I nod and walk to the door. As I open the door, I stop and look at the old poker table that Rose and I had spent many hours at. On top of the table is a mess of scattered cards. I put my head down and walk out of the room. As I drive home, I make a frown. I try to brush it away, but it's too strong. I start to cry. I let it out. I let it all out.

Back home. I sit on the patio with a beer on the table. The patio is next to an old wooden fence. Branches from the trees give it some shade, but the sun shines through and onto my weary face. My eyes are red as I look through to nothing. A high pitch hum is heard. I don't know where from, maybe in my head.

This is the lowest point in my life. You wouldn't know just by looking. I'm just some guy sitting alone, drinking a beer, and smoking a cigarette. *One man or woman's inner demons cannot be measured or judged by another. Someone always has it worse than you do. This is important for me to say, for it has gotten me through some of my weaker days.* Today though, it doesn't mean shit. Today I hate myself more than anyone in the world. I'm not quite sure why, but I do. Not only that but there was nothing to blame for who I was. I wanted to blame my shitty companions for everything. They have never left me and are a constant reminder from the time I wake to the time I sleep. I remember, at a young age, hoping that Tic would leave me, but he never did. Much like waiting

422

out a common cold or flu. I just wanted to be me again. I know it was so long ago, but I remember what it felt like. Not only would my shitty companions stay to torment me, but they would become me. If I hate them and blame them, I will always hate myself. Either way, I'll never give up.

Among other things, I was confused and frustrated about why Rose had left. I was good to her and had few doubts about spending the rest of my life with her; today, there were zero. A feeling that I can't describe was tearing me apart. I have heard that a man cannot truly love another until he can love himself. For whatever reason, just then, sitting in that chair looking out to the sun, I was able to do just that. But it was too late.

I lay in my bed, looking at the ceiling. The moonlight shines across. All the anger of Rose's departure had left. When this happened, I was able to see the little things I could improve. Either way, I wasn't letting her go without a fight. Morning time. I still lay awake and look at the ceiling. I was going after her. There was nothing that couldn't be undone. I had to tell her everything. I jump up and grab my keys. The sun had risen, and I couldn't wait any longer. I had no clue what I would say to her. No matter what happens, I needed one more chance to show her how much she meant to me.

Rose's house. I get out of my car as Rose walks to meet me. We sit on two logs in the clearing by the ruins of her old tree fort. I am done with what I needed to say. We look at each other, both with serious faces. A long moment passes before Rose stands up and walks to me. She sits in my lap, smiles, and hugs me. It ends with a kiss. The most important kiss of my life.

THE DINING ROOM

Mom and Dad's house. The house I grew up in has its windows open, and a sweet summer breeze flows over the dining room table where Rose and I eat dinner with my family. Voices and laughter fill the table as we eat. Fred Jr and a baby girl named Leah sit by Sis. Every so often, I think of where I would be without the parents I was given. I can't think of any scenario where I would still be alive. Faith finished college with a history degree. She has always shared the same sense of adventure as Sis and me, and I'm sure she will follow it as far as it takes her. The boy sitting next to her is her new boyfriend. I've only known him a week, but I'm guessing he'll be around for a while. After so many years of helping others for free, my sister Cecelia got a job as a social worker. Fred Jr likes to build things, and little Leah can't talk yet, but something tells me she's going to have a good sense of humor.

The inside of a front door to an old-style small house. The door's stained-glass window has blue and purple flowers. As for Rose and me. The front door opens, and I come in wearing a shirt and tie. "Baby-az!" I shout. Eggs and bacon cook as the morning sun shines through the kitchen window directly on Rose. She's wearing a T-shirt with flowers on it and yoga pants. A tiny kitten chews on my foot as I put my work bag down. "Ah, Hey! Get out of here." I gently push it by the butt with my foot. Rose enters the living room of the small house, which looks to not yet be fully furnished. Some plants, chairs, and my Hawaiian sling hang on a wall next to the old wooden Jamaican man's head. A small brown couch and a TV are set up as well.

"Hey, love!" I say while getting a kiss from Rose as the kitten chews on our feet. "Is Faith ever going to come back for this guy?" Rose asks. "Something tells me he's ours now," I answer. "Aw, she doesn't want him?" Rose asks as she picks up the kitten. "I think it's more like she got it and now can't have it," I tell Rose with a smirk. "Mmm, smells good," I say. "Come and get it!" Rose shouts. "Ok, give me five," I say as I go into the bathroom and turn on the shower. I open the closet door and pull an engagement ring out of my pocket. I reach up and hide it in the lip of the closet. The water runs down my face in the shower. I get out and put on boardshorts, flips, and a tank top. "Aw, that's better," I say as I come out to the dining room and sit with Rose as we drink orange juice and eat bacon and eggs. "How was work?" Rose asks, "I thought you said you would be late today." "They canceled," I answer. "Nice! Well, I already told my sisters that I would have a girl's day. I'm sorry." Rose says. "It's all good. I'll find someone to hang with." As I answer, I see something on the shelf in the living room. "What?" I get up and walk over to it. "Oh, No! It was supposed to be a surprise!" She tells me. "Where did you find this!?" I ask as I pick up the plaque. "Your mom found it in the attic." Rose says, "Shit, I knew I should have hid it. I was going to frame it for you." "You're the best," I tell her. The plaque has a picture of a bison, and under it reads. *Best Director, Mike Devaney*. On the shelf are also some VHSs and a glossy sheet with images of my high school films. Rose puts her chin on my shoulder. "Is that you?" She says as she points to a picture of me backflipping off a roof. "Yup." I laugh. "Now I know why your lower back always hurts," Rose says with a smile. "Who are you shooting at?" Rose asks. "Bad Guys," I state. "I can't believe you never showed me these," Rose says as she heads to the bedroom. "I thought I lost them." "Well, tonight, I say we have a marathon in the game room!" She shouts as I nod, "It's a date." "And write some new ones. I want to make movies!" Rose shouts from the bedroom. "You're going to be my star?" I ask. "Hell yea!" Rose answers. "Ok then," I say with a smile as I check out the images. "Tim and I had some epic fight scenes," I tell her. "What are the other movies about?" Asks Rose. I think for a second before answering. "Well. High School." I see a pic of Jeb strapped with homemade blood packets and laugh. "Time chasers, though, was the..." I stop mid-sentence. "Shit, Jeb! I have to go, right..." Rose comes in and gives me a look. "I'm sorry, Hunny," Rose says. "SHIT!" I yell. "They left this morning." I'm such an asshole!" I shout. "No, you're not! He understands." Rose tells me. "I can't believe I missed him," I say. "We can visit!" "Yeah, but I should have been here when he stopped by," I say aloud. "He left you something." Rose mentions. "Oh, the cash!? I told him not to worry about that," I say as I shake my head. "It's in the game room. Go check it out." Rose says with a grin.

Later that morning, I find myself in a chair in the backyard. The hot sun shines down on me as I scroll through my contacts for a playmate. I sip my cold fruit smoothie and stare at Jeb's name on my phone. Remembering what Rose had told me, I head inside and walk to the game room. The game room. Hundreds of old game cartridges and consoles cover a wall. I open the door and look around. I see something on the TV stand by the window. The window is open, and the summer breeze blows the blinds causing them to gently tap on the wood window frame. The sunlight shines through and onto a small laptop with white, yellow, and orange butterflies painted on the front. A green sticky note is stuck on the top of the closed laptop. I walk up, look at the computer, grab the sticky note and read it.

I sit now in the living room on the couch. With the laptop on a chair, I open it up. The screen saver pops up, and I instantly smile. It's a picture of our old tree fort in its prime. I look away and rub my chin as a wind chime is heard through a screen window in my living room. I open up the word pad and start to type with two fingers. The day moves on as I take breaks to make coffee, eat and chug water. I rub my chin, and I'm back to typing. Around five o'clock, I crack a beer and lean on the fridge before sitting back down to type. As the sun sets, Rose, walks through the door. "Hey, whatcha doing?" She asks as I stare at the screen with bloodshot eyes. Rose jumps on me and looks at the screen, "Hey, pretty. Nothing, just writing down some funny shit me and Jeb did as kids." I say. "I'm done for now, though. My brain hurts. "Strange Times with Mike and Jeb." She reads. "No, it's a working title," I add. "Aw, you don't like it?" Asks Rose. "Maybe, I don't know. It sounds like we're butt fucking." Rose laughs out loud. "Well, I know you'll think of something." She says as she gets up and heads to the kitchen. "You eat yet?" "Not really," I answer while thinking to myself. I look over and see the kitten playing with the sticky note from Jeb. I get up and walk over to it as the kitten runs away. After picking it off the floor, I sit back at the laptop and look at the note. It reads...

What's up I GOT TICS BOYA!? I hope this comes in handy. Talk to you soon, bro. Your best friend, JEB.

I look back at the screen and erase the title I had before typing a new one. Now satisfied, I type under the title. *Chapter One* You know what? I think I'll save this last section for the end. With that said, I believe it's time for me to say goodbye. These next few paragraphs are the last that will be set in stone for the moments after will be my future. If you're still with me, I thank you. In a strange way, it's as though you have been with me my entire life. If you are one of the rare handful of people who actually have been, then I thank you from the bottom of my heart. A pan in the kitchen drops to the floor, and I look up at Rose. I will close this laptop, head into the kitchen, grab Rose and kiss her. I'm an in-the-moment kind of guy, after all.

I GOT TICS BOYA

Springtime. An old man splits wood with an ax by the entrance of the woods that leads to the old mansion. As the old man takes some wood inside, a young woman peeks her head around the corner of his house. She sneaks through the weeds and comes to a rusty old metal grill in the back of the yard. She opens the grill and puts in an envelope that sticks halfway out. The envelope reads *MAP # 2* This young woman happens to be my mom.

Blue skies hang above a group of kids on the railroad tracks in Bakersfield, New Jersey. Cousin Matt helps us dig with our hands through some rocks as Hill balances on the tracks. "There's nothing here, dude," Matt claims. "It's definitely the tracks, man." Jeb holds a paper with a homemade map that looks like the tracks. Satch, Holly, and Mason Tepper rummage through some discarded scrap by the tree line. "You guys find anything?" Tepper shouts. "Nothing here." Yells Satch. "Hey Mikey, there's some flat pennies over here." Says Hill. We all run over. I see a pile of rocks near the flattened coins. We pull them away and find *Map # 7*. "That's it!" I open the map, and we all study it. "Hm, some woods, a broken window," Jeb says. "It's got to be the deadly swamp." Says Tepper. "We were there already." Adds Matt as he shields his eyes from the sun. Jeb starts to jab at the map with his pointer finger. "That's my Dad's BOAT!" Sis, Cassie, and Jess look under a pile of rotten wood in the woods by the tracks. I peek my head through the trees. "It's at Jeb's house!" I yell. The three girls drop the wood and run towards me. A shovel breaks through some dirt. We start to get excited as we hit something. Our hands come in and clear dirt off a cardboard box that has been placed in the ground. Jeb rips it open with his hands, and we all cheer. Water guns, candy, quarters, switchblade hair combs, confetti poppers, yo yo's, a whoopie cushion, and silly string are pulled out by the tiny hands.

Sitting at the dining room table back at my house, we all eat ice cream cake that holds Eight candles. Dad and Mom sit in the living room with the grownups. *Over the Hills and Far Away* plays low on the house stereo. My friends, Sis, and my cousins talk amongst ourselves. I do my eye tic and pinch my nose. "What are you doing?" Asks Satch. "What?" I ask while doing my eye tic. "That! Cut it out." Satch says. "He caaan't." Mocks Jeb as he makes a face. "What do you mean?" Satch asks. "They're his tic's. He can't help it, Jeb." Sis yells, "Tic's?" Asks Satch." Yea, he's got lots of them." Says Holly. "I don't have that many!" I state. "He says it's like an itch," Says Sis. "But he's gotta do it until it hurts," Jeb Replies. Hill laughs. "I like his cough." "I like when he smashes his face in the DESK!" Yells Tepper. "No way, ready. I Got Ticks Boya!" Jeb says the loudest. "That one's the best!" Matt agrees, giving Jeb a hi-five. "Mike does it the best, though," Jeb says. "Let's hear it, Mike." He adds. "I don't feel like it," I tell them. "Oh, come ooon!" Complains Jeb. "Fine, I got Ticks Boya." "BOOOOO!" "NOO" Hill holds her nose to add to my failed attempt.

The song has ended, and Dad changes the vinyl record and walks back into the living room, leaving us kids alone once again. After getting a disappointing review from my friends, I crack a smile and stand up as the crowd starts to chant. "DO IT!" "DO IT!" I stand on the chair and climb onto the dining room table. I look around the room with confidence before taking a deep breath. With two clenched fists held out by my side, I put my head back and yell with all my might. "I GOT TICS BOYAAAAAAAAAAAAA!! The crowd throws their fists in the air and cheers as *Touch Me* plays on the stereo. "That's the ONE!" Jeb yells as the cheers turn back into conversations. I wear a grin and look around the room at my lifelong companions before jumping down to join them.

THE END